PCs

FOR

DUMMIES®

7TH EDITION

PCs FOR DUMMIES®

7TH EDITION

by Dan Gookin

IDG Books Worldwide, Inc.
An International Data Group Company

Foster City, CA ◆ Chicago, IL ◆ Indianapolis, IN ◆ New York, NY

PCs For Dummies,® 7th Edition

Published by
IDG Books Worldwide, Inc.
An International Data Group Company
919 E. Hillsdale Blvd.
Suite 400
Foster City, CA 94404
www.idgbooks.com (IDG Books Worldwide Web site)
www.dummies.com (Dummies Press Web site)

Library of Congress Catalog Card No.: 99-65865

ISBN: 0-7645-0594-7

Printed in the United States of America

10 9 8 7 6 5 4 3 2

7B/QS/QZ/ZZ/IN

Distributed in the United States by IDG Books Worldwide, Inc.

Distributed by CDG Books Canada Inc. for Canada; by Transworld Publishers Limited in the United Kingdom; by IDG Norge Books for Norway; by IDG Sweden Books for Sweden; by IDG Books Australia Publishing Corporation Pty. Ltd. for Australia and New Zealand; by TransQuest Publishers Pte Ltd. for Singapore, Malaysia, Thailand, Indonesia, and Hong Kong; by Gotop Information Inc. for Taiwan; by ICG Muse, Inc. for Japan; by Intersoft for South Africa; by Eyrolles for France; by International Thomson Publishing for Germany, Austria and Switzerland; by Distribuidora Cuspide for Argentina; by LR International for Brazil; by Galileo Libros for Chile; by Ediciones ZETA S.C.R. Ltda. for Peru; by WS Computer Publishing Corporation, Inc., for the Philippines; by Contemporanea de Ediciones for Venezuela; by Express Computer Distributors for the Caribbean and West Indies; by Micronesia Media Distributor, Inc. for Micronesia; by Chips Computadoras S.A. de C.V. for Mexico; by Editorial Norma de Panama S.A. for Panama; by American Bookshops for Finland.

For general information on IDG Books Worldwide's books in the U.S., please call our Consumer Customer Service department at 800-762-2974. For reseller information, including discounts and premium sales, please call our Reseller Customer Service department at 800-434-3422.

For information on where to purchase IDG Books Worldwide's books outside the U.S., please contact our International Sales department at 317-596-5530 or fax 317-596-5692.

For consumer information on foreign language translations, please contact our Customer Service department at 1-800-434-3422, fax 317-596-5692, or e-mail rights@idgbooks.com.

For information on licensing foreign or domestic rights, please phone +1-650-655-3109.

For sales inquiries and special prices for bulk quantities, please contact our Sales department at 650-655-3200 or write to the address above.

For information on using IDG Books Worldwide's books in the classroom or for ordering examination copies, please contact our Educational Sales department at 800-434-2086 or fax 317-596-5499.

For press review copies, author interviews, or other publicity information, please contact our Public Relations department at 650-655-3000 or fax 650-655-3299.

For authorization to photocopy items for corporate, personal, or educational use, please contact Copyright Clearance Center, 222 Rosewood Drive, Danvers, MA 01923, or fax 978-750-4470.

is a registered trademark under exclusive license
to IDG Books Worldwide, Inc. from International Data Group, Inc.

About the Author

Dan Gookin got started with computers back in the post vacuum tube3 age of computing: 1982. His first intention was to buy a computer to replace his aged and constantly breaking typewriter. Working as slave labor in a restaurant, however, Gookin was unable to afford the full "word processor" setup and settled on a computer that had a monitor, keyboard, and little else. Soon his writing career was under way with several submissions to fiction magazines and lots of rejections.

The big break came in 1984, when he began writing about computers. Applying his flair for fiction with a self-taught knowledge of computers, Gookin was able to demystify the subject and explain technology in a relaxed and understandable voice. He even dared to add humor, which eventually won him a column in a local computer magazine.

Eventually Gookin's talents came to roost as a ghostwriter at a computer book publishing house. That was followed by an editing position at a San Diego computer magazine. During this time, he also regularly participated on a talk show about computers. In addition, Gookin kept writing books about computers, some of which became minor bestsellers.

In 1990, Gookin came to IDG Books Worldwide with a proposal. From that initial meeting unfolded an idea for an outrageous book: a long overdue and original idea for the computer book for the rest of us. What became *DOS For Dummies* blossomed into an international bestseller with hundreds of thousands of copies in print and many translations.

Today, Gookin still considers himself a writer and computer "guru" whose job it is to remind everyone that computers are not taken too seriously. His approach to computers is light and humorous yet very informative. He knows the complex beasts are important and can help people become productive and successful. Gookin mixes his knowledge of computers with a unique, dry sense of humor that keeps everyone informed — and awake. His favorite quote is "Computers are a notoriously dull subject, but that doesn't mean that I have to write about them that way."

Gookin's titles for IDG Books include *Word 2000 For Windows For Dummies, C For Dummies, Buying a Computer For Dummies,* and the *Illustrated Computer Dictionary For Dummies.* All told, he's written more than 50 books about computers, some of which he's written more than once. Gookin holds a degree in communications from the University of California, San Diego, and lives with his wife and four boys in the hinterlands of Idaho.

Dan can be contacted by e-mail at dang@idgbooks.com.

ABOUT IDG BOOKS WORLDWIDE

Welcome to the world of IDG Books Worldwide.

IDG Books Worldwide, Inc., is a subsidiary of International Data Group, the world's largest publisher of computer-related information and the leading global provider of information services on information technology. IDG was founded more than 30 years ago by Patrick J. McGovern and now employs more than 9,000 people worldwide. IDG publishes more than 290 computer publications in over 75 countries. More than 90 million people read one or more IDG publications each month.

Launched in 1990, IDG Books Worldwide is today the #1 publisher of best-selling computer books in the United States. We are proud to have received eight awards from the Computer Press Association in recognition of editorial excellence and three from Computer Currents' First Annual Readers' Choice Awards. Our best-selling ...*For Dummies*® series has more than 50 million copies in print with translations in 31 languages. IDG Books Worldwide, through a joint venture with IDG's Hi-Tech Beijing, became the first U.S. publisher to publish a computer book in the People's Republic of China. In record time, IDG Books Worldwide has become the first choice for millions of readers around the world who want to learn how to better manage their businesses.

Our mission is simple: Every one of our books is designed to bring extra value and skill-building instructions to the reader. Our books are written by experts who understand and care about our readers. The knowledge base of our editorial staff comes from years of experience in publishing, education, and journalism — experience we use to produce books to carry us into the new millennium. In short, we care about books, so we attract the best people. We devote special attention to details such as audience, interior design, use of icons, and illustrations. And because we use an efficient process of authoring, editing, and desktop publishing our books electronically, we can spend more time ensuring superior content and less time on the technicalities of making books.

You can count on our commitment to deliver high-quality books at competitive prices on topics you want to read about. At IDG Books Worldwide, we continue in the IDG tradition of delivering quality for more than 30 years. You'll find no better book on a subject than one from IDG Books Worldwide.

John Kilcullen
Chairman and CEO
IDG Books Worldwide, Inc.

Steven Berkowitz
President and Publisher
IDG Books Worldwide, Inc.

Eighth Annual
Computer Press
Awards ≥1992

Ninth Annual
Computer Press
Awards ≥1993

Tenth Annual
Computer Press
Awards ≥1994

Eleventh Annual
Computer Press
Awards ≥1995

IDG is the world's leading IT media, research and exposition company. Founded in 1964, IDG had 1997 revenues of $2.05 billion and has more than 9,000 employees worldwide. IDG offers the widest range of media options that reach IT buyers in 75 countries representing 95% of worldwide IT spending. IDG's diverse product and services portfolio spans six key areas including print publishing, online publishing, expositions and conferences, market research, education and training, and global marketing services. More than 90 million people read one or more of IDG's 290 magazines and newspapers, including IDG's leading global brands — Computerworld, PC World, Network World, Macworld and the Channel World family of publications. IDG Books Worldwide is one of the fastest-growing computer book publishers in the world, with more than 700 titles in 36 languages. The "...For Dummies®" series alone has more than 50 million copies in print. IDG offers online users the largest network of technology-specific Web sites around the world through IDG.net (http://www.idg.net), which comprises more than 225 targeted Web sites in 55 countries worldwide. International Data Corporation (IDC) is the world's largest provider of information technology data, analysis and consulting, with research centers in over 41 countries and more than 400 research analysts worldwide. IDG World Expo is a leading producer of more than 168 globally branded conferences and expositions in 35 countries including E3 (Electronic Entertainment Expo), Macworld Expo, ComNet, Windows World Expo, ICE (Internet Commerce Expo), Agenda, DEMO, and Spotlight. IDG's training subsidiary, ExecuTrain, is the world's largest computer training company, with more than 230 locations worldwide and 785 training courses. IDG Marketing Services helps industry-leading IT companies build international brand recognition by developing global integrated marketing programs via IDG's print, online and exposition products worldwide. Further information about the company can be found at www.idg.com.

1/24/99

Author's Acknowledgments

I would like to express my thanks and appreciation to Andy Rathbone, for his contributions to earlier editions of this book.

Thanks to Maryann Yoshimoto, for her medical assistance with the text.

Thanks also to the many readers who write in with questions, which prompts me to write a better and better book each time. Cheers!

Publisher's Acknowledgments

We're proud of this book; please register your comments through our IDG Books Worldwide Online Registration Form located at http://my2cents.dummies.com.

Some of the people who helped bring this book to market include the following:

Acquisitions, Editorial, and Media Development

Senior Project Editor: Kyle Looper

Acquisitions Editor: Andy Cummings

Copy Editor: Kim Darosett

Technical Editor: Richard Graves

Editorial Manager: Leah Cameron

Media Development Manager: Heather Heath Dismore

Editorial Assistant: Beth Parlon

Production

Project Coordinators: E. Shawn Aylsworth, Regina Snyder

Layout and Graphics: Angela F. Hunckler, Kate Jenkins, Barry Offringa, Brent Savage, Jacque Schneider, Mary Jo Weis, Dan Whetstine

Proofreaders: Vickie Broyles, Nancy L. Reinhardt, Rebecca Senninger

Indexer: Christine Spina Karpeles

General and Administrative

IDG Books Worldwide, Inc.: John Kilcullen, CEO; Steven Berkowitz, President and Publisher

IDG Books Technology Publishing Group: Richard Swadley, Senior Vice President and Publisher; Walter Bruce III, Vice President and Associate Publisher; Steven Sayre, Associate Publisher; Joseph Wikert, Associate Publisher; Mary Bednarek, Branded Product Development Director; Mary Corder, Editorial Director

IDG Books Consumer Publishing Group: Roland Elgey, Senior Vice President and Publisher; Kathleen A. Welton, Vice President and Publisher; Kevin Thornton, Acquisitions Manager; Kristin A. Cocks, Editorial Director

IDG Books Internet Publishing Group: Brenda McLaughlin, Senior Vice President and Publisher; Diane Graves Steele, Vice President and Associate Publisher; Sofia Marchant, Online Marketing Manager

IDG Books Production for Dummies Press: Michael R. Britton, Vice President of Production; Debbie Stailey, Associate Director of Production; Cindy L. Phipps, Manager of Project Coordination, Production Proofreading, and Indexing; Tony Augsburger, Manager of Prepress, Reprints, and Systems; Laura Carpenter, Production Control Manager; Shelley Lea, Supervisor of Graphics and Design; Debbie J. Gates, Production Systems Specialist; Robert Springer, Supervisor of Proofreading; Kathie Schutte, Production Supervisor

Dummies Packaging and Book Design: Patty Page, Manager, Promotions Marketing

◆

The publisher would like to give special thanks to Patrick J. McGovern, without whom this book would not have been possible.

◆

Contents at a Glance

Cartoons at a Glance

By Rich Tennant

page 239

page 371

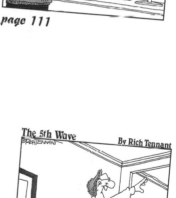

page 111

page 5

page 39

page 389

page 289

Fax: 978-546-7747 • E-mail: the5wave@tiac.net

Table of Contents

Introduction

*W*elcome to *PCs For Dummies,* the all-new 7th Edition. This is the book that answers the question, "How does a computer turn a smart person like you into a dummy?"

Computers are useful, yes. And a fair number of people — heaven help them — fall in love with computers. But the rest of us are left sitting dumb and numb in front of the box. It's not that using a computer is beyond the range of our IQs; it's that no one has ever bothered to sit down and explain things in human terms. Until now.

This book talks about using a computer in friendly, human — and often irreverent — terms. Nothing is sacred here. Electronics can be praised by others. This book focuses on you and your needs. In this book, you'll discover everything you need to know about your computer without painful jargon or the prerequisite master's degree in engineering. And you'll have fun.

What's New in This Edition?

This book is a near total rewrite of the previous edition. Old information has been thrown out! New information has been cheerfully added and updated! All the stuff that's important to today's PC user can be found right here betwixt these covers.

In this edition, you can find the following new and exciting topics:

- Using a UPS
- Information on Zip, Jaz, CD-R, CD-RW, and DVD drives
- The latest information on USB ports
- Using more than one monitor in Windows 98
- The latest in modem technology (stuff that you can buy now)
- All about graphics software
- Scanning images and using a digital camera
- AOL coverage
- A massive dose of currently hot Internet topics: shopping, auctions, investing, stocks, travel, game playing, chatting, e-mail attachments, uploading a Web page, and more

Plus you'll continue to find the kind of soothing, basic information told in gentle tones that calm even the most panicked beginner.

Where to Start

This book is designed so that you can pick it up at any point and start reading — like a reference. There are 34 chapters. Each chapter covers a specific aspect of the computer — turning it on, using a printer, using software, kicking it, and so on. Each chapter is divided into self-contained nuggets of information — sections — all relating to the major theme of the chapter. Sample sections you may find include:

- Your Basic Hardware (A Nerd's-Eye View)
- Learning which buttons you can ignore
- "My taskbar is gone!"
- General Commands for All Reasons
- Exiting a program
- Turning off the computer

You don't have to memorize anything in this book. Nothing about a computer is memorable. Each section is designed so you can read the information quickly, digest what you've read, and then put down the book and get on with using the computer. If anything technical crops up, you'll be alerted to its presence so you can cleanly avoid it.

Conventions Used in This Book

This book works like a reference. Start with the topic you want more information about; look for it in the table of contents or in the index. Turn to the area of interest and read the information you need. Then, with the information in your head, you can quickly close the book and freely perform whatever task you need — without learning anything else.

Whenever I describe a message or information on the screen, it looks like this:

```
This is a message on-screen.
```

If you have to type something in, it looks like this:

Type me in

You would type the text **Type me in** as shown. You'll be told when and if to press the Enter key.

Windows menu commands are shown like this:

Choose File⇨Exit.

This means to choose the File menu and then choose the Exit command. You can use your computer's mouse, or you can press the Alt key and then the underlined keys, F and then X in the preceding example.

Key combinations you may have to type in are shown like this:

Ctrl+S

This means to press and hold the Ctrl (control) key, type an *S,* and then release the Ctrl key. It works just like the way pressing Shift+S on the keyboard produces an uppercase *S.* Same deal, different shift key.

What You Don't Need to Read

A lot of technical information is involved with using a computer. To better insulate you from it, I've enclosed such material in sidebars that are clearly marked as technical information. You don't have to read that stuff. Often, it's just a complex explanation of information already discussed in the chapter. Reading that information will only teach you something substantial about your computer, which is not the goal here.

Foolish Assumptions

I am going to make some admittedly foolish assumptions about you: You have a computer, and you use it somehow to do something. You use a PC (or are planning on it) and will be using Windows as your PC's operating system or main program.

This book covers all the basic information about Windows 98, with a lot of Windows 95 stuff thrown in just because I'm a nice person. If information relates to a specific version of Windows, I'll name the version. Otherwise, when I use the term "Windows," it applies to both Windows 95 and 98.

(This book no longer covers Windows 3.11 or DOS. For Windows 3.11 coverage, refer to the 4th Edition or earlier. I cover DOS in the first two editions.)

Icons Used in This Book

This icon alerts you to needless technical information — drivel added because I just feel like explaining something totally unnecessary (a hard habit to break). Feel free to skip over anything tagged with this little picture.

This icon usually indicates helpful advice or an insight that makes using the computer interesting. For example, when pouring acid over your computer, be sure to wear a protective apron, gloves, and goggles.

Ummm, I forgot what this one means.

This icon indicates that you need to be careful with the information presented; usually, it's a reminder for you not to do something.

This is a new icon with this edition. Because I list my e-mail address in this book, I often get letters from readers who need more information or help. I've culled through those letters and posted some of my replies in the "Ask Dan" sidebars. Speaking of which. . . .

Getting in Touch with the Author

My e-mail address is listed here if you'd like to write me on the Internet. I promise that I'll personally respond to every e-mail message I get. But while I can answer most questions, please don't try to stump me! Remember that you paid your dealer for technical support and you should try there first.

    dan@wambooli.com

Where to Go from Here

With this book in hand, you're now ready to go out and conquer your PC. Start by looking through the table of contents or the index. Find a topic, turn to the page indicated, and you're ready to go. Also, feel free to write in this book, fill in the blanks, dog-ear the pages, and do anything that would make a librarian blanch. Enjoy.

Part I
Say Hello to Mr. Computer

The 5th Wave   By Rich Tennant

In this part . . .

In the early Cro-Magnon days of the computer (say the late 1940s), one of the pioneers of that age stated flatly that the world of the future would need five, maybe seven computers tops. That's it.

We've come a long way.

Today there are millions of computers, and each person can have his own. They no longer occupy a city block or require thousands of vacuum tubes or an army of men in white lab coats to keep them going. Anyone who's willing or merely curious can use, enjoy, or even conquer the computer. It's simple — painless, even.

This part of the book gets you up to speed on some very basic computer concepts, even if you don't have a computer or are just setting out to buy one. Or maybe you just bought a shotgun and need to know what to shoot at. Whatever the case, this part of the book is for you.

Chapter 1

PC 101

Sometime in the near future, personal robots will become the rage. You'll open the box, and your PR (personal robot) will pop out, introduce itself, and say, "I'm here to serve your every whim!" Like an electronic genie, it will do whatever you say. Surely that will be bliss.

Then, of course, the Robot Rebellion will take place, and not too long after that, intelligent chimpanzees will take over and hunt us into extinction. But before that, you have to deal with a rather rude personal servant known as *the computer* or *PC*. If your PC popped out of the box, shook your hand, and gave you a big hug, then this book wouldn't be necessary. Until then, this book starts with this introductory chapter on understanding personal computer basics.

✔ If you don't already own a PC, I can recommend a great book: *Buying a Computer For Dummies*, written by yours truly and available from IDG Books Worldwide, Inc. It covers the basics of the PC, how to select one just right for you, and how to set it up for the first time.

✔ This book tries its best to be jargon free or at least explain terms before using them. Other books and magazines cannot make the same promise, so I can recommend a good computer dictionary: *The Illustrated Computer Dictionary For Dummies*, also available from IDG Books Worldwide, Inc.

✔ I promise not to plug any of my other books for the remainder of this chapter.

What Exactly Is a PC?

A PC is a personal computer, named after its earliest ancestor the IBM PC. IBM (International Business Machines) created the PC (Personal Computer) after years of making larger, more impersonal computers (IPs).

Today, any PC you can buy for yourself or for the office is dubbed a PC. This is true no matter what brand name the computer has. In fact, even the Macintosh is a PC, though Mac people turn all strawberry, tangerine, orange, lime, and blueberry when you accuse their computers of being PCs (because *PC* first identified the IBM-type of personal computer).

- ✔ Technically, a PC is a large calculator with a better display and more buttons.

- ✔ PCs are as adept with words as they are with numbers. It's the software that controls things, which is covered later in this chapter.

- ✔ All Macintosh computers — the G3, PowerBook, iMac, and earlier models — are PCs, though I don't specifically cover them in this book. PC here means (mostly) "it runs Windows."

- ✔ Laptops and notebook computers are lighter and more portable versions of the PC. They allow people to play computer games on airplanes. Although a laptop may not be your first PC, I mention various laptoppy things throughout this book just to amuse my managing editor.

- ✔ I just made up the term IP (for impersonal computer). Larger computers are called *mainframes*. Feel free to ignore them.

- ✔ Computers are not evil. They harbor no sinister intelligence. In fact, when you get to know them, they're rather dumb.

What does a PC do?

Computers defy description. Unlike other tools that have definite purposes, a computer can do a number of different things, solving an infinite number of problems for an infinite number of people. Just about anything that can be done with words, numbers, information, or communication can be done with a computer.

In a way, a computer is just another electronic gadget. Unlike the toaster and your car's fuel injection system, which are programmed to do only one thing each, a personal computer can be *programmed* to do a number of interesting tasks. It's up to you to tell the computer what you want it to do.

- The computer is the chameleon of electronic devices. Your phone can be used only as a phone, your VCR only records and plays videos, and your microwave oven only zaps things (food, mostly). A computer's potential is limitless.

- Computers get the job done by using *software.* The software tells the computer what to do.

- No, you never have to learn about programming to use a computer. Someone else does the programming, and then you buy the program (the software) to get your work done.

- Your job, as the computer operator, is to tell the software what to do, which then tells the computer what to do.

- Only on cheesy sci-fi shows does the computer ever tell *you* what to do.

- You can always *verbally* tell the computer what to do with itself. This happens millions of times a day, by programmers and nonprogrammers alike.

- Software is only half of the computer equation. The other side is *hardware,* which I cover later in this chapter.

What does a PC not do?

The PC does not give off a pleasing odor, nor does it hum. And while it can do many things at once, it just cannot chew gum.

A PC is happy to do Windows, but it won't clean the house. It makes an okay companion, but it's not really a spouse.

With your PC you can play games, interactive and chess. But if you need a hug, the computer could care less.

The PC does work, calculating, storing, and retrieval. But while it may seem really smart, it's certainly not evil.

And above all, remember this handy PC rule of thumb: It's not *you* but the computer that's really dumb, dumb, dumb, dumb.

Hardware and Software

Two separate things make up a computer: hardware and software. They go hand in hand. You cannot have one without the other. It would be like romance without the moon, lightning without thunder, macaroni without cheese, Rosencrantz without Guildenstern.

Hardware is the physical part of a computer, anything you can touch and anything you can see. Yet, hardware is nothing unless it has software to control it. In a way, hardware is like a car without a driver or a saw without a carpenter; you need both to make something happen.

Software is the brains of the computer. It tells the hardware what to do. Without software, hardware just sits around bored and unappreciated. You must have software to make a computer go. In fact, software determines your computer's personality.

- ✔ If you can throw it out a window, it's hardware.

- ✔ Computer software is nothing more than instructions that tell the hardware what to do, how to act, or when to lose your data.

- ✔ Computer software is more important than computer hardware. The software tells the hardware what to do.

- ✔ Although computer software comes on disks (CDs or floppy disks), the *disks* aren't the software. Software is stored on disks just as music is stored on cassettes and CDs.

- ✔ Without the proper software, your computer is merely an expensive doorstop.

Your Basic Hardware (A Nerd's-Eye View)

Figure 1-1 shows what a typical computer system looks like. I've flagged the most basic computer things you should identify and know about. These are the basics. The rest of this book goes into the details.

Console: The main computer box is the console, though geeky types call it the *system unit.* It's a box that contains your computer's guts plus various buttons, lights, and holes into which you plug the rest of the computer system.

Monitor: The monitor is the TV-set-like thing on which the computer displays information. It sits to the right or left of the console, or if you put the console beneath the table, the monitor sits on top of the table. (Putting the monitor beneath the table is a silly idea.) I cover monitors in detail in Chapter 12.

Keyboard: It's the thing you type on. Clackity-clack-clack. Chapter 14 cusses and discusses the computer keyboard.

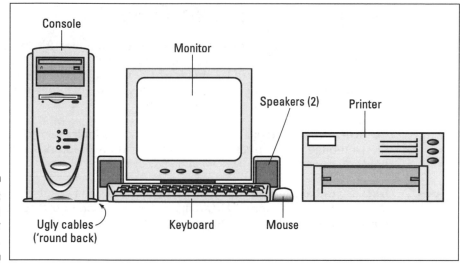

Figure 1-1:
Basic
computer
things.

Mouse: Ah, the computer mouse. No rodent or pest, it's a helpful device that lets you work with graphical objects that the computer displays on the monitor's screen. See Chapter 13 for more mouse information.

Speakers: Most PCs can bleep and squawk through a set of stereo speakers, either external jobbies you can set up, as shown in Figure 1-1, or the speakers may be built into the console or the monitor. Pay more money, and you can even get a subwoofer to sit under the desk. Now *that* will scare the neighbors.

Printer: It's where you get the computer's output: the printed stuff, also called *hard copy.* Sashay off to Chapter 15 to increase your PC printer knowledge.

Lots of ugly cables: One thing they never show you — not in any computer manual and especially not in advertisements — is the ganglia of cables that lives behind each and every computer. What a mess! These cables are required to plug things into the wall and into each other. No shampoo conditioner on earth can clean up those tangles.

✔ These parts of the computer are all important. Make sure that you know where the console, keyboard, mouse, speakers, monitor, and printer are in your own system. If the printer isn't present, it's probably a network printer sitting in some other room.

✔ A computer really exists in two places. Most of the computer lives inside the console. Everything else, all the stuff connected to the console, is called *peripherals.* See Chapter 18 for more information about peripherals.

Stuff on the console (front)

The console is the most important part of your computer. It's the main thing, the Big Box. Every part of your computer system either lives inside the console or plugs into it. Figure 1-2 shows what a typical PC console may look like. I've flagged the more interesting places to visit, although they may appear in a different location than shown in the figure.

CD-ROM or DVD drive: These high-capacity discs look exactly like musical CDs, although they contain computer information. Chapters 5 and 10 cover how you use and abuse CD-ROM and DVD drives and discs.

DVD drives have the DVD symbol on them. If you don't see the DVD symbol, then your PC has a mere CD-ROM drive. That's okay for now, because little software is available exclusively on DVD discs.

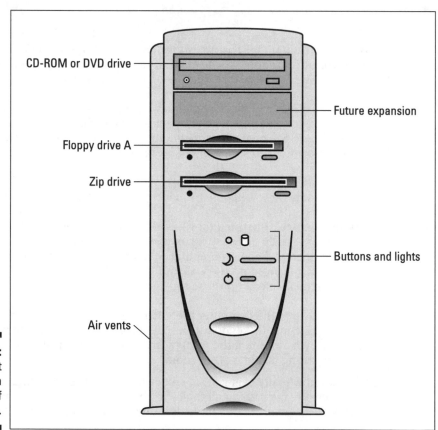

Figure 1-2: Important doodads on the front of the console.

CD-ROM or DVD drive

Future expansion

Floppy drive A

Zip drive

Buttons and lights

Air vents

Future expansion: Ah, potential! You can add a whole grab bag of goodies to a computer, and most consoles have plenty of room for it. Any blank spots or covers on the front of your computer means that you can add even more junk later. Such a space may already be taken, filled with such goodies as a tape backup unit, Zip drive, another CD-ROM drive, another hard drive, or an assortment of other computer things many folks eagerly spend their hard-earned money on.

Floppy drive: This slot eats floppy disks. Some software comes on floppy disks, and you can use these disks to move files from one PC to another.

Zip drive: A common option found on many PCs is the Zip drive, which is like a super-dooper floppy drive. On a Zip disk, you can store the equivalent of 100 floppy disks worth of information. Not every PC has a Zip drive, however.

Air vents: Okay, this one isn't truly important, but most consoles sport some type of air vent on the front. Don't block the air vents with books or sticky notes! The thing has gotta breathe.

Buttons and lights: Most of the computer's buttons are on the keyboard. A few of the more important ones are on the console, and these buttons on fancier PCs are accompanied by many impressive tiny lights. These buttons and lights include the following:

> ✔ **On-off button:** The PC's main power button, the one you use to turn the darn thing on. A light usually accompanies the on-off button, although computers make enough racket that you can usually hear when they're turned on.

> ✔ **Reset button:** Allows you to restart the computer without going through the bother of turning it off and then on again. Chapter 2 explains why anyone in his right mind would want to do that.

> ✔ **Sleep button:** A feature on some newer PCs and most laptops. Pressing this button causes your PC to go into a coma, suspending all activity without turning the computer off. Read all about this trick in Chapter 2.

> ✔ **Hard drive light:** Flashes when the hard drive is working. Because the hard drive lives inside the console, this light is your reassurance that it's alive, happy, and doing its job.

Other fun and unusual things may live on the front of your console. These include other types of removable drives, locks and keys, turbo buttons, and the various stickers that say "I was built to run Windows 98" or "A Pentium lurks inside this box." Rarely, if ever, will you find a Panic button.

> ✔ The console isn't the only part of your computer system that sports an on-off switch. Your PC's monitor, printer, modem, and almost everything else also have their own on-off switches. See Chapter 2 for more information about turning everything on.

- ✔ The on-off symbol just shown may indicate the reset button on some computers, so much for international symbols! Check with your computer manual to be sure.

- ✔ Try not to block the air vents on the front of the console. If you do, the computer may literally suffocate. (Actually, it gets too hot.)

- ✔ If your computer does have a lock and key, don't count on using it for security purposes: I have several computers in the office from different manufacturers, and the same key works with all the locks.

- ✔ A hard drive light can be red or green or yellow, and it flickers when the hard drive is in use. Don't let it freak you out! It's not an alarm; the hard drive is just doing its job. (Personally, I find the green type of hard drive light most comforting — reminds me of Christmas.)

Stuff on the console (back)

The back of the console is where you find the computer's busy side. That's where you find various connectors for the many other devices in your computer system: a place to plug in the monitor, keyboard, mouse, speakers, and just about anything else that came in the box with the PC.

Figure 1-3 illustrates the typical PC's rump, showing you where and how the various goodies can connect. Your computer should have most of the items shown in the figure, although they'll probably be in different locations on the PC's backside.

Power connector: This thing is where the PC plugs into a cord that plugs into the wall.

 Keyboard connector: The keyboard plugs into this little hole. The wee li'l picture is supposed to be a keyboard. Note that some keyboard holes may be labeled KBD or even say *Keyboard* with all the vowels and the *R*.

 Mouse connector: It's generally the same size and shape as the keyboard connector, although this hole has a mouse icon nearby to let you know that the mouse plugs in there.

 USB port: Plug snazzy USB devices into these Certs-size slots. You can find out more about what can be plugged into a USB port in Chapter 9.

 Serial, or COM, ports: Most PCs have two of these ports, labeled COM1 and COM2. They're where an external modem or sometimes a mouse is plugged in.

 Printer port: The PC's printer plugs into this connector.

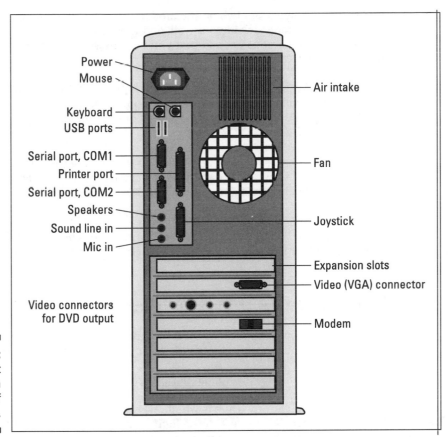

Figure 1-3:
Important
doodads on
the back of
the console.

Labels (left side, top to bottom): Power, Mouse, Keyboard, USB ports, Serial port, COM1, Printer port, Serial port, COM2, Speakers, Sound line in, Mic in, Video connectors for DVD output

Labels (right side, top to bottom): Air intake, Fan, Joystick, Expansion slots, Video (VGA) connector, Modem

Joystick port: This port is used mainly for scientific applications. The port may be identified by an image (shown in the margin), or it may say *Joystick* or *Game controller.*

Monitor connector: Your PC's monitor plugs into this hole. Sometimes the hole is on an expansion slot and is unlabeled. If so, you can tell what the monitor connector is because it has 15 little holes in it — more than the serial port, which is the same size but has only 9 holes.

Speaker/sound-out jack: It's where you plug in your PC's external speakers or where you would hook up the PC to a sound system. (If you have USB speakers, then you should use the USB port for external speakers.)

Line-in jack: This jack is where you plug in your stereo or VCR to the PC for capturing sound.

Microphone jack: The computer's microphone plugs into this hole.

Modem: Two connectors live on the modem. One is for connecting the modem to the phone jack in your wall, and the other is to connect a telephone (the kind humans use) so that you can answer the phone. More on modems in Chapter 16.

S-Video out: If your PC sports a DVD drive, it probably has several additional connectors for video output. The S-Video connector allows you to connect an S-Video-happy TV to your PC. Other video connectors let you pump a DVD movie out to a TV set or VCR.

In addition to the ports, jacks, and holes on the back of the console are expansion slots. They're the backsides of various expansion cards you plug into your PC. Some expansion slots have connectors for other PC goodies as well.

The good news? You connect all this stuff only once. Then your PC's butt faces the wall for the rest of its life, and you never have to look at it again.

"So where is my A drive?"

The A drive is your computer's first floppy drive. It's the only floppy drive if you have one, and it's typically the *top* floppy drive if you have two.

Then again, it could be the *bottom* floppy drive.

To find out which floppy drive is which, watch them when your PC starts up. The first floppy drive, drive A, has a light on it that lights up for a few moments after the PC starts. Immediately write *Drive A* on that drive by using an indelible marker or use a label maker to create a label for the drive.

The Cheat Sheet inside the front cover of this book includes space for you to jot down your drive A location. That way, you always remember.

- ✔ You need to know which is your A drive because lots of software and various computer manuals refer to it. Labeling it now saves you from frustration later.

- ✔ Zip drives don't have a specific drive-lettering scheme, though when you find out which letter is attached to your Zip drive, you should label it just as you did the floppy drive.

- ✔ Chapter 7 describes all this disk-drive-lettering nonsense in crystal-clear detail.

⚡☉★ᵻ⚓◯✈»✳︎☌♉◯♋☉✿♏✝︎♓♌(☉∴

(Know your sign language)

International signs are all the rage! These are the symbols you see on the highway and at airports and at all the very cosmopolitan places. You've seen them: universal signs for *no* and *food* and *the moving walkway is ending.*

Similar international signs have tried to find their way on your PC. But as with anything on a computer, the signs make no sense. Apparently *universal language* means *language from another universe* to the computer. Oh well. Figure 1-4 should help you decipher things.

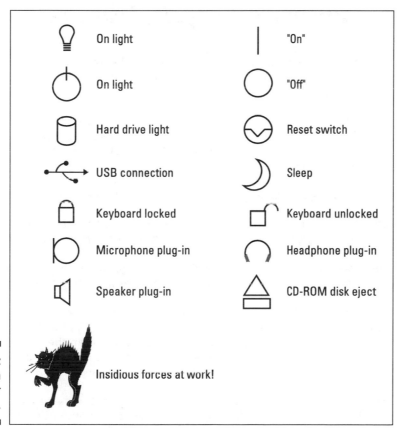

	On light		"On"
	On light		"Off"
	Hard drive light		Reset switch
	USB connection		Sleep
	Keyboard locked		Keyboard unlocked
	Microphone plug-in		Headphone plug-in
	Speaker plug-in		CD-ROM disk eject
	Insidious forces at work!		

Figure 1-4:
Common computer hieroglyphics.

✓ Forget seeing *on* or *off* on a computer switch. Computers use a bar for on and a circle for off (as shown in Figure 1-4). You can remember which is which by keeping in mind that a circle is an O and the word *off* starts with the letter *O*. (Then again, so does *on*. Just don't think about it.)

✓ To drive this confusing point home: Most PCs now have a dual on-off switch with *both* symbols on it. Press once to turn it on, and press again to turn it off. *Sigh*. . . .

✓ Most consoles have a little light that lets you know that the computer is on. This little light is accompanied by a special symbol. Figure 1-4 shows three *the computer is on* symbols. Why? Wouldn't it just be simpler to teach everyone English? What's the Esperanto word for *on* anyway?

Variations on the typical computer theme

Not all computers look like the image shown in Figure 1-1. The type of PC shown there is currently the most popular, called the *mini-tower*. It can sit upright on your desk or be tucked away out of sight beneath the desk. And it's sleek and sexy.

PCs need not all be configured as mini-towers. For the first ten years or so of the PC's life, the desktop model was the most popular. Other models exist as well, each with an orientation, size, and enough blinking lights to please any particular person.

The following list describes the various types and models of PCs:

Mini-tower: The most popular PC configuration, where the computer sits upright on a desktop or beneath the desk (refer to Figure 1-1).

Desktop: Formerly the most popular PC configuration, with a slab-like console lying flat on the table top with the monitor squatting on top.

Desktop (small footprint): A smaller version of the desktop, typically used in low-priced home systems. (A PC's *footprint* is the amount of desk space it uses. A small footprint desktop model is just tinier than the full-size desktop model. Of course, in the end it makes no difference: The amount of clutter you have always expands to fill available desk space.)

Notebook/laptop: A specialty type of computer that folds into a handy, lightweight package, ideal for lugging around airports. Laptop PCs work just like their desktop brethren; any exceptions are noted throughout this book.

Towers: Essentially a full-sized desktop standing on its side, making it tall, like a tower. These PCs have lotsa room inside for expansion, making them the darling of power-mad users. They typically sit on the floor, usually propping up one end of the table.

Your Basic Software

Computer software doesn't get the credit it deserves for running your computer, which is probably why it's overpriced. In any event, you need the software to make your hardware go.

The operating system (Or "Who's in charge here?")

The most important piece of software is the *operating system*. It's the computer's number-one program — the head honcho, the big cheese, Mr. In Charge, Fearless Leader, *le roi*.

The operating system rules the computer's roost, controlling all the individual computer components and making sure that everything gets along well. It's the actual brains of the operation, telling the nitwitted hardware what to do next.

The operating system also controls applications software (see the next section). Each of those programs must bend a knee and take a loyalty oath to the operating system.

- The computer's most important piece of software is the operating system.

- The operating system typically comes with the computer when you buy it. You never need to add a second operating system, although operating systems do get updated and improved from time to time. See Chapter 19 for information about upgrading the operating system.

- When you buy software, you buy it for an operating system, not your brand of PC. In the olden days (the 1980s), you would walk to the Apple or IBM or Commodore section of the software store. Today you browse either in the Macintosh or Windows aisles.

- For the PC, the most popular operating system used to be DOS. Now it's Windows. Although other popular operating systems exist, Windows is pretty much king of the heap. Bill Gates knows this fact every time he reviews his monthly bank statement.

- Chapter 3 chitty-chats about Windows.

Software that actually does something

The operating system is merely in charge of the computer. By itself, an operating system doesn't really do anything for you. Instead, to get work done, you need an application program. *Application programs* are the programs that do the work.

Application programs include word processors, spreadsheets, and databases. Whatever it is you do on your computer, you do it using an application program.

Other types of programs include utilities and games and educational and programming software. And then there are all the Internet applications: Web browsers, e-mail programs, and software of that ilk.

Some Consoling Words of Advice

The biggest problem I encounter with people new to the world of computers is that they quickly blame themselves when something goes wrong.

Honestly, people! It's not your fault!

Computers goof up. Programs have bugs. Things go wrong, and sometimes they would do so even if you weren't sitting there at the controls.

Please, don't assume you've goofed up or somehow wrecked something. True, that does happen. But a good deal of the time, the computer is just acting dumb.

- ✔ Blame the computer or the software first! The stuff sometimes doesn't work.

- ✔ See Chapter 30 for more information on troubleshooting your PC should it do something wrong or happen to explode.

Chapter 2

The Big Red Switch

*T*urning on a car takes more steps than turning on a computer. Computers have only one switch (which is neither big nor red). Cars have ignition switches, plus you have to take them out of gear and often press on the brake pedal. And if you screw up, the car could lurch forward or back, making various ugly grinding noises. By contrast, computers are far easier to get going.

This chapter covers the basics of turning on a computer. More than flowers and poems about the moon, you turn on a computer simply by flipping its power switch. Of course, that would make for a rather short chapter, so I've tossed in information about what to do *after* flipping the switch, plus important info on when (if ever) to turn the computer off.

To Turn the Computer On, Throw the Switch

Click.

Perhaps the toughest part of turning the computer on is *finding* the switch. Most PCs put the switch on the front of the console. On others, you may find the switch on the side or even the back.

Some switches are the on-off flip or *rocker* type. Other switches are push buttons that turn the system on and turn it off.

- The power switch on your PC is most likely labeled in the international manner. Refer to Chapter 1 for various symbols that may represent *on* or *off* on a computer.

- Laptop computers have strange on-off switches. Some of them are on-off push buttons beneath a stiff rubber top. Other switches may be a "slide-and-release" job. And there's no telling which side of the slab it's on; just get used to wherever the button is.

- If the computer doesn't turn on, check to see whether it's plugged in. If it still doesn't turn on, refer to Chapter 30.

- Two nerdy terms for turning on a computer: power-on and power-up.

- Make sure there isn't a floppy disk in drive A when you start your computer. If there is, then the computer doesn't start from the hard drive like it's supposed to. Keep drive A empty.

- See Chapter 5 for more information about drive A.

Oops! Other things to turn on

Just about everything connected to your PC has an on-off switch, which sometimes means that turning on the console by itself doesn't complete the job. Instead, you should turn on other devices you may need.

Here is the list of things you should turn on in the general order they should be turned on:

1. **The monitor.** Get this warmed up and ready to display text.

2. **Peripherals.** Turn on any external devices you plan on using: scanners, external disk drives, CD-Rs, digital cameras, and so on. Turning these on now means the computer will *see* them once it gets up and running.

3. **The console.** Turn this on last.

"The manual tells me to boot my computer: Where do I kick it?"

Oh, don't be silly. Booting a computer has nothing to do with kicking it. Instead, *booting* simply refers to turning on a computer. To *boot a computer* means to turn it on. Rebooting a computer is the same as pressing the Reset button. It's all weird nerd talk.

Or you can turn everything on at once, which is okay. Generally speaking, however, the console should come on last.

- These devices each have their own on-off switches.

- The largest button on the front of the monitor turns it on. Some older models may have the on-off switch in back.

- You don't need to turn on an external modem right away. Don't bother turning it on until you're ready to use it. Or, you can be like me and just leave the external modem on all the time.

- You don't need to turn on your printer until you're ready to print something. Or (again), you can be like me and leave your printer on all the time. (I have one of those *power-saving* printers, so it's environmentally safe and all that.)

- Another no-need-to-turn-on-at-first item is the scanner. You need to switch on most scanners only just before you plan on scanning a photo or document (though some of the newer scanners are on all the time).

The best solution for turning on a PC

Because the computer has so many devices that must be plugged in and turned on, most people buy a power strip, as shown in Figure 2-1. The power strip comes with six (more or less) sockets into which you can plug every part of your computer. Then you just plug the power strip into the wall. Flipping the switch on the power strip then turns on the console, monitor, and everything.

Here are some power strip hints and suggestions:

- Set everything up by plugging each of your PC's parts into the power strip: console, monitor, modem, scanner, printer, and so on.

- Don't plug laser printers into a power strip. The laser printer draws too much juice for that to be effective — or safe. Instead, you must plug the laser printer directly into the wall socket. (It says that in your laser printer's manual, if you ever get around to reading it.)

- Try to get a power strip with surge protection. They're a little more spendy than plain-old power strips, but they offer a level of power protection that could save your PC should a power surge occur.

- For even more protection, get a UPS, which I cover in the next section.

- I recommend the Kensington SmartSockets power strip. Unlike cheaper power strips, the SmartSockets lines up its sockets in a perpendicular arrangement, making it easier to plug in bulky transformers.

- Plugging everything into a power strip sure solves the problem of "which part of the computer do I turn on first?"

✔ Honestly, the order you turn things on doesn't matter, though I recommend turning on the console last; when the other devices are on and ready, turning the console on last ensures that the computer's guts will find and recognize all its peripherals.

✔ With a power strip, you can turn on your computer system with your foot (providing that the power strip is on the floor). Or if you take off your shoes, use your big toe. And if you're really classy, use your big toe sticking out of a hole in your sock.

✔ The medical name for your big toe is hallux.

An even better power solution

Perhaps the best thing to plug your computer into is a UPS or Uninterruptable Power Supply. It's like a large battery that keeps your computer running even if the power goes out.

Depending on the number of outlets on the UPS, you can plug in your monitor and console plus other items in your computer system. For example, I also plug my external modem and external CD-R drive in my UPS (it has four sockets). That setup keeps me up and running during minor power outages.

Figure 2-2 illustrates one approach to how a UPS could work along with a power strip to power your computer system.

Figure 2-1:
A power
strip.

The urge to surge

Q: I am a bit unsure of how you feel about surge protectors. I was under the impression that most computer gurus think everyone should have a surge protector, even if the power in the area is usually stable and lightning doesn't strike more than normal. Maybe the big chain stores just push surge protectors to make more money; I'm not sure. So, do you think everyone who buys a PC should also purchase a surge protector?

A: Yes. Buying a power strip with surge protection kills two birds with one stone: It gives you more sockets to plug things into, and it adds surge protection. I don't believe the surge protector is a must-have item, though; you can avoid lightning strikes with *spike* protection. But if you need the extra sockets, you may as well go with a surge-protected power strip.

Despite their reputation, UPSs aren't your ticket to computing in the dark. Whenever the power does go out, you should immediately save your work and shut down your computer. That's the true protection a UPS provides; contrary to the advertising, most UPS boxes give you only three to five minutes of power. So saving and shutting down is best.

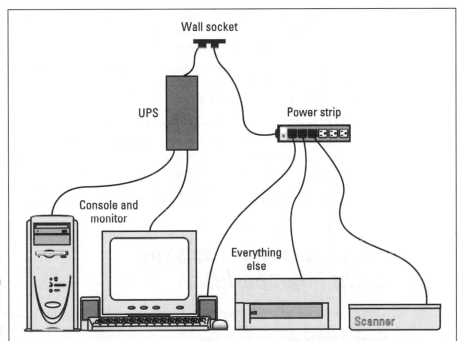

Figure 2-2:
Using a
UPS.

- ✔ A UPS works best for brief power outages. For example, those little power burps that may just flicker the lights can reset your PC. A UPS prevents that reset.

- ✔ In addition to emergency power, a UPS also provides higher levels of electrical protection for your equipment. Many models offer surge, spike, and dip protection, which keep your PC running smoothly despite any nasties the power company may throw your way.

- ✔ Don't bother plugging your printer into a UPS. Printing can wait until after the power is back on.

Here Comes Windows!

After starting your computer (the hardware), the operating system (the software) takes over. Remember that the software controls the hardware, and the main piece of software is the operating system. So the operating system (Windows) is the first program that your computer runs.

As Windows comes to life, you see various messages displayed on the screen. Whatever. Just sit and watch; most of it has low entertainment value, kind of like a long list of credits before a good film . . . or a mediocre film, in this case.

- ✔ For everyone reading this book, the operating system is Windows, either Windows 95 or more likely Windows 98. This book is geared toward Windows 98, which is nearly identical to Windows 95. When the operating systems behave differently, I note those exceptions.

- ✔ If you have an older PC, the information in this book may not apply to you. In that case, I encourage you to get an earlier edition of *PCs For Dummies;* anything prior to the 4th edition should help you.

- ✔ Lots of chaos occurs as Windows loads. Don't fret over any of it.

- ✔ Some monitors may display text as Windows starts up or even before your computer is turned on. My Hitachi monitor, for example, tells me `Invalid Sync` whenever it's on and the computer is off. Your monitor may also display various numbers and values as it changes video modes. It's nothing to concern yourself with; just enjoy the show.

"My computer was shut down improperly?"

There's a right and wrong way to do everything. For shutting down a computer, you don't just throw the big red switch the other way. A few years back, that was okay. Today, however, you have to shut down properly. If you don't, Windows may warn you when you first start the computer.

Don't fret over the warning. It's actually a good thing that Windows catches an improper shutdown. The warning tells you that the ScanDisk program is about to run, which fixes any problems caused by the improper shutdown.

 ✔ If ScanDisk finds any errors, fix them by pressing the Enter key.

 ✔ You don't need an _undo disk,_ so select the Skip Undo option if you ever see it offered.

 ✔ See the section "Turning the Computer Off," later in this chapter, for information about how to properly turn off your computer.

"My computer says 'Non-system disk.' What gives?"

It happens frequently, even to Bill Gates!

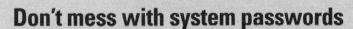

```
Non-system disk or disk error
Replace and strike any key when ready
```

Remove the floppy disk from drive A and press the Enter key. Your computer then starts up normally.

The reason you see the message is that you or someone else has left a floppy disk in your PC's drive A. The computer has tried to start itself up by using software on that disk and — whaddya know? — no software is on that disk! The software (your PC's operating system) is really on your PC's hard drive, which can't be loaded until you remove that dern floppy disk from drive A and whack the Enter key.

Don't mess with system passwords

Some PCs have the capability to have a system password. I don't recommend using it because forgetting the password can lead to lots of trouble.

The system password sounds nifty: A prompt appears right after you turn on your computer, preventing unauthorized access. If you don't

know the password — or you forget it — you can't use the computer. A password is great for security, but it's a serious risk should your brain suddenly forget it.

My advice: Don't bother with system passwords.

Getting rid of the Windows password

Providing your computer is not on a network, getting rid of the Windows password is a cinch:

1. **Open the Control Panel. Choose Settings⇨ Control Panel from the Start menu.**

   The Control Panel opens.

2. **Open the Passwords icon.**

   The Password Properties dialog box shows up.

3. **Click the Change Windows Password button.**

A special dialog box appears where you enter the old password and the new password twice.

4. **Type in the current password, whatever it is.**

5. **Leave the New password and Confirm New Password boxes blank.**

6. **Click OK.**

"What is this annoying password box?"

The final step Windows takes in its long startup journey is to ask for a password (see Figure 2-3). This request happens for several reasons:

- To log you and your computer onto a peer-to-peer network (mostly at the office or, if you're *really* into computers, at your home)

- To identify you as one of several people who use the same computer

- To annoy the bejeezus out of you

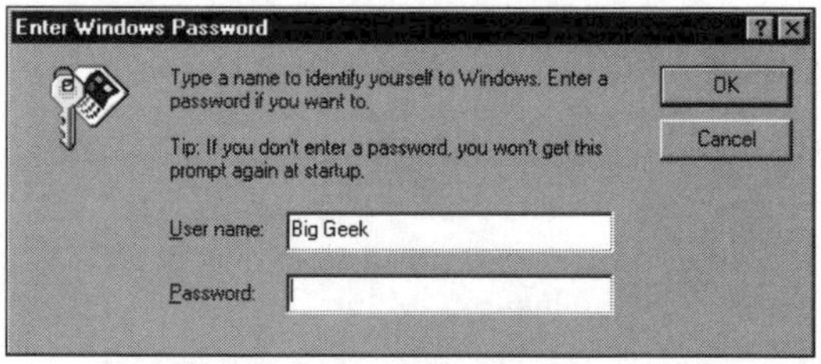

Figure 2-3: Who are you and what do you want?

Enter Windows Password

Type a name to identify yourself to Windows. Enter a password if you want to.

Tip: If you don't enter a password, you won't get this prompt again at startup.

User name: Big Geek

Password:

OK

Cancel

You probably identify most with the third reason. Unless your computer is on a network or configured for multiple users, you don't need a password. It's just an extra step that gets in the way. See the sidebar "Getting rid of the Windows password" for details on eliminating this irksome step.

- ✔ Windows probably already knows your username and displays it proudly for you, as shown in Figure 2-3. Your job is merely to enter the proper password.

- ✔ Press the Tab key to move between the User Name and Password text boxes.

- ✔ The Windows password really offers no security. If you're not on a network, then the password is merely a stumbling block; anyone can click the Cancel button or press the Esc key to gain access to the computer.

- ✔ If you *really* want the password, then note that Windows gives you two chances to type it in correctly. After two changes, Windows goes ahead and lets you use the computer anyway.

- ✔ If you're on a network, then you *need* to type in the password to access network devices. Network passwords offer *real* security.

- ✔ Telling the network who you are is technically called *logging in*. It has nothing to do with cutting timber.

- ✔ If they guarded the crown jewels as feebly as Windows guards itself, we would all be wearing funny, expensive hats.

It's about time this operating system showed up

Eventually — and I'm not talking time to form cobwebs but at least long enough to get a cup of coffee or shave — Windows presents itself as ready for you to use. What you see on the screen (see Figure 2-4) is the desktop, Windows' main screen, or home plate, if you will. Windows is finally ready for you to use. Time to get to work.

- ✔ As part of the startup process, various messages or windows appear on the screen. Some of them disappear, and others require you to click an OK or Cancel button to get rid of them. (See Chapter 13, which talks about using the mouse, if the point-and-click stuff seems strange to you.)

- ✔ Chapter 4 offers more information about Windows and getting to work.

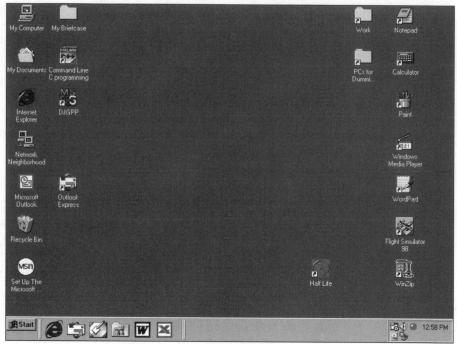

Figure 2-4:
This isn't
your father's
operating
system.

Getting Your Work Done

Between turning your computer on and off, you should do something. Get work done. Do it now.

- ✔ Refer to Part IV of this book for more information on using software.

- ✔ Also refer to Part V for information on using the Internet, which is like using software but also involves using a modem.

Turning the Computer Off

Computers are fussy things. One of the ways you can keep them happy is to be sure you *properly* shut them off. Flipping the power switch to the *off* position just doesn't work. Unfortunately, that's just not polite enough for your computer. It's rude. Windows insists that you shut down properly, or it gets really, really sore.

Before you can feel the satisfaction of flipping that big red switch, heed these steps to properly furl the Windows sails:

1. **Summon the Start menu.**

   If you can see the Start button on the taskbar (refer to the bottom-left corner of Figure 2-4), click that button with your mouse.

   The best and most reliable way to make the Start menu appear is to press the Ctrl+Esc key combination. It works every time, whether you can see the Start button or not.

2. **Choose the Shut Down menu item.**

   Click it with the mouse.

   The Shut Down Windows dialog box appears, as shown in Figure 2-5, filled with even more options for shutting down your PC.

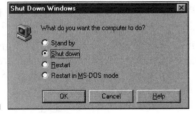

Figure 2-5:
This dialog box is the Windows exit door.

3. **Ensure that the Shut Down option is selected.**

   The option is properly selected in Figure 2-5. If it's not selected on your screen, then click the Shut Down item with the mouse.

4. **Click the OK or Yes button.**

   Windows is outta here! Bye-bye.

   If you haven't saved any information in any programs, you're told about it. Go ahead and save everything.

   If you've been running some older DOS programs, the whole operation stops. You must quit your DOS programs *before* you shut down Windows. (It's a sibling rivalry thing.)

   Eventually, after more disk commotion than seems necessary, you see a screen that tells you, and I quote, "It's now safe to turn off your computer." Look, Ma, no sparks!

5. **Flip the big red switch off.**

   Click. You're done.

Some PCs may actually shut themselves off automatically. If so, you don't need to do Step 5. You may still have to switch off your monitor, printer, and other devices around the PC.

✔ Yes, you shut down by first pressing the Start button. Such logic. . . .

✔ The Stand By option in Figure 2-5 appears only if you have a computer capable of sleeping. See the section "Placing Your PC in Suspended Animation," later in this chapter.

✔ Another option for shutting down a computer is to log in as a different user. This item appears in the Shut Down Windows dialog box in Windows 95 and as a separate menu item on the Start menu in Windows 98. Choose that option if you're one of several people using the same PC and you want to keep Mr. Computer on for someone else to use.

✔ Never turn off a computer when you're in the middle of something! Always quit your programs and then shut down Windows properly. The only time you can safely turn off your PC is when the screen tells you that it's *safe* to do so. An exception is when your computer has gone totally AWOL. When that happens, refer to Part VI of this book.

✔ If you're familiar with DOS (where you could shut down the computer at any time), be wary of seeing that friendly C:\> on the screen and thinking, "Golly, it's okay to shut down the computer now." Not so with Windows! You must first *quit* DOS, which you do by typing the EXIT command:

```
C> EXIT
```

This command makes your DOS prompt vanish, and, lo, you're back in Windows.

✔ It's a good idea to wait at least 10 to 20 seconds before turning the computer on again. That gives the computer's hard drives time to slow down and stop. (Basically, it's just a bad idea to flip the PC's power switch rapidly from On to Off to On again.)

Turn offs

Q: You state in your book not to turn the computer off but leave it on all the time. I don't have a fancy PC that sleeps, so does it really matter if I turn it off — after Windows says so, that is.

A: If you're going to be away from the computer for more than two days, turn it off. Otherwise,

you don't really need to shut down. I leave mine on all the time, mostly because I think computers take too long to start. But if you've gone through the trouble of shutting the system down, feel free to turn it off. Or press the reset button or the Ctrl+Alt+Delete key combination to restart.

"I Want to Leave My Computer Off All the Time"

Hey, I'm with you.

"I Want to Leave My Computer On All the Time"

The great debate rages: Should you leave your computer on all the time? Anyone who knows anything will tell you, "Yes." Leave your computer on all the time, 24 hours a day, 7 days a week, and 14 days a week on the planet Mars. The only time you should turn a system off is when it will be unused for longer than a weekend.

Computers like being on all the time. You leave your refrigerator on all night or when you're away on trips, so why not your PC? It doesn't increase your electrical bill much, either.

Whatever you do with your PC, it's always a good idea to turn its monitor off when you're away. Some monitors can *sleep* just like PCs, but if they don't, turning them off can save some electricity.

✔ A screen-dimming program *(screen saver)* can *blank out* the monitor after your PC has been idle a specific length of time. Screen savers are located in the Control Panel. From the Start menu, choose <u>S</u>ettings➪ <u>C</u>ontrol Panel and then double-click the Display icon with the mouse. Click the Screen Saver tab and do whatever is necessary there, which I don't have time to explain here. See Chapter 12.

✔ If you do leave your computer on all the time, don't put it under a dust cover. The dust cover gives the computer its very own greenhouse effect and brings the temperatures inside the system way past the sweltering point, like in a sweaty Southern courtroom drama.

What about turning off the monitor?

Q: You recommend leaving the computer on rather than turning it on and off frequently. So I have a dumb question; do you mean for only the computer to stay on? Should the monitor be turned off? I was turning my machine on and off several times daily.

A: Leave your PC on, and you'll get started quickly "several times daily." Turn the monitor off when you leave your desk or just use a screen saver. (See Chapter 12 for screen saver information.)

Placing Your PC in Suspended Animation

This is a trick I no longer recommend, primarily because I've gotten too many complaints about it not working properly. First, however, the general idea.

As an alternative to leaving your PC on all the time, you may consider giving it a coma instead. It isn't anything evil, and your PC doesn't have an out-of-body experience while it's down. Instead, you just tell your PC to take a nap. The computer shuts off power to the screen and disk drives, but maintains enough juice to remember what it was doing last.

When you wake the computer up, either by pressing a key on the keyboard or jiggling the mouse, all systems return to full power, and the computer is instantly on (though it was never really off).

The reason I don't recommend this approach any more is that many PCs enter an eternal slumber from which they cannot be wakened. Jiggling the mouse or pressing any key (or pounding the keyboard on the desktop) does not wake the PC up. Instead you have to reset, which is a rather dreadful act.

Why do the PCs stay in a coma? I don't know. But I've had it happen to me a few times, and I've received enough e-mail about it to not recommend the full coma approach. Even so, the following sections elaborate.

Why not just sleep the monitor?

Instead of putting the whole PC to sleep, suspending the monitor seems to be a worthy alternative. In this mode, the PC simply stops sending a signal to the monitor, which shuts it off and saves power after a period of inactivity.

To configure your monitor this way, follow these steps:

1. **Open the Control Panel.**

   From the Start menu, choose Settings⇨Control Panel.

   This action displays the Control Panel window, which contains various icons for controlling every tid and bit of your computer.

2. **Open the Power Management icon.**

   This action displays the Power Management Properties dialog box, as shown in Figure 2-6.

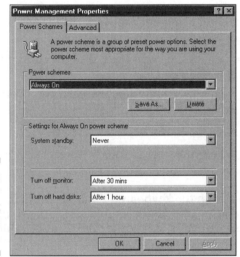

Figure 2-6:
The Power
Management
Properties
dialog box.

3. **Select a time for shutting down the monitor.**

   Locate the Turn Off Monitor item near the bottom of the dialog box. Next to it is a drop-down list displaying various time periods. Select one. After that time period (30 minutes in Figure 2-6), the monitor automatically shuts down.

4. **Click OK to close the Power Management Properties dialog box.**

5. **Close the Control Panel.**

Now your PC's monitor will sleep after a given period of inactivity.

This setting does not turn the monitor off. (On a few PCs it will, but on most it does not.) Instead, it merely stops displaying an image. You still need to push the monitor's on-off button to turn it off.

Sleeping the whole PC (if you dare!)

If you really want to suspend your PC, putting it to sleep instead of turning it off, follow these steps. Remember, I do not recommend this.

1. Pop up the Start menu.

Click the Start button on the taskbar or press the Ctrl+Esc key combination.

2a. Choose the Suspend menu item.

This item appears in Windows 95. Click it with the mouse or press the N key because this is the *N*.

In Windows 98, the Suspend menu item appears in the Shut Down Windows dialog box as `Stand By`.

2b. Choose the Shut Down menu item and then click Stand By in the Shut Down Windows dialog box. Click OK.

If you don't see either command, you cannot suspend your PC (only some newer models can).

3. Watch as your PC sleeps.

Fwoot! (The sound you hear may vary.) Your PC looks like it has just switched off, but it's not off. It's almost better than off.

To revive your PC, press a key on the keyboard (Enter or the spacebar are my choices) or jiggle the mouse. That action should revive the thing. If not, then your PC has entered sleep-death, and you'll need to reset, which I cover in the next section.

✔ You don't have to save your work before you use the Suspend command — although it's still a good idea to always save your work whenever you're leaving your PC.

✔ To reanimate your computer, you merely touch a key or move the mouse. Everything snaps back to the way it was.

✔ On a laptop, you enter suspend mode by closing the lid with the power on, or activating a keyboard command, or choosing the proper command from the Start menu.

✔ Some desktop PCs have a sleep button on the console, which lets you suspend the computer instantly. The button typically has a moon icon on it or nearby. Press the button again to wake it back up.

Resetting Your PC

Resetting your computer is a way to turn it off and on again without having to actually click the on/off button twice (and it's healthier for the PC than kicking the power cord from the wall, despite the satisfying feeling you get). When you *reset,* you're restarting the computer while it's on.

You can reset in three ways, two of which I don't recommend, as I explain in a minute. The third technique, which I recommend, is covered in the next section.

The first not-recommended way: If your computer has a reset switch, you can push it. Ka-chinka! The computer stops whatever it's doing (or not doing) and starts all over again.

The second not-recommended way: Press the Ctrl, Alt, and Delete keys at the same time. You have to do it twice in a row in Windows because Windows doesn't like for you to press Ctrl+Alt+Delete, the reasons for which I get into in the following section.

- ✔ Ctrl+Alt+Delete is known as the three-finger salute, or Control-Alt-Delete.

- ✔ Ctrl+Alt+Delete is also called the *Vulcan nerve pinch* because your fingers are arched in a manner similar to Mr. Spock's when he rendered the bad guys unconscious.

- ✔ A reset is often called a *warm boot.* It's like a cold boot that has been sitting in front of the furnace all night.

- ✔ As when you turn a computer off, you shouldn't reset while the disk drive light is on or while you're using an application (except when the program has flown south). Above all, do not reset to quit an application. Always quit your programs properly and wait until Windows tells you that it's safe, before you turn off your computer.

- ✔ Remember to remove any floppy disks from drive A before resetting. If you leave a disk in there, the computer tries to start itself from that disk.

The proper way to reset in Windows

If you can, you should reset using the Shut Down Windows dialog box (refer to Figure 2-5). Follow the steps to shut down as you normally would but select Restart from the dialog box instead of Shut Down.

If you cannot get to the Shut Down Windows dialog box — and, by golly, you've made every effort in the world — then you have to press your PC's reset button. Dink! That's almost the same as turning off the power and starting over, but not as time-consuming.

✔ Resetting should be a last resort. Only if you cannot, no way, uh-uh, no how, kaput, cannot use the computer should you even consider it.

✔ In Windows 95, the command to reset may be shown as `Restart the computer` instead of just `Restart`.

✔ If your PC lacks a reset button (Hello, IBM!), you have to turn off the power switch. Wait. Then turn the system back on again.

✔ Any time you reset and start the computer again, Windows warns you that the system was not properly shutdown. See the section "My computer was shut down improperly?" near the start of this chapter.

Pressing Ctrl+Alt+Delete in Windows

Hey DOS users! Windows won't let you press Ctrl+Alt+Delete to reset. The reason is probably that it's a bad idea to reset in the middle of something — and Windows is always in the middle of something. So rather than use a reset command, Windows uses Ctrl+Alt+Delete to kill off programs that run amok.

If you press Ctrl+Alt+Delete in Windows, you see a Close Program dialog box, like the one shown in Figure 2-7. Because it's best not to mess with this dialog box, click the Cancel button or press the Esc key.

Figure 2-7:
The
Windows
Close
Program
dialog box.

✔ Don't press Ctrl+Alt+Delete in Windows unless you want to kill off a program. If you want to kill off a program, see the section in Chapter 30 about killing off a program run amok.

✔ In the old version of Windows (before Windows 95), Ctrl+Alt+Delete also killed off a program, but only the program you were using. This process was confusing for everyone, which is a good reason not to use Ctrl+Alt+Delete in the older version of Windows.

Part II
Using Your PC

The 5th Wave — By Rich Tennant

DANGER
HIGH VOLTAGE
POWER LINES

"Hurry, Stuart!! Hurry!! The screen's starting to flicker out!!"

In this part . . .

In a way, a computer can be like the sweet and annoying little kid who says, "I've got a secret." The computer knows something and, like the dear little tot, it's not going to tell you exactly what the secret is. After a while, the game becomes frustrating. You *know* the information is in there, and you know the computer (or the little kid) should freely be able to tell you. But what sorts of dances must you spin to get the information out?

The key to using your PC is using software — primarily the computer's operating system. Granted, it's not obvious. Whereas microwave ovens have a Popcorn button and TVs have a nifty pad for changing channels, the computer offers no clues. Fortunately, you have the chapters in this part of the book. They're designed to familiarize you with using your PC and show you how to get something done. Pain is minimal. Information is top notch. Entertainment is by the way.

Chapter 3

Your PC's Operating System

*A*re operating systems necessary? Being curious, I had to know. So the first thing I did when I got my old DOS computer was type ERASE DOS, just to see what would happen.

Nothing happened. Well, I got a File not found error. Luckily for me, DOS didn't get erased.

Windows, like DOS, is an operating system. It's necessary to run your computer. It's the software that controls everything — all the hardware and all the other software you use. To use your PC, you need to know your operating system.

✔ Your primary duty with Windows is to tell it to run your software. I cover this task in Chapter 4.

✔ As a secondary duty, you use Windows to manage the many files and documents you create. That's another aspect of an operating system: organizing all your computer junk and storing it properly on the hard drive. Chapter 6 covers this subject.

✔ Your tertiary (meaning *third*) duty in Windows is to run your computer. It's the geeky aspect, the thing that drives too many people over the edge. I might cover it in this book. Might not. I haven't made up my mind.

Windows, Your PC's Real Brain

The main program in charge of your PC is Windows. Ideally (which means that it could never happen in real life), a computer's operating system should be quiet and efficient, never getting in the way and carrying out your instructions like a dutiful and grateful servant.

In reality, Windows is far from being dutiful or grateful. It's the kid who has the only baseball, making you play the game by rules he invents as he goes along. Windows is like the hustler who lures you into a game of pool or poker, neither of which you play well. Yes, Windows is in charge, by golly. And you must play the game by Windows' rules simply because Windows rules.

Oh well. To get started (and to eventually dominate Windows), you should know three basic parts of the operating system: the desktop, the taskbar, and the Start button.

"Where is the desktop?"

Windows is a graphical operating system. It uses graphical images, or *icons,* to represent everything inside your computer. These graphics are all pasted on a background called the *desktop.* Figure 3-1 shows the desktop with the famous Windows clouds background.

You control everything by using your computer's mouse. The mouse controls the pointer on the desktop, which looks like an arrow-shaped UFO in Figure 3-1. You use the mouse and its pointer to point at things, grab them, drag them around, punch 'em, scratch 'em till they bleed, and other mouse-y things like that.

Oh, you can also use the keyboard, although graphical operating systems such as Windows love mice more than they love keyboards.

- ✔ The *desktop* is merely the background on which Windows shows you its stuff — like an old sheet you hang from the wall to bore your neighbors with your Cayman Islands vacation slide show.

- ✔ The little pictures are called *icons.*

- ✔ Doesn't look much like a real desktop, does it? That's because Windows is based on the Macintosh, which is based on the ancient Lisa computer. On the Lisa, the desktop *really did* look like a desktop, with paper, a clock, glue, scissors, and other desktop-y things. We've come a long way. . . .

- ✔ Figure 3-1 shows what Windows *may* look like. On your computer, it looks different (probably because your computer doesn't like you).

✔ Refer to the end of Chapter 13 for more information about using a mouse, including all those mouse activities and their associated terms.

✔ I cover using your keyboard somewhat in Chapter 14.

Control things with the taskbar

The desktop is kind of an ethereal, lost-in-space sort of thing. Or, put another way, with your icons in the clouds, how can you get down to earth and actually *do something* with the computer?

The answer is the taskbar. It's that gunboat-gray strip along the bottom of the desktop. The taskbar serves as the Windows control center.

On the left end of the taskbar is the Start button, as shown in Figure 3-2. Yes, the Start button is where you start programs in Windows. You can also shut down Windows by using the Start button. Start. Stop. Microsoft can't make up its mind.

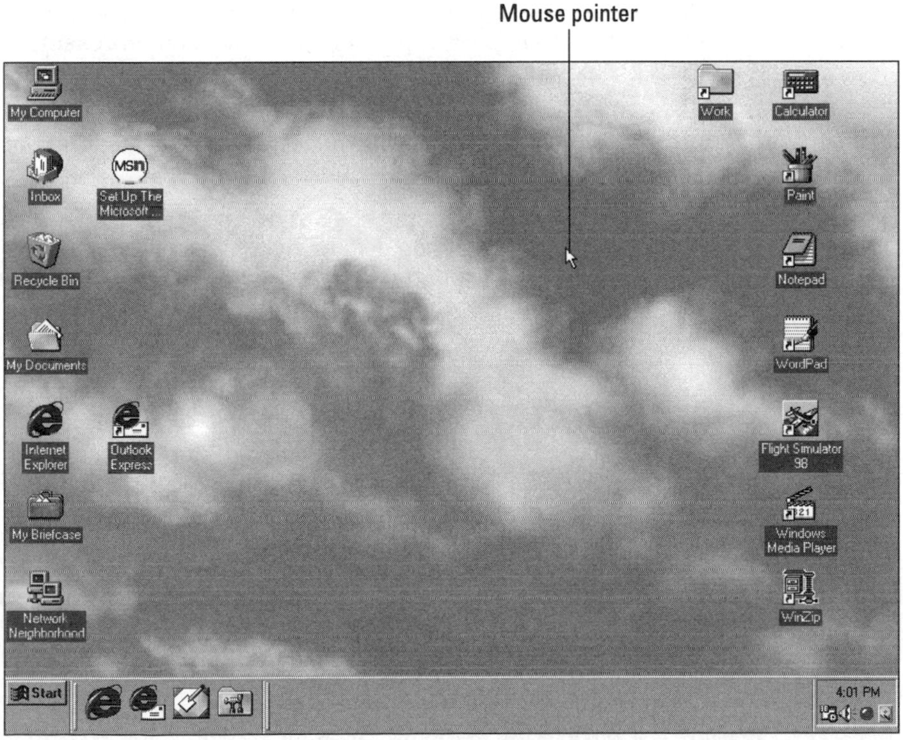

Mouse pointer

Figure 3-1:
The
Windows
desktop.

Start button   Quick Launch bar   Window buttons   System tray

Figure 3-2:
The taskbar.

On the right end of the taskbar is the *system tray*. I like to call it the *loud time* because it typically looks like a speaker shouting out the time of day. Other items may show up on the system tray, depending on the various little programs you have running in your PC.

The Quick Launch bar is the part of the taskbar that contains buttons to quickly start various programs. Figure 3-2 shows buttons for Internet Explorer, Outlook Express, Word, Excel, and others. Clicking one of these buttons starts the associated program (one of several ways to start programs in Windows).

Finally, the taskbar can contain buttons representing open windows or applications on the screen. Figure 3-2 shows a button for the My Computer window.

- ✔ To see what the system tray's various little icons represent, just point the mouse at one. Hovering the mouse over an icon eventually causes a little bubble to appear, explaining what the icon represents or does. For example, pointing at the time in the system tray displays the full date.

- ✔ If you don't have a sound system in your PC, the speaker doesn't show up. If you're computing on the international date line, the time doesn't show up either.

- ✔ The taskbar can float on any edge of the desktop; use your mouse to drag the taskbar to the top, left, or right sides of the screen. (Point the mouse at a blank part of the taskbar to drag it.) Most folks leave it on the bottom, which is where this book assumes that it lies.

The almighty Start button

Humans have a belly button; Windows has the Start button. The Start button is where everything starts in Windows. It's located on the left side of the taskbar, which isn't a navel-like center like your belly button, but it's handy.

Clicking the Start button with your mouse produces a heavy-duty pop-up menu on which you find various commands and programs and ways to control, manipulate, and fuss with Windows.

There. That's it for the Start button discussion in this chapter. For more information, see the section in Chapter 4 about starting a program in Windows.

"My taskbar is gone!"

The taskbar tends to wander. It can not only go up, down, left, and right, but also get fatter and skinnier. Sometimes it can get so skinny that you can't see it anymore. All you see is a thin, gray line at the bottom of the screen. That can drive you batty.

That thin, gray line is still the taskbar. It's just that someone has shrunk it to Lilliputian size. To make the line thicker, hover the mouse pointer over the taskbar's edge. The mouse pointer changes to a this-way-or-that-way arrow. Then drag the taskbar to a nicer, plumper size. You can even use this trick to make the taskbar fatter when it's crowded with too many buttons.

Another way the taskbar can disappear is if you tell it to hide. You perform this vanishing act in the Taskbar Properties dialog box: Right-click your mouse on the taskbar and select Properties from the pop-up shortcut menu. In the Taskbar Properties dialog box, make sure that the Auto Hide option doesn't have a check mark by it (click in the box next to Auto Hide to remove the check mark). Click the OK button to go on your merry way.

If you've really lost the taskbar, try this set of keystrokes: Press Ctrl+Esc, Alt+Enter, and S, and then press the up-arrow key a few times to see the taskbar. Press the Esc key when the taskbar is fully visible.

Remember: You can always get at the Start menu by pressing Ctrl+Esc. This keystroke works whether the taskbar is visible or has been sent by Houdini to some other realm.

- To pop up the Start menu, click its button by using your mouse. Click.

- If you would rather use your keyboard, press the Ctrl+Esc key combination. This action is guaranteed to work, popping up the Start button's menu even when you can't otherwise see the Start button.

- Some newfangled keyboards sport a Windows key (two of them, actually). The key cap has the Windows flag logo, and the key sits just outside the Alt key on either side of the spacebar. Pressing that key also raises the Start menu.

The My Computer and Explorer Programs

The second chore of an operating system is to work with the files, documents, and other junk stored on your computer. Two programs tackle this job: My Computer and Explorer.

My Computer is a more window-oriented approach to viewing files. The Explorer program is more of a disk tool, but with a lot of features from Internet Explorer blended in.

It's My Computer

My Computer has Macintosh written all over it. It's a program that displays information in your computer as pretty little icons, each of them grouped into folders.

You start My Computer by double-clicking the little My Computer icon in the upper-left corner of the desktop. This effort displays a list of goodies inside your computer, primarily your disk drives, as shown in Figure 3-3.

Figure 3-3: Open My Computer and see what lurks inside your PC.

If you double-click one of your system's disk drives, such as drive C, it opens to reveal a window full of folders and icons, as shown in Figure 3-4. The icons represent files on your system. You can open folders (by double-clicking) to display another window chock-full of more files and folders. It can get insane!

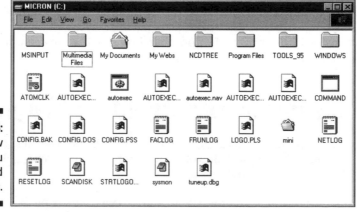

Figure 3-4: This window shows you files and folders.

- You double-click an icon to open it. Double-clicking some icons runs (opens) programs. For folders, the double-click opens the folder, revealing its contents.

- Icons represent files on your computer, which can be files you create, program files, or other files that sprout from certain fungi.

- Folders are simply storage places for more icons and files.

- See the section "Closing a window," later in this chapter, for information about closing windows opened in My Computer.

The disk Explorer

Explorer (which is called Windows Explorer, although I use the term *Explorer*) works just like My Computer, except that Explorer displays information in a different way. (Microsoft just couldn't make up its mind here: "Which way should we have people see files on their computers? Hey! Why not two utterly different and confusing ways?")

Start Explorer by clicking the Start button and choosing Programs⇨ Windows Explorer from the menu.

Unlike My Computer, Explorer has only one window, as shown in Figure 3-5. The disk drives and folders on your computer appear on the left side of the window; files and folders appear on the right.

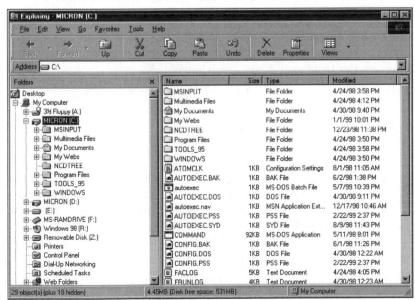

Figure 3-5: Explorer in action.

Okay. Enough of Explorer. Choose File⇨Close to quit the program because there's no sense in wasting screen real estate with something so ugly.

✔ Computer nerds prefer Explorer. I recommend using My Computer first, until you get used to it. Then use Explorer, which can be quicker.

✔ A quick way to start Explorer is to press the Windows and E keys together — like pressing Shift+E to get a capital E (for Explorer), but use the fancy Windows key rather than Shift.

✔ I discuss the My Computer and Explorer programs in more detail in the other chapters in Part II of this book.

✔ Windows sports another explorer, Internet Explorer. I cover it in Part V of this book.

Control Panic, er, Panel

Each of the icons in the Control Panel represents some aspect of your computer, something for Windows to control. By opening an icon, you see a window, or *dialog box,* with more information, more controls, more chaos. . . .

My advice: Leave this one to the experts.

Close the Control Panel window by choosing File⇨Close from the menu.

✔ Open an icon in the Control Panel by double-clicking it.

✔ I have no idea what most of the things in the Control Panel do. In fact, they frighten me.

✔ Various chapters in Part III of this book have you mess with parts of the Control Panel. Mostly, you leave it alone.

Windows Gizmos

Windows is a graphical candy store of fun things to play with, stuff to drive you crazy, and interesting toys over which you waste colossal amounts of time. It has tiny buttons you push with the mouse, graphics that slide and stretch, things to poke, and stuff that drops down. In other words, *gizmos* are on the screen, most of which control the way the windows look and how programs in Windows operate.

Changing a window's size

Your windows can be just about any size, from filling the entire screen to too small to be useful and everything in between.

To make a window fill the entire screen — which is where it's most useful — click the *Maximize* button in the window's upper-right corner. (When a window is maximized, the Maximize button changes to the *Restore* button, which is used to return the window to its demure size before maximizing.)

To turn a window into a mere button on the taskbar, click the *Minimize* button in the upper-right corner of the window. This action shoves the window out of the way, shrinking it to a button on the taskbar — but it isn't the same as quitting. To restore the taskbar button to a window, click the button.

When a window isn't maximized, you can change its size by grabbing an edge with the mouse: Hover the mouse over one side of the window or a corner, and drag the window in or out to a new size. Release the mouse button to snap the window into place.

✔ Enlarging a window to full-screen size is called *maximizing*.

✔ Shrinking a window into an icon is called *minimizing*.

✔ Positioning a window *just so* on the screen and then having Windows move it for no reason is called *frustrating*.

✔ If you use your imagination, the Maximize button looks like a full-screen window, and the Minimize button looks like a button on the taskbar. Then again, if you use your imagination, Windows looks like a bright, sunny day with green grass and birds chirping in the meadow.

Moving a window around

Windows puts its windows wherever Windows wants. To move a window to a new position, drag the window by its title bar (the topmost strip on the window, typically above the menu bar). This action is akin to the myth of a caveman dragging his woman around by her hair. That never really happened, of course, not after the women started carrying their own clubs, anyway.

✔ By the way, you cannot move a window around when it's maximized (filling the screen). Refer to the preceding section to find out how to maximize a window.

✔ By the way (Part 2), you cannot move Uncle Arny around when he's maximized after a holiday meal. It's the same concept Microsoft borrowed for maximized windows.

Scrolling about

Often, what you're looking at in a window is larger than the window. For example, imagine you're in a tall building, and King Kong is standing just outside. If you ride up in the elevator, and the elevator has a window, you see only a small bit of Kong at a time. That's kind of how scrolling in Windows works, but in Windows you're looking at a long document or large graphic on the screen and not some mass of black hair.

To facilitate scrolling a window around, you use one or two scroll bars. The *scroll bar* is a long, skinny thing, with an arrow at both ends and an elevator-like box in the middle like you see below. You use the arrows and elevator to move the window's image up and down or left and right, revealing more of the total picture.

Accessing a menu

All the commands and whatnot of the Windows application are included on a handy — and always visible — menu bar. It's usually at the top of a window, right below the title bar and down the street from Ed's Bar.

Each word on the menu bar — File and Edit, for example — is a menu title. Each title represents a drop-down menu, which contains commands related to the title. For example, the File menu contains Save, Open, New, Close, and other commands related to files, as shown in Figure 3-6.

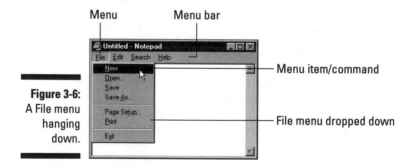

Figure 3-6:
A File menu hanging down.

To access these commands, click the menu title with the mouse. The menu drops down. Then choose a menu item or command. If you don't like what you see, click the menu title again to make the menu go away, or choose another menu.

🖙 You can access the menus with your keyboard, if you like. Press either the Alt or F10 key. This action highlights the first menu on the menu bar. To choose a menu or item on a menu, press the underlined letter, such as the F key for File. The letters to press are underlined in this book, just as they are in Windows.

🖙 In this book, I use the format File⇨Close to represent menu choices. To access that command on the menu, you press Alt, F, C.

🖙 To choose the File⇨Close command, you can also press Alt+F (the Alt and F keys together, and then release both keys) and then C.

🖙 Oh, bother. Just use your mouse. Point. Click. Click. Sheesh.

Closing a window

☒ Closing a program's window is the same as quitting the program; you make it disappear. The most common way to close a window is to click the X button in the upper-right corner of the window.

Another striking way to close a window — striking because it's obvious — is to choose the Exit or Close command from the File menu. This action also quits the program you're running.

You can't quit Windows by closing a window, which is how it worked in the old version of Windows. Instead, use the Shut Down command on the main Start menu. See Chapter 2 for more information.

Struggling with a Dialog Box

When it comes to making choices, Windows displays a specialized type of window called a *dialog box*. A dialog box contains gadgets and gizmos that you click, slide, and type in, all of which control something or set certain optional options. Clicking an OK button sends your choices off to Windows for proper digestion.

If all that sounds complicated, consider the old DOS-prompt way of doing things:

```
C> FORMAT A: /S /U /F:144 /V:FLIPPY
```

That's a real, honest-to-goodness DOS command. In Windows, a dialog box lets you do something similar but in a graphical way. Figure 3-7, in fact, shows you how the same command looks.

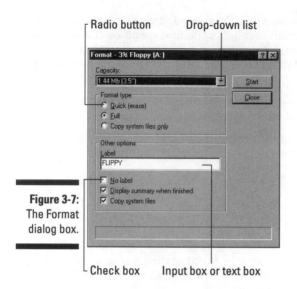

Radio button   Drop-down list

Check box   Input box or text box

Figure 3-7:
The Format
dialog box.

All the doojobbies shown in Figure 3-7 are manipulated with the mouse. What they do isn't important right now. What the doojobbies are called *is* important. All the following definitions refer to Figure 3-7:

Drop-down list: Under the word *Capacity* is a drop-down list. You drop down the list by clicking the down-pointing arrow button to the right of the list. This action displays a list of choices, one of which you point at and click with the mouse. If the list is long, it has a scroll bar to one side, which you can use to scroll up or down.

Radio button: The round buttons in a dialog box are radio buttons. They're grouped together into families, such as the three shown in Figure 3-7. Like in an old car radio, you can punch only one of the buttons at a time. To punch a button, click it once with the mouse. A round dot fills the one button that is *on*.

Input box or text box: Any box or area you can type in is an input box, also called a text box. In Figure 3-7, it's the box under the word *Label*.

Check box: The square buttons in a dialog box are check boxes. Unlike with radio buttons, you can click the mouse in as many or all of the check boxes as necessary. A check mark appears in the box if an option is on. To remove the check mark and turn the option off, click the mouse in the box again.

After you've made your selections, you typically click an OK button. (In Figure 3-7, the OK button is called Start.) If you don't like your choices, click Close.

To get help, click the question mark button in the dialog box's upper-right corner. This action changes the mouse pointer into the combination arrow-pointer and question-mark thing. When that happens, point and click any part of the dialog box to see a pop-up cartoon bubble supposedly offering help. Click the mouse to make the cartoon bubble go away.

- ✔ Pressing the Enter key in a dialog box is usually the same as clicking the OK button with your mouse.

- ✔ Pressing the Esc (escape) key on your keyboard is the same as clicking the Cancel button in a dialog box.

- ✔ You can press the F1 key to get help with whichever part of the dialog box you're messing with.

- ✔ Some dialog boxes feature an *Apply* button. It works like an OK button, except that it enables you to see your changes without closing the dialog box. If you like the changes, you can then click OK. Or, if the changes stink, you can reset them or click the Cancel button. See? Microsoft is being nice here. Make a note of it on your calendar.

- ✔ If more than one input box appears in a dialog box, press the Tab key to move between them. Don't press the Enter key because that's the same as clicking the OK button and telling Windows that you're done with the dialog box.

- ✔ Another type of list, similar to the drop-down list and not shown in Figure 3-7, is a *scrolling list*. It works the same as the drop-down list, except that the list is always visible inside the dialog box.

- ✔ If you like a mental challenge, you can use your keyboard to work a dialog box. Look for the underlined letter in each part of the dialog box (such as *p* in Capacity in Figure 3-7). Pressing the Alt key plus that key is the same as choosing that command with a mouse.

Squeezing Windows for Help

Help in Windows is always handy. And though it makes no sense, the F1 key is the key you press for help. F1. F one needs help? Find help first? F'wonder where the help key is? Oh, I give up. . . .

When you press F1, you activate the Windows Help system, as shown in Figure 3-8. This key works for both Windows itself as well as various programs you'll use. The Help system lets you look up topics, search for topics, or see related items, all by properly using your mouse.

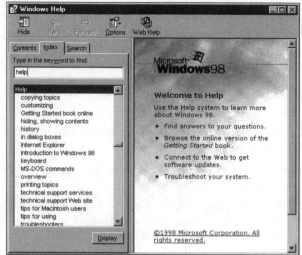

Figure 3-8:
The
Windows 98
Help
system.

The help engine is divided into three panels, as shown in Figure 3-8: Contents, Index, and Search (or Find in Windows 95). Here are some hints:

✔ The Contents panel shows you information just like the yechy manual, with chapters and pages and text written by Ph.D.'s for Ph.D.'s.

✔ The Index panel is the most useful. Click the word Index to see that panel, and then type your topic, such as **Shortcut**, in the box at the top of the panel. In the bottom part of the panel, click a subtopic and then click the Display button to read all about it.

✔ Ignore the Search panel.

✔ Some programs, such as those that come with Microsoft Office, employ a different Help system. It works similarly but looks different on the screen. You still use the F1 key to activate it.

✔ Most of the helpful information is displayed as a list of steps or tips.

✔ You can click the underlined text to see more information about related topics.

✔ To get general Windows help, choose Help from the main Start menu.

✔ You can click green underlined text (with a dotted underline) to see a pop-up window defining the term.

The help engine is its own program. When you're done using help, remember to quit: Click the X close button in the upper-left corner of the window.

Error message mayhem

Q: You wouldn't happen to have a book somewhere like *"Messages your computer sends to you in the dialog boxes that are nowhere in any book" For Dummies* do you?

A: Alas, no. Way back in the early '90s, Microsoft came out with DOS Version 5. It had so many error messages that Microsoft published a book full of them, explaining what each one meant. (A whole book!) Microsoft got mixed reviews.

Some people chastised the company for having so many error messages, many of which were repetitive and most of which didn't make any sense. On the other hand, Microsoft was being nice in letting everyone have a reference. Whether due to the criticism or not, Microsoft dropped the published error list for DOS 6 and for all versions of Windows. We just have to suffer. Sorry!

Soothing Windows Words of Advice

Use your mouse. If you don't have a mouse, you can still use Windows — but not as elegantly. Ack, who am I kidding? You need a mouse to use Windows!

Have someone organize your Start menu items for you. Ask this person to put your most popular programs on the desktop as *shortcut icons*. Offer a bag of Doritos or a vat of peanut butter as a bribe.

Keep in mind that Windows can run several programs at the same time. You don't have to quit one program to start another. You can switch between the programs by clicking the buttons on the taskbar or using the Alt+Tab keyboard shortcut.

Always quit Windows properly. Never just turn your PC off or punch the reset button. Review the steps in Chapter 2 for properly shutting down Windows if you've forgotten how.

Chapter 4

Getting Your Work Done

• •

In This Chapter

▶ Starting a program

▶ Making your program's window fill the screen

▶ Switching programs

▶ Cutting, copying, and pasting

▶ Using common Windows program commands

▶ Quitting your program

• •

*E*ver notice that people in soap operas don't really do any work? Sure, they all have jobs. You may even see them "at work." But no one is ever productive — there is no idle conversation between Phyllis and Ernestine as they stitch together basketball sneakers. Instead, you just see idle people meeting and not really working. Talking. Whispering. Gossiping. No work, though. They say, "Steve might have an evil twin," and not, "That better not be a personal call!" or "Since James is out of prison Eva is leaving the convent," and not, "If you've got time to lean, you've got time to clean." No, they just aren't productive in soap operas.

Because you don't live in a soap opera, you need to get work done. While soap opera–type activities may come and go, your basic function most of the day is to produce something and get work done. That's the job of software, which this chapter helps to explain.

Starting a Program in Windows

Windows is like a structure, a building. The building isn't anything until you fill it with businesses and people to meet. Spinning your wheels in Windows is not working. But starting software in Windows is the first step to working. Here are the rest of the steps:

1. **Pop up the Start menu.**

   Click the mouse on the taskbar's Start button. Up pops the menu. Pressing the Ctrl+Esc key combination does the same thing.

2. **Choose Programs.**

   Click the word Programs, and you see the slippery Programs submenu appear, such as the one shown in Figure 4-1.

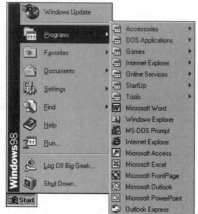

Figure 4-1:
The
Programs
submenu.

3. **Pluck out your program from those listed on the submenu.**

   For example, in Figure 4-1 you would point and click the words *Microsoft Word* to start that program.

   If your program doesn't appear on the list, try one of the other sub-menus listed; Accessories, Internet Explorer, Games, and others contain even more programs. Yes, and you even see sub-sub-submenus (and on and on) with even more programs.

   You gots programs comin' outta yer ears!

4. **Your program starts; the Start menu goes away.**

   ✔ At times, the program you want to start may appear right on top of the main Start menu. If so, point and click, and the program starts up.

   ✔ The menus are rather slippery. They pop up and disappear as your mouse roves over them. So be careful! It can be aggravating if you're a sloppy mouse mover or your mouse is too sensitive.

   ✔ Refrain from beating your mouse into your table when it behaves erratically.

✔ Quickly start any recently worked-on stuff by using the Documents sub-menu: Pop up the Start menu and click Documents. Look for your document on the list. If it's there, click it to start it. If it's not there, you can take the day off and watch your favorite soap.

Starting your program from an icon on the desktop

A quick way to start a program without playing slip-and-slide with the Start menu is to find the program's icon floating on the desktop. This method works for any icon on the desktop, whether it represents a program or a file you created.

Find the shortcut item you want and then open it by double-clicking its icon with the mouse.

Placing a shortcut icon on the desktop

To place an icon of your favorite program on the desktop, fire up the Explorer or My Computer program. Locate your program in its proper folder or wherever it's stashed. (You can refer to the section in Chapter 7 about finding wayward files and programs if you need help.)

After you find the program, use the _right_ mouse button to drag its icon from the Explorer or My Computer window out to the desktop. Figure 4-2 shows what this process may look like, though you can't see my finger on the right mouse button in the figure (but it's there!).

After you release the right button (pointing at the desktop), a pop-up short-cut menu appears, just like the one shown in Figure 4-2. Select the item Create Shortcut(s) Here. Lo, the shortcut is created on the desktop, available for easy access.

Remember to use the right mouse button to drag the icon and create a short-cut. The right button is not the button you normally press.

Using the Quick Launch bar

Windows 98 sports many, many toolbars you can slap down on top of the taskbar. Although most of them are a joke, one that's really handy is the Quick Launch bar.

Program icon

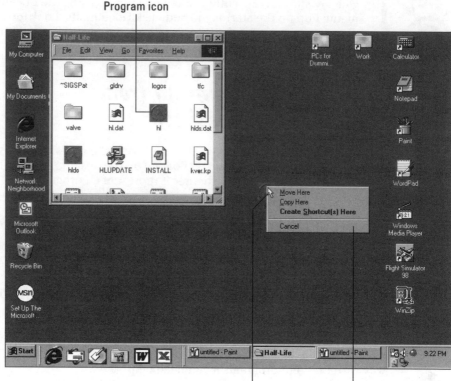

Right dragged to here   Pop-up menu

Figure 4-2:
Right-
dragging
an icon to
the desktop
to create a
shortcut.

To display the Quick Launch bar, right-click on the taskbar and choose
Toolbars⇨Quick Launch from the pop-up menu.

You can add new icons to the Quick Launch bar by dragging them there from
a My Computer window or from Windows Explorer — similar to the way you
drag icons to the desktop, as I describe in the preceding section.

The beauty of the Quick Launch bar is that the icons that appear there need
only one click to start. So put all your very, very most favorite programs on
the Quick Launch bar for easy access.

✔ Windows 95 does not have a Quick Launch bar unless you upgrade to
  Internet Explorer 4.0 (or later).

✔ To see the Quick Launch bar displayed with large icons, right-click on
  the Quick Launch bar (on the left side, where the vertical bar is) and
  choose View⇨Large from the pop-up menu.

✔ Try to put only a handful of icons on the Quick Launch bar. The way I see it, *everything* should be on the Start menu, but only the programs you use all the time should have a spot on the Quick Launch bar. On my PC, I put only four icons there. Well, five since I did the Excel book.

Maximizing Your Work

This section has nothing to do with self-help, nor will a tall, charismatic man with big teeth come out to empower you. Instead, you may find it useful to maximize your program's window after it starts. Some programs start in full-screen mode right off. Other programs start as only a measly window on the screen. Blech! Who needs that?

To make your program's window fill the screen — and get every dollar per pixel you paid for on that monitor — click the window's Maximize button (the middle button in the upper-right corner, or the image shown in the margin).

✔ Some windows can't be maximized. Some games, for example, have a fixed window size you can't change. Don't be greedy.

✔ If you have a humongous monitor, you may opt to run your programs without switching them to full screen.

✔ If you have two monitors on your PC (and this is crazy, but possible), then know that maximizing a window fills it to only one screen.

✔ If you're working with several programs, you may want to arrange their windows on-screen so that each is visible. To do that, right-click on the mouse on a blank part of the taskbar or right-click on the time (on the right side of the taskbar). From the menu that pops up, select either Tile Horizontally or Tile Vertically to arrange your windows on-screen.

Multitasking

In Windows, you can run several programs at one time, doing several things at the same time, all without any knowledge of juggling or balancing skills. This is known as *multitasking*.

Multitasking is something the computer does. It can run a copy of Word, a copy of Excel, and have Internet Explorer online and viewing a live picture of the I-5/805 exchange in Sorrento Valley, California, all at the same time. Why bother? Well, the idea is primarily that you don't have to sit and wait for things.

For example, you could be running a monster sort in Microsoft Access, and while the computer is busy doing that, you can catch up on your e-mail. Or you can be viewing two different Web pages at a time. Or you can be playing a game and then quickly switch back to your word processor when your supervisor wanders by.

- ✔ Running several programs at once is called multitasking.

- ✔ Of course, you can only *use* one program at a time, so you spend most of your time switching between programs, which I cover in the next section.

- ✔ The program you're currently working on — the *active window* — is in the *foreground*. The other programs, those that are running but on which you're not actively working, are said to be in the *background*.

- ✔ Windows can multitask several programs at once. The limitation is the amount of memory (RAM) in your PC. If your PC starts to run slowly (with lots of hard disk crunching sounds), then you've probably exceeded the limits of multitasking. Better quit some programs to *free up* memory.

- ✔ The idea behind multitasking is that you don't have to quit one program to start another. Especially if you're working between two programs, you just keep switching back and forth and not quitting and restarting every few minutes.

Switching between Programs

Granted, the computer is capable of doing several things at once, but you as a human (and I assume you are) are capable of doing only one thing at a time. So what you end up doing is switching between the several running programs, as opposed to attempting to work on them all at once — which is next to impossible, even for the multi-headed and thousand-tentacle beings of the Planet Bromaxum.

To switch to another program, you have several options:

The quick way: The quickest way to switch programs is to grab the mouse and click in another program's window, as long as that window is visible. Clicking in a window brings that window to the top of the pile.

The quick way if you can't see the window: Look for a button on the taskbar corresponding to the window you want. Click that button. Thwooop! The window stands before you, eager to please.

 The shove-aside way: Minimize the current window, shrinking it to a button on the taskbar. This action doesn't quit the program; it just shoves it aside, enabling you to access whatever other windows lie behind it. You accomplish the minimization process by clicking the Minimize button in the upper-right corner of the window (see the image in the margin).

Non-mouse-y ways: If you run out of mouse methods for switching programs, try one of the two keyboard methods. They're hard to remember, although I'm fond of the Alt+Tab key combination approach.

- ✔ **Alt+Tab:** Press and hold the Alt and then tap the Tab key. This action summons a little picture box in the center of the screen that displays icons for your windows and programs. Keep holding down the Alt key and tap the Tab key until the icon representing your program or window is in the box. Then release the Alt key.

- ✔ **Alt+Esc:** Press (and hold) the Alt key and then tap the Esc key. Release both keys. This action switches you to the next program you have active (in the order in which you use the programs). You may have to press Alt+Esc a few times to find the program or window you want.

- ✔ To switch to another window, click it.

- ✔ You can use two key combinations to switch to another window or program: Alt+Esc or Alt+Tab.

Minimizing a window by clicking the Minimize button in the upper-right corner of the window does not quit that application. Instead, the program shrinks to icon size at the bottom of the screen. Double-click that icon if you want to access the program's window.

General Commands for All Reasons

Windows programs all do things in similar ways. This is one of the supposed advantages of Windows: Learn one program, and you won't have trouble learning the rest. And that claim is somewhat true, but not true enough that Microsoft still boasts about it on the box.

One of the ways Windows makes all programs similar is in the common commands they share. These commands also include the Cut, Copy, and Paste commands, which allow you to share information between two or more dissimilar programs. Ah, yes, more productivity boosting, thanks to Chairman Bill and the merry Microsoft minions.

Copy

To copy something in Windows, select it with the mouse: Drag the mouse over some text, or click a picture or an icon with the mouse, or drag the mouse around the object. This action highlights the text, picture, or icon, which means that it has been *selected* and is ready for copying.

After selecting the whatever, choose Edit⇨Copy. This step puts a copy of the whatever into the secret Windows storage place, the *Clipboard,* from whence it can be pasted (see the "Paste" section, later in this chapter).

The quick-key shortcut for this step is Ctrl+C. That's easy to remember because *C* means copy.

✔ After you copy your text or picture, you can paste it into the same program or switch to another program for pasting.

✔ When you copy something, Windows puts in into the Clipboard. Unfortunately, the Clipboard holds only one thing at a time. Whenever you copy or cut, the new item replaces whatever was already in the Clipboard. (Such a Clipboard doesn't seem very handy, but Microsoft would like me to remind you here of all the time you're saving in Windows.)

✔ The programs in the Microsoft Office 2000 suite have a multiple pasting capability called Collect and Paste. You can cut or copy several things in a row and then paste them into other applications selectively or one at a time. Other programs may also use this feature.

Cut

Cutting something in Windows is just like copying: You select a picture or some text or an icon, and then choose the Edit⇨Cut menu command. Unlike with Copy, however, the picture or text you cut is copied to the Clipboard and then deleted from your application.

The quick-key shortcut for this trick is Ctrl+X. You can remember it because when you cut something, you "X it out." (I know, I'm pushing it here, but the Ctrl+C key combination is already taken.)

Paste

You use the Paste command to take text, a picture, or an icon stored in the Clipboard, and slap it down into the current application. You can paste a picture into text or text into a picture, and icons can go just about anywhere. Ah, the miracle of Windows.

To paste, choose the Edit⇨Paste command. Or you can press Ctrl+V, the Paste key combination, from the keyboard. The *V* must stand for vwapp! or voom! or vomica or something.

- ✔ You can paste text or a picture from the Clipboard back into the current application, or you can switch to another application for pasting.

- ✔ You can paste material cut or copied from any Windows application into another Windows application.

- ✔ You cannot paste graphics into a program that cannot accept graphics. Likewise, you cannot paste text into a program that works only with graphics. When this happens, you'll try to Paste, but the command won't work (or the menu will appear *dimmed*). Oh well.

- ✔ You may be wondering, "Why didn't they just make Ctrl+P the Paste shortcut key?" Alas, Ctrl+P is the Print command's shortcut key.

Undo

The powers at Microsoft have graced sloppy Windows users (meaning all of us) with the blessed Undo command. This command undoes whatever silly thing you just did.

To undo, choose Edit⇨Undo from the menu. Undo just happens to be the first item on the list. How convenient. The key command is Ctrl+Z; the Z means, "Zap that mistake back to Seattle!"

- ✔ Undo undoes just about anything you can do: unchange edits, replace cut graphics, and fix up a bad marriage, for example.

- ✔ If you look at your keyboard (and you shouldn't, if you're a touch-typist), you see that the Z, X, C, and V keys are all together on the left side of the bottom row, as shown in Figure 4-3. Hey! These are the common Windows shortcut keys, which may explain why the letters don't make much sense.

Figure 4-3:
The Undo,
Cut, Copy,
and Paste
keys on your
keyboard.

Save

After you've etched your brilliance into silicon and the phosphor on the screen glows warmly in your eyes, you need to save your work to disk. Not only does the computer keep your stuff nice and tidy on disk, but you can also open it up later to work on it again.

You save a file by choosing File⇨Save. This step summons the Save dialog box, which you then use to save your work to disk. (Chapter 6 officially presents the Save dialog box.)

The Save shortcut key is the logical Ctrl+S key combination.

✔ Always save your work. I save my stuff every five minutes or so.

✔ Save! Save! Save! Remember that.

✔ Jesus saves.

✔ The first time you save something to disk, you must give it a name and tell Windows where to put it (which you can read about in Chapter 6, so don't think that I'm being crude here). After that, you just use the Save command to continue to save the file to disk; you don't have to give it a name again. Just save!

✔ A variation of the Save command is Save As. This command works like Save, although it allows you to give the file a new name when you save it. Choosing a new name keeps the original version intact.

Open

After something has been saved on disk, you retrieve it with the Open command. This command lets you find your stuff on disk and open it up like a present on your birthday. Your stuff then appears in the program's window, ready for you to do something with it.

To open something on disk, choose the File⇨Open command or use the handy Ctrl+O keyboard shortcut. This command displays the Open dialog box, where you use the various controls and whatnots to grab your file from disk.

Chapter 6 covers the Open dialog box in morbid detail.

Print

The Print command takes your lovely work that you see on-screen and causes something similar-looking to spew forth from the printer.

To print, choose the File⇨Print command. It displays the Print dialog box, which has a bunch of hocus-pocus in it, so you usually click the OK button, and your something then prints. The keyboard shortcut for the Print command is Ctrl+P. Easy 'nuff.

✔ Make sure that the printer is on, has paper, and is ready to print before you try to print something.

✔ Chapter 15 covers the details of printing something.

Quit (or Exit or Close)

When you're done working, quit your program and wander off to do something else. This command is perhaps the best one of any Windows program.

To quit, choose the File⇨Exit command. Alas, some programs may not have a File menu, let alone an Exit command. If so, the last command (at the bottom) of the first menu typically does the trick.

The keyboard combination to quit any Windows program, and to close any window, is bizarre: Alt+F4. It's just too strange to think up anything clever to say about it.

✔ If your application doesn't have a File⇨Exit command, you can quit by clicking the program window's X button in the upper-right corner.

✔ Sometimes the command is File⇨Close.

✔ You don't have to quit. If you're working on something and want to put it aside for later, you can minimize the program. See the section "Switching between Programs" earlier in this chapter, for the details.

Literacy lore

Q: Can you tell me which books cover the subject of computer literacy? Is anything available on CDs?

A: Well, what type of computer literacy are you talking about? The broad definition is "to be able to use an ATM machine," though many narrow it down to "programming a computer." So it depends on how you define it.

Remember, *computer literacy* was an advertising slogan originally. It was designed to scare parents into buying expensive toy computers for their kids. It still exists as a buzzword, though specific books on the subject just aren't written.

If you just want to know more about computers, then any introductory book on computers (such as this one) should get you started. From there, take off on whatever interests you. Operating a computer is easy, but if you want to know more (hardware, software, programming, and so on), then you have to buy specific books or take courses at a community college. That's what I'd recommend.

Chapter 5

Know Your Disk Drives

● ●

In This Chapter

▶ Finding disk drives on your PC

▶ Disk drives and drive letters

▶ Understanding all about CD-ROM and DVD drives

▶ Ejecting a CD

▶ Playing a music CD or video

▶ All about floppy disks

▶ Formatting floppy disks

▶ Discovering Zip drives

● ●

*A*nother one of Windows many jobs is to manage all the information you store in your computer. All those pictures of your sister's cat she e-mails you; the catalog of what your baseball card collection would be worth today had you not thrown it out in a fit of rage when you were 14; the four-dozen attempts you've made at starting a novel; and the notes you took when you phoned the Psychic Stock Market Pal Network. You have to put it all somewhere.

Your PC most likely has at least three types of disk drives, possibly more. You use them for storing stuff. They store the operating system, programs, and all the many wonderful things you create on your PC. This chapter tells you how to work with those disk drives in Windows. Chapter 6 continues the discussion, and Chapter 10 covers disk drives from a purely hardware point of view.

✔ The term disk drive and disk are often used interchangeably. Storing something *on disk* means to save it to a disk drive somewhere in your computer system.

✔ Watch out for the ugly term *disk memory*. While technically correct, it's confusing. Memory (or RAM) is where your computer does the work. The disk is where your work is stored. Disk memory is just another term for disk or storage on a disk drive, but it's confusing to many beginners. So when you see *disk memory* just think *disk drive*.

Why Use Disk Drives?

So why bother having disk drives? I mean, the computer has memory (RAM), right? Many PCs are sold with 32, 64, or more megabytes of RAM. That seems to be enough memory. Why bother with disk storage?

The reason is that disks are for long-term storage. They're storage in addition to the memory (RAM) inside your computer. That memory, which is often called *temporary memory,* is used when you're running a program and creating something. The computer *works* in RAM.

When you're done creating, you can *save* your work by making a permanent copy on a disk drive. That's long-term storage, also called permanent storage.

Computer memory (RAM) is temporary storage because RAM is erased each time you turn the computer's power off. But if you save your stuff to disk, it's there the next time you turn your computer back on.

- ✔ A *megabyte* is a million bytes, or enough storage space to hold 1 million characters, 1,000 pages of information, or several hundred graphics files. It's a lot of space.

- ✔ You use disks to store information long-term. You can then open the information, or *files,* later for another peek, to reedit, to show to friends, or just because.

- ✔ Chapter 11 discusses computer memory, or RAM.

- ✔ Like memory (RAM), disk storage is measured in bytes, mostly *megabytes* and *gigabytes.* See Chapter 11 for more information about what these terms measure.

- ✔ Your computer can't use the information directly on a disk. Instead, it copies the information to memory (RAM). From there, the computer can manipulate the data, send it to the printer, or occasionally lose it. Because the computer is working only with a copy of the data, the original data is still safe on the disk.

- ✔ Saving information to disk (making a permanent copy) is called *saving* or *saving a file* or even *saving a document.* When you use that file again, you *open* it. These are common Windows terms you'll get used to in no time.

- ✔ Never worry whether the file on disk is larger than your PC's memory. For example, you can view a 12GB (billion byte) movie on a PC with only 48MB of RAM. Now that would seem like squeezing a 6,000-pound elephant into a pair of nylons, but it's not an impossible task for the PC! Amazing devices, those computers.

Finding Your Disk Drives

Windows keeps a representation of all your PC's disk drives in one handy place: the My Computer window.

Open the My Computer icon on the desktop. (Click the icon twice with the mouse.) The window that appears lists all the disk drives in your computer system, similar to what's shown in Figure 5-1.

Figure 5-1:
Disk drives shown in the My Computer window.

The various types of disk drives are covered in Chapter 10. Specifically, you should be able to locate the following disk drives in the My Computer window:

3½ Floppy (A:)

Drive A. This is your PC's first floppy disk.

[C:]

Drive C. This is your PC's main hard disk drive. Your computer may also have a hard drive D and possibly even a hard drive E. If so, they'll have the same icon (shown in the margin).

[R:]

CD-ROM drive. On most PCs, this is the CD-ROM or DVD drive. It usually has the letter following the last hard drive, which is drive D on most PCs. Even if it's another letter on your PC, it has the same icon. In Figure 5-1, the DVD drive is shown as drive R. (Both DVD and CD-ROM drives have the same icon.)

Zip 100 [Z:]

Other drives. Other drives may exist in your system, such as the Zip drive (drive Z) in Figure 5-1.

Here are the answers to some questions you may have about this disk drive madness:

- Each disk drive has an icon, a letter, and an optional name.

- The icon tells you which type of disk drive it is: hard disk, floppy disk, CD-ROM/DVD. Icons even exist for removable disks, 5¼-inch floppy disks, RAM drives, network drives, and other interesting storage devices.

- Yes: CD-ROM, DVD, CD-R, and CD-RW drives all use the same CD-ROM drive icon. (Read more about these types of disk drives in Chapter 10.)

- The disk's optional name can be changed. For example, the manufacturer placed the name MICRON in Figure 5-1.

- The following section explains more about drive letters.

- The little hand-holding drives C and D in Figure 5-1 indicate that those drives are being shared on a computer network. (You'll have to visit another Dummies book for networking information. I can recommend Doug Lowe's *Networking For Dummies,* published by IDG Books Worldwide, Inc.)

- Any drives you see with pipes beneath them (shown in the margin) are disk drives on network computers. You access these disk drives like other drives on your PC, though they exist on other computers elsewhere on the network. (The subject of networking disk drives is beyond the scope of this book, though seeing and using the drives works as described here.)

- The various folders in the My Computer window represent other interesting things Windows controls. If you point the mouse button at the folder and hold the mouse still, a pop-up description of the folder appears.

- The Web Folders icon (shown in Figure 5-1) is not a disk drive, but rather a shortcut to a folder on the hard drive where Web pages are stored. It's boring, really.

Drive letters from A (skipping B) to Z

In Windows, disk drives are known by their letters, from A (skipping B), C, D, and on up to Z. These letters are how the drives are known to Windows and your software.

Drives A and C are special. Drive A in all PCs is the first floppy drive. Drive C in all PCs is the first hard drive.

Drive B is reserved for the *second* floppy drive. Back in the early days, when hard drives were outrageously expensive, most PCs were sold without hard disks. The second floppy drive served as a cheap form of extra storage. Today you don't need it, though letter B is set aside just in case.

After drive C, drive letters are up in the air! For instance, no hard and fast rule exists that says drive D *must* be the CD-ROM drive. Don't ever expect computers to make that much sense.

If you have any extra hard drives in your PC, then they're given drive letters D on up. Figure 5-1 shows *three* hard drives: C, D, and E. Newer PCs may have only one hard drive C. But if you add a second hard drive, it becomes drive D. In the disk-drive pecking order, the hard drive always gets first dibs on the next available drive letter.

After the last hard drive letter comes your CD-ROM or DVD drive. This could be drive D or E or anything on up to Z.

Other disk drives in the system are given other letters after the CD-ROM drive.

What does all this naming stuff mean? It means you can never count on anything being identical from PC to PC. This is why software instructions may say: "Insert the CD into your CD-ROM drive, which may be drive D or drive E or even drive *n* where *n* is the letter of your CD-ROM drive." Sheesh.

✔ If you do add a second floppy drive to your PC, it becomes drive B. I can think of no sensible reason to add a second floppy drive, however.

✔ People pronounce *A:* as "A-colon," as in:

Alex Trebek: People use this to digest food.

You: A colon.

Alex: I'm sorry, you must phrase that response in the form of a question.

✔ Don't neglect your hard drive D (or E or F)! It offers more storage for your stuff. There's nothing wrong with installing software or saving your stuff to another hard drive.

✔ On my computers, I typically install games on drive D. I have no reason for it, other than it forces me to use drive D. (And drive D usually sits empty on most people's PCs.)

✔ Fill in this book's Cheat Sheet with the names and locations of your computer's disk drives and their letters. If you have a label maker, label your removable drives: Put *A* on drive A, *E* (or whatever) on your CD-ROM drive, and *F* (or whatever) on your Zip drive (if you have one), and so on.

✔ Knowing your system's disk drives helps with some software installation programs. For example, they may ask you to type your CD-ROM drive's letter.

✔ You can change the letters for removable drives in your system. I
changed my drive letters; in Figure 5-1 you see that the DVD drive is
letter R, and the Zip drive is letter Z. The steps to change the letters are
complicated, though I list them on this book's companion Web page.
Visit the following address:

```
www.wambooli.com/PCs_for_Dummies/Chapter.5/
```

✔ Don't always depend on a PC's CD-ROM drive to have the same drive
letter on every computer!

How much space is left on the disk drive?

Like closets and attics, disk drives fill up. To see how much space is available
on a disk, follow these steps:

1. **Open the My Computer window.**

   Follow the steps at the start of this chapter in "Finding Your Disk Drives."

2. **Right-click on a disk drive.**

   Select a disk drive by clicking it once with the mouse using the right
   mouse button. A pop-up menu appears.

   If you select a floppy disk, CD-ROM, or any removable disk, ensure that a
   disk is in the drive before continuing.

3. **Select Properties.**

   The disk's Properties dialog box appears, which lists — right there in
   the General tab — the amount of space used and free for that disk.
   Figure 5-2 shows something similar to what you see on your screen.

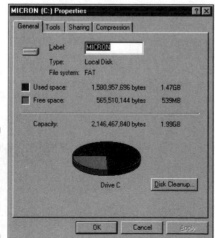

Figure 5-2:
Information
found in
a disk's
Properties
dialog box.

4. **Gawk.**

   Either squirm with excitement over all the space you have yet to fill, or gasp in desperation as you see the disk fill up!

5. **Click OK to close the disk's Properties dialog box.**

Some disks, such as CD-ROMs and DVDs, are always full! That's because these disks can only be read from, not written to.

If your disk looks full (which means only a small purple slice of the pie is left), click the Disk Cleanup button (Windows 98 only). This button is one quick way to eliminate a lot of repetitive and useless files on your hard drive.

In Windows 98, you can preview the disk size by choosing View⊏>As Web Page from the menu. You may need to re-size the window to see the disk's size-pie-thing on the left side. This method is quicker than choosing the Properties command, as described in the preceding steps; it lets you click any disk drive to see its used/free ratio instantly. Figure 5-3 illustrates how things should look.

Figure 5-3:
Previewing
disk size
using the
Web view.

Using the CD-ROM/DVD Drive

CD-ROM drives eat special CD-ROM discs, which I call CDs, or computer CDs. The computer CDs look exactly like music CDs, although they store megabytes and megabytes of computer information. The CD-ROM drive can access that information, making it available to you just like it was on a hard disk or floppy. Oh and it can play music CDs as well.

A DVD drive (also called a DVD-ROM drive by those who have more time to type than I do) looks and acts just like a CD-ROM drive. But in addition to reading computer CDs and music CDs, the DVD drive can access computer DVD and video DVD disks.

- ✔ The *RO* in CD-ROM means Read-Only. You can only read information from a CD-ROM disc. You cannot add new information to the disc or erase or change information already on the disc.

- ✔ Ditto for DVD disks: You can only read from them. You cannot record new information on a DVD disk.

- ✔ Special CD-ROM and DVD drives are available, which allow you to create your own CDs or DVDs. Chapter 10 covers these devices.

Inserting a computer CD into a CD-ROM drive

Computer CDs go into CD-ROM drives in one of three ways: slide-in, tray, or caddy. DVD drives use either the slide-in or tray method. Only older CD-ROM drives use the caddy method.

Slide in. The first way (my favorite) is just to slide the CD into the CD-ROM drive, similar to the way some car CD players work. Pushing the CD into the slot causes some gremlin inside the drive to eventually grab the CD and suck it in all the way. Amazing.

Tray. The second way to put a CD in the drive is by setting it into a sliding tray that pops out of the CD-ROM drive like a little kid sticking out his tongue. Press the CD-ROM drive's eject button to pop out the tray (often called a *drink holder* in many computer jokes). Drop the CD into the tray, label up. Gently nudge the tray back into the computer. The tray should slide back in the rest of the way on its own.

Caddy. The third way to slip a computer CD into a CD-ROM drive — my least favorite way — is to use the *caddy* or container. The disc goes into the container label up, so you can see the label through the container's clear cover. Close the container and then shove it into the drive. I'm not a fan of this type of drive because putting the CD-ROM in the caddy is an extra step that I'd rather not do.

When the disc is in the drive, you use it just like any other disk in your computer.

✔ If you have the caddy type of CD-ROM drive, it behooves you to go out and buy a whole bunch of extra caddies. That way, you can keep all your CD-ROM discs in their own caddies, which saves you time when you need to swap them in the CD-ROM drive.

✔ If you don't have the caddy-type of CD-ROM drive, you might want to go out and buy some extra *jewel cases* in which to store your computer CDs; unfortunately computer CDs do not come in jewel cases for the most part. To keep them safe, It's best to store them in jewel cases.

✔ Many DVDs are double-sided. For example, the TV version of a movie may be on one side, and the wide-screen or letterbox version on the other. Make sure you put the proper side in, label up, when you use the disk.

Ejecting a CD or DVD disk

Follow these steps to eject a computer CD from the CD-ROM or DVD drive:

1. **Locate the CD-ROM drive icon by using the My Computer program.**

   Open the My Computer icon on the Windows desktop by double-clicking it with the mouse. A window appears showing you all the disk drives in your computer, plus a few token folders.

(R:)

2. **Point the mouse at the CD-ROM drive icon.**

   A sample of what the icon looks like appears in the margin.

3. **Click the mouse's right button.**

   This step displays the shortcut menu for the CD-ROM drive, as shown in Figure 5-4.

Figure 5-4:
A CD-ROM
drive's
shortcut
menu.

4. **Select Eject from the menu.**

   Point at the word *Eject* with your mouse and click.

   The disc spits from the CD-ROM drive.

✔ These steps also work for most types of removable disks — but not floppy disks.

✔ If your floppy disk is a Super Disk, then this trick works. In fact, it's the only way to get the disk out of the floppy drive.

✔ Oh, and you can always eject a CD by pushing the manual eject button on the CD-ROM drive. Note that some model CD-ROM drives require you to press two buttons simultaneously to eject.

Playing a music CD

To play a music CD in your computer's CD-ROM or DVD drive, just stick the disk into the drive. In a few seconds, the Windows Media Player (or a custom CD player) appears, as shown in Figure 5-5, and the music plays.

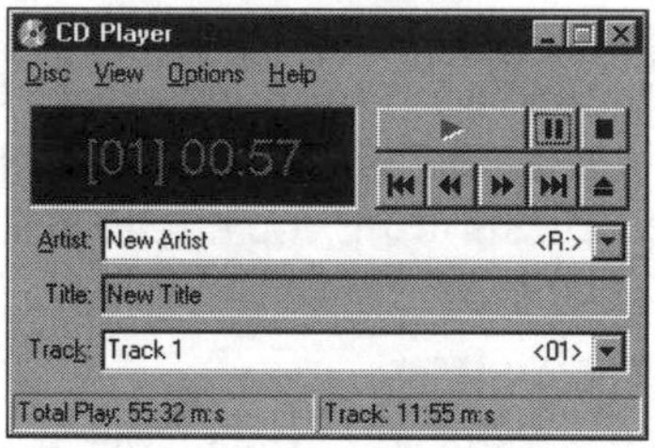

Figure 5-5:
The CD
Player.

Buttons on the Media Player (or your custom CD player) mimic those found on common CD players, such as Play, Stop, Pause, and Skip Track. An eject button allows you to switch discs.

Note that some CD players start automatically as a button on the taskbar. You need to click that button to adjust the CD.

Audio CD (R:)

When you put a music CD into your CD-ROM drive, the CD icon in the My Computer window changes to a musical CD icon, shown in the margin.

Playing a video

Viewing a DVD movie on your PC is as easy as listening to a CD: Just put the DVD movie into your PC's DVD drive. The movie player software should start up at that point and play the movie.

Various controls on the movie player software let you manipulate the movie the same way you manipulate a movie played on your VCR. However, with DVD movies, you have the options for separate audio tracks and subtitles.

(I'd show you a picture of Windows' DVD Player program, but it doesn't recognize my DVD drive. Also, due to copyright restrictions, it's impossible for me to take a screen shot of a movie playing. Oh well.)

Using the Floppy Drive

The most important thing to remember about using your floppy drive is to put a formatted floppy disk into it before you do anything. Floppy drives need floppy disks the way CD-ROM drives need CDs. (However, you can both read and write to floppy disks.)

"Are floppy drives really necessary?"

Back in 1981, when the PC made its debut, the question was "Are hard drives really necessary?" After all, floppy disks gave you 180K of storage — more than enough for anyone! DOS came on a single floppy disk, with room to spare. Hard drives? Don't kid around. . . .

Today, floppy drives stick around not only because of tradition but also because they're handy. Lots of programs still come on floppy disks. Driver files for new hardware that you may add to your PC often come on floppy disks. And you can use floppy disks to move files between two computers. (Not large files, but most files.)

Beyond a few instances, however, you probably won't use your floppy drive much. Even the chore of backing up your files, one of the key reasons for having a floppy drive, is now done by tape drives and other devices. Oh well. Still, there are some floppy issues to discuss.

In and out goes the floppy disk

Floppy disks are flat, 3½-inch square coasters on which you can store about 1.5MB of information. To use the floppy disk, you must insert it into your PC's floppy drive.

Be careful not to insert the floppy disk into the Zip drive slot. The Zip drive slot is larger than the floppy drive slot. If you have both, be sure you put floppies in the floppy drive.

Stick the floppy disk into the drive label up, with the shiny metal piece going in first. The disk should make a satisfying *thunk* noise when it's in place.

To remove the floppy disk, push the button beneath and slightly to the right-of-center of the floppy drive slot. This action ejects the disk out of the drive about an inch or so (depending on how vigorously you push the button). Grab the disk and put it away.

Always make sure the computer is not writing to the floppy disk before you eject it. The floppy drive's blinking access light should be off. Also, make sure you're not currently using any files on the floppy drive; before you eject the disk, close any files you may have accessed. If you don't, Windows asks you to reinsert the floppy disk so that it can finish writing information.

Formatting floppies

All floppy disks must be formatted. Unless you were smart enough to buy preformatted floppy disks, you have to format them at some point. A disk must be formatted before you can use it.

If the disk isn't formatted and you try to access it, Windows spits up an ugly error message, similar to the one shown in Figure 5-6. If this message appears, click the Yes button and get ready for formatting.

Figure 5-6:
The
nefarious
"disk is un-
formatted"
error
message.

1. **Stick an unformatted disk in drive A.**

   You can stick a new disk or an old disk into the drive. If you use an old disk, be aware that formatting erases *everything* on the disk. This is a devastating act. Be careful.

2. **Open the My Computer icon.**

Double-click the My Computer icon, sitting all by itself in the upper-left corner of the desktop.

This step displays a list of disk drives in your computer, plus some odd-ball folders (refer to Figure 5-1).

3. Select drive A.

Point the mouse at drive A's icon and click once. This step highlights that disk drive, selecting it for action.

4. Choose File⇨Format.

The Format dialog box appears, as shown in Figure 5-7.

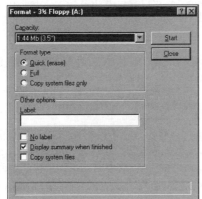

Figure 5-7:
The Format
dialog box.

5. Click the Start button.

Ignore those dialog box options! Point at the Start button and click the mouse.

The formatting process takes a minute or longer, so count the holes in the ceiling tiles for a while. When Windows finishes formatting . . . nothing happens. Well, you may see a summary screen. Press Esc to close the dialog box, and you're ready to use the disk.

✔ The floppy drives in the My Computer window have little floppy disks on their shoulders.

✔ If your PC sports a B floppy drive, you can format the disks in it by using the same steps just described.

✔ Magneto-optical (MO) drives are formatted using the same steps as I just described.

✔ After the disk is formatted, slap a label on it. You can use one of the sticky labels that came with the disk. Be sure to write on the label *before* you slap it on the disk.

✔ Don't use sticky notes as disk labels. They fall off when you're not looking and can sometimes get stuck inside your disk drives.

Sending a file to drive A

You access drive A just like any other disk in your PC: After inserting a floppy disk, just open the drive A icon in the Windows Explorer or My Computer window, or access it from any Save As or Open dialog box. Files on drive A exist just like files on any other disk, though drive A doesn't have a lot of room for storing stuff.

A quick way to send a file to drive A is to use the Send To⇨Drive A shortcut. Find and select the file (or group of files) you want to copy to drive A. Then choose File⇨Send To⇨3½ Floppy (A) from the menu. Don't forget to put a formatted floppy disk in drive A before you choose this command!

✔ The typical floppy disk stores 1.44MB of information. Those disks get full fast! And if you try to copy too many files or a file that's too large, Windows tells you with the appropriate insulting error message.

✔ To copy files *from* drive A, double-click the My Computer icon on the desktop and then double-click the drive A icon in the My Computer window. Then drag or select and copy the files you want to put somewhere else. See Chapter 7 for more information on copying files from one place to another.

✔ Floppy disks are great for storage and transportation. Please do not run your programs from them, nor should you save your work directly to the floppy disk. Instead, work on the hard drive and only copy files to the floppy disk as a safety measure.

Floppy foibles

Q: This error message appears anytime I try to do anything with my floppy disk, save or retrieve: `A:/ is not accessible the device is not ready. Retry. Cancel.` Any ideas?

A: A floppy disk must be in the drive before you can access the drive. Further, the floppy disk must be formatted. Also ensure the disk is *all the way* into the drive.

Using a Zip Drive

Zip drives are becoming popular alternatives and supplements to the traditional PC floppy disk. You can store 100MB or 250MB of information on a single Zip disk, depending on which Zip drive model you have. That's around 70 or 170 times the capacity of a junky old floppy disk.

- ✔ Zip drives come with many new PCs and are available as options to other PCs.

- ✔ You can add a Zip drive to your PC at any time. Some models are installed internally; others can be attached to your PC via a cable.

- ✔ 100MB Zip drives can read only 100MB disks. You must have a 250MB Zip drive to read the 250MB disks; these drives can also read the 100MB disks.

- ✔ Zip disks are a great way to move lots of information or massive files between two computers.

- ✔ Zip disks are expensive. Yowie! Buy them in bulk to get any deal on them. And make sure you buy the PC-formatted Zip disks, not the Macintosh Zip disks.

- ✔ No physical difference exists between Macintosh and PC Zip disks, but they are formatted differently. If you plan on taking your graphics files to a service bureau, make sure it can read PC Zip disks; most places can read only Macintosh Zip disks.

- ✔ The information in the following sections also applies to Jaz disks. Jaz is a 1GB or 2GB removable disk, available from Iomega, the same company that produces the Zip disks. Jaz drives don't come preinstalled as often as Zip disks, but Jaz drives can be added later. And the speed and large capacity of Jaz disks makes them ideal for backing up information or storing humongous files.

Inserting a Zip disk

Zip disks go into the drive just like floppy disks: label up, with the shiny metal part stuck in first.

Don't force the Zip disk in! If it doesn't fit, then you have the disk in the wrong orientation. Inserting the disk is especially frustrating if the disk drive is mounted sideways.

You must push the Zip disk all the way into the drive. After a certain point the disk becomes locked into place. Stop pushing at that point.

Only when the Zip disk is in the drive can you read or write information to it.

Ejecting a Zip disk

You can eject Zip disks using the menu (which I cover in the next section) or with the push button.

The push button is located beneath the slot in the Zip drive, to the right of center. Push the button once to eject the disk.

Looking at the Zip menu

Zip drives have their own special menu. After you insert a Zip disk into the drive, right-clicking on the Zip disk icon in the My Computer window displays a detailed menu with special Zip menu items, as shown in Figure 5-8.

Figure 5-8:
A Zip drive's
special
menu.

Note the special commands flagged by the *I* (for Iomega, Zip's manufacturer). These are Zip-drive-only commands. For example, the Format command is particular to Zip drives. Also notice the Eject command, which ejects a Zip disk automatically.

Chapter 6

Organizing Your Files

- -

In This Chapter

▶ Dealing with hard drive organization

▶ Understanding the folder

▶ Creating a folder

▶ Deleting folders

▶ Working the Open dialog box

▶ Working the Save As dialog box

- -

*T*he ancient Greek seer Tiresias was both blessed and cursed. He was blessed in that he knew the future. He was cursed in that whenever he told someone the future, they wouldn't believe him. Such is the life of a mystic. Gurus around the world utter truths every day. Yet sometimes the answers are so simple that no one believes them. So the madness goes on.

Here is your PC prophesy of the day: Computers can be much easier to deal with if you organize your files in *folders*. It's a very simple truth, but one few people pay attention to. This chapter tries to expand upon that wisdom nugget. Just read along, smile, and follow a few steps, and you too will soon enjoy the benefits of having an organized hard drive.

"Why Should I Bother Organizing Files on My Hard Drive?"

The truth is, you don't have to organize anything. Most people don't. They use their computers for months and never create or bother with a folder. But problems crop up quickly:

✔ Without folders, files just go anywhere. Although you may be able to find them, you probably won't.

✔ Different programs stick their files in different folders. Who knows where your stuff is?

✔ Ever pull your hair out trying to find a lost file? It's probably because you didn't care much about folders when you created and saved the file.

✔ With folders, you neatly tuck your files into areas with similar files. You can organize your stuff by project, by type of file, or however you see fit.

The true problem is that Windows, honestly, doesn't give a hoot whether you use folders. If you do, you'll be organized and always be able to find your stuff. If you don't, working on the computer takes longer, but everything still works.

Personally, I'd rather be organized and keep those clumps of hair that look *great* on my head.

Using Folders

A *folder* is a storage place for files in your computer's hard drive specifically. Folders keep files together — like barbed wire keeps prisoners, vicious animals, and kindergartners from wandering off.

Folders can hold, in addition to files, more folders. They're just another level of organization. For example, you can have a folder named Finances and in that folder have other folders, one for 1999, one for 2000, and on up until the year you die.

✔ Folders contain files, just like folders in a filing cabinet contain files. Golly, what an analogy.

✔ All files on disk go into various folders. When you save something in Windows, you're really placing it in a specific folder somewhere on your hard drive.

✔ The key is to put files into folders *you* create for specific purposes.

The root folder

Every disk — even a lousy floppy disk — has at least one folder. That one folder — the main folder — is called the *root folder*. Like a tree (and this isn't a dog joke), all other folders on your hard drive branch out from that main, root folder.

✔ The root folder is simply the main folder on the disk drive.

✔ Had computer scientists been into construction instead of growing trees, they might have called it the *foundation folder* instead of the root folder.

- ✔ The root folder does not have a cutesy icon associated with it.

- ✔ When you open a disk drive in My Computer or in Explorer, the files and folders you see are all stored in the root folder.

- ✔ The root folder may also be called the *root directory*. This term is merely a throwback to the old days of DOS (which is a throwback to the days of UNIX, which King Herod used).

The My Documents folder

My Documents

A special folder in Windows 98 is the My Documents folder. It's the place where you will save your document most of the time in Windows. Most of the applications in Windows and other programs attempt to save files first in the My Documents folder.

Having a My Documents folder is a blessing. Even though it's not required for you to save things, immediately you have a place just for your files.

- ✔ If you're using Windows 95, you may or may not have a My Documents folder. (You have it if you've installed Microsoft Office 95 or later.) If you don't have a My Documents folder, you can create it.

- ✔ All your new documents should be created in the My Documents folder.

- ✔ Yes, you'll be creating more folders inside the My Documents folder to keep things *organized*.

- ✔ In the United Kingdom, you'll keep things *organised* instead.

Viewing the tree structure

The whole mess of folders on your hard drive is organized into something the computer nerds call the *tree structure*. The folders all start at the root, branching out to more folders and folders, and eventually you end up with files, kind of like the leaves on a tree. There are no aphids in this simile.

The Windows Explorer program illustrates this tree structure thing. Start the Windows Explorer by choosing it from the Start menu, Programs⇨Windows Explorer. (You can also start the Windows Explorer by pressing the Windows key plus the E key on your keyboard: Win+E is how I would write that.)

Figure 6-1 shows the Explorer as Windows 98 shows it, which looks much like the Internet Explorer program. In Windows 95, the Explorer looks subtly different, although it still works the same. Choose View⇨Toolbar from the menu in Windows 95 Explorer to see the toolbar.

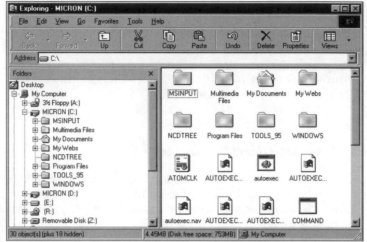

Figure 6-1:
Explorer in
action.

Adjust the size of the Explorer window, if necessary, to see all of the toolbar: Use the mouse to grab a corner of the window and drag the window out to a larger size.

The Explorer window is divided into two parts, or panels. On the left is the tree structure — the way your hard drive is organized from the desktop down to the lowliest folder. On the right are the contents of whatever you have highlighted on the left.

You can open part of the tree structure by clicking the plus (+) by a folder. This action displays a *branch* of the tree structure.

Click the minus (-) by a folder to close the branches of the tree structure.

 When you're done with Explorer, close its window by clicking its wee little X close button in the upper-right corner.

✔ If you don't see the Explorer toolbar, choose View➪Toolbars➪Standard Buttons. You may also want to choose Address Bar and Text Labels from the Toolbars submenu.

✔ What you're looking at in the right panel of the Explorer window is the contents of whatever is highlighted on the left. In Figure 6-1, you see the contents of drive C, the root folder.

✔ The Views button on the far right side of the Explorer toolbar in Windows 98 lets you see files and icons displayed in four different ways. If you have oodles of time to waste, click the button once to see a different view. Click again to see another view.

> ✔ Windows 95 has four buttons to the right of the Explorer toolbar. Clicking each button displays the files in a different view.
>
> ✔ President Ulysses Grant played the part of Desdemona in an 1865 all-soldier production of Shakespeare's *Othello.*

Creating a Folder

Creating a folder is easy. Deciding where to create it is the hard part. As an example, the following steps create a folder named Stuff in the My Documents folder on drive C:

1. Open the My Documents icon on the Windows desktop.

My Documents

Double-click the My Documents icon on the Windows desktop. This step opens a window detailing all the documents in your computer.

Note that this is the My Documents icon, not My Computer!

If you don't have a My Documents icon on the desktop (as is probably the case in Windows 95), do this instead: Open the My Computer icon, open drive C, and then open the My Documents folder.

If you don't have a My Documents folder, create one now! Open the My Computer icon and then open drive C. Right there — in the root folder — create the My Documents folder.

2. Choose File⇨New⇨Folder.

New Folder

This step places a new folder in the window, looking something like the icon in the margin. (The icon may look different, depending on which view you've chosen from the View menu.)

Ta-da! There's your new folder.

3. Give the folder a name other than the silly New Folder.

Type a new name for the folder. In fact, the folder is ready and willing to be renamed anything other than New Folder.

TIP

Be clever with the name! Remember that this folder will contain files and possibly other folders, all of which should relate somehow to the folder's name. If you can't think of anything useful for this tutorial, type the nondescript name **Stuff**.

Use the Backspace key to back up and erase if you make a mistake.

If you need additional information to complete this step, check out the sidebar "Type it where?"

See Chapter 7 for information about naming and renaming files. The same rules apply when you're naming or renaming a folder.

4. **Press Enter to lock in the name.**

See? Wasn't that easy? The new folder is ready and waiting for you to place new and interesting files into it.

Now the folder is ready for play. You can double-click the new folder's icon to open it. A blank window appears because it's a new folder and has no contents. Time to fill it up!

- You can create more folders or copy and paste files and folders into the new folder.

- You can always create a new folder and move files there. Go on an organizational frenzy!

- Chapter 7 covers copying and pasting files.

- Also see Chapter 7 for information on naming and renaming icons in Windows.

- If you've just created the Stuff folder and have no use for it, kill it off! See the section "Removing a Folder," just a few millimeters from this very spot.

Removing a Folder

Find the folder you want to trash by using either the Explorer or My Computer program. Drag that folder across the desktop and drop it on the Recycle Bin icon.

Fwoosh! It's gone.

Type it where?

Q: So here I am on Step 3 of creating a folder, and I can't seem to find the dialog box to type in a new name.

A: No dialog box, gentle reader. Just click any icon once to select it, file or folder. The icon becomes highlighted, turning a different color on the screen. Then press the F2 key to select the icon's name, and you can type in whatever name you like. When creating a new folder, you can name it only if you type *immediately* after creating it, as outlined in the steps nearby.

✔ Death to the folder!

✔ A warning box may appear, telling you that you're about to delete a folder and only bad people do that and are you sure you don't want to change your mind? Click Yes to trash it.

✔ If you can see the toolbar, you can click the Delete button to zap a selected folder.

✔ You can also use the Undo command to immediately undelete a folder. This command works only immediately after the folder is deleted, so be timely. Choose Edit⇨Undo Delete, press Ctrl+Z, or click the Undo button on the toolbar.

✔ Deleting a folder kills off everything in that folder — files, folders, and all the files and folders in those folders. Egads! It's mass carnage! Be careful with this one, lest you have to confess to some hard drive war-crimes tribunal.

✔ You can rescue anything Windows deletes. Chapter 7 covers this topic.

Using the Open Dialog Box

You'll often find yourself digging through folders when you use the Open command to fetch a file from disk. In most applications, choosing File⇨ Open summons an Open dialog box, which is a tool used to find the file. In Windows, all Open dialog boxes work the same, which I find a refreshing blessing.

Figure 6-2 shows a typical Open dialog box. Here is how you would work it to find a file for opening on disk:

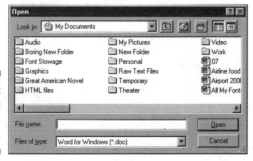

Figure 6-2:
The typical
Open dialog
box.

1. **Look for your file. If it's there, open it.**

   In the big list in the center of the dialog box is a buncha file icons. If you find your file there, double-click it to open it. That file then appears, ready for tweaking in your favorite program.

   You may need to use the scroll bar at the bottom of the list to see more files.

2. **If you can't find your file, look in another folder.**

   If you can't find your file, look for a folder in the big list. Double-click the folder to open it, and look in there for the file.

   Keep opening folders to find the one you want. (If your hard drive is organized and your folders cleverly named, it should be a snap.)

   If you find your file, open it!

3. **If you still can't find your file, switch disk drives.**

   Use the Look In drop-down list at the top of the dialog box. Click the down arrow to the right of the list to display it. Then pluck out a disk drive from the list, such as drive C, to start looking there.

   The contents of the big list in the center of the dialog box change to show you the files on drive C (in the *root folder*).

   If you find your file, open it!

    If you want to go back up to the preceding folder, click the handy Up One Level button (shown in the margin).

By opening a file, you're copying it from disk into the computer's memory, where you can work on the file. You can view it, edit it, modify it, print it — whatever. But you must open the file (or *document,* which sounds much more lofty) before you can do anything with it.

✔ At the bottom of the dialog box is a drop-down list titled Files of Type. It can help you narrow the types of files displayed in the Open dialog box's big list. For example, in Figure 6-2, only files of the Word for Windows (*.doc) type appear in the big list. Another option is All Files, which displays every type of file available.

✔ You find the Open command on the File menu: File⇨Open.

✔ You can also access the Open command by pressing the Ctrl+O key combination.

 ✔ And you can open things by clicking the Open button, which graces toolbars in most applications.

✔ Some Open dialog boxes are more complex than the one shown in Figure 6-2. For example, the Open dialog box in Microsoft Word is a doozy. It still works the same; it just has more annoying options to ignore.

✔ The Desktop button (fourth from the right in Figure 6 2) minimizes all open windows to display only the desktop. This button appears only with Windows 98; the button doesn't appear in the Open dialog box if you're using Windows 95.

✔ The Browse dialog box is similar to the Open dialog box. It appears whenever you click a Browse button to go hunt down a file for Windows.

✔ You can also open a file by clicking it once and then clicking the Open button. I find that if you're going to click it once, you may as well rapidly click it twice and forget the Open button.

✔ You can use the Files of Type drop-down list to narrow down the list of files displayed by the Open dialog box. In Figure 6-2, only Word for Windows (*.doc) files are displayed. Use the drop-down list to view other types of files in the Open dialog box. (Note that not every application can open or view every type of file.)

✔ If you're nerdy, you can type the file's full pathname (if you know it) in the File Name box. It's a very DOS-y thing to do. Cover your mouse's eyes if you try it (you don't want to shame him).

Using the Save As Dialog Box

The Save As dialog box is the most important dialog box you'll ever use in Windows. It's the key to organizing your files in a sane manner. You'll feel almost as nifty as those people who buy that California Closet organizer or the Wonder Purse.

You summon the Save As dialog box, shown in Figure 6-3, by using the File➪Save As command. (If you haven't yet saved your stuff to disk, then the File➪Save command also works.) Here's how you go about working it:

Figure 6-3:
The typical
Save As
dialog box.

Sneaky information about the Open and Save dialog boxes

Both the Open and Save dialog boxes display a list of files, just like the Explorer or My Computer windows. That's obvious. What often isn't obvious is that the list of files works exactly like the list of files displayed in the Explorer or My Computer windows.

For example, you can rename a folder or file displayed in an Open or Save As dialog box. You can right-click on a file and copy it or cut it. You can open a file by double-clicking it. Just about anything you can do with files in Windows can be done in that wee, tiny Open or Save As dialog box. This is a handy trick to use when organizing files.

1. **Most important: Make sure that you're in the proper folder.**

   See which folder the Save As dialog box wants to put your document in by checking the Save In drop-down list. In Figure 6-3, it says My Documents — that's the folder in which your document will be saved. If that folder isn't what you want, move on to Step 2.

   If the folder is okay, skip to Step 4 to give the file a descriptive name.

   In Windows 98, the Save As dialog box initially puts your document in the My Documents folder. That's fine, unless your PC doesn't have a My Documents folder or uses some other folder instead. If so, keep reading with Step 2.

2. **Hunt for the folder in which you want to save your stuff.**

   The best way to find a folder is to start at the root. To get to the root folder, you must select a hard drive from the Save In drop-down list (at the top of the dialog box.)

   Click the down arrow on the right side of the Save In drop-down list. You'll see a drop-down list of disk drives and other places in your PC. Select the proper disk drive from the list (such as drive C) to display that drive's root directory.

   Notice that the contents of the big list in the center of the dialog box change to show you the files in the root folder on drive C.

   I don't recommend saving your file in the root folder; that rule would have been the 14th Commandment had Moses not broken that tablet.

3. **Open a folder.**

   Locate the folder in which you want to save your stuff, or the folder that contains the folder (and so on). For example, open your Work folder or the My Documents folder.

   As you open various folders, the contents of the file list in the center of the dialog box change.

   When you find the folder you want — the perfect folder for your stuff — move on to the next step. Otherwise, keep opening folders.

 You can also click the New Folder button in the Save As dialog box to create a new folder. Name the folder and then open it to save your masterpiece right then and there.

4. **Type a name for the saved file.**

   In the File Name input box, type a name. It's the name for your saved file, the name you should be able to recognize later and say (out loud), "Say! That's my file. The one I want. I am so happy I saved it with a short, clever name that tells me exactly what's in the file. Oh, joy."

   See Chapter 7 for more information about naming files. Basically, you can name a file anything you want, although being brief and sticking to letters and numbers is best.

   If you give the file an unacceptable name, you can't save it. Windows is stubborn about filenames.

5. **Click the Save button.**

   Click! This last, official act saves the file to disk, with a proper name and in a proper folder.

   If the Save button appears to be broken, you probably typed an improper filename. Try giving the file a new name (refer to Step 4).

After you save your stuff once, you can use the File⇨Save command to resave your file to disk again. This command is a quick way to update the file on disk without having to work the Save As dialog box again.

If you want to save your file to disk in another spot, or give it a new name, or save it as another type of file, you need to use the Save As dialog box again. In that case, choose File⇨Save As from the menu.

The shortcut for saving a file is Ctrl+S.

 You can also use the Save button that appears on the toolbar in many applications.

As with the Open dialog box, some Save As dialog boxes are more complex than the one shown in Figure 6-3. The same business goes on; they just have more things to get in the way.

"What the heck is a pathname?"

A *pathname* pinpoints a file's location on a certain disk drive and in a certain folder. Long. Technical. Complex. It's a wonder that anyone has to deal with these things.

As an example, consider the file named Red Blocks.bmp. This file typically lives in the Windows folder on drive C. Therefore, its full, ugly pathname is

    C:\WINDOWS\RED BLOCKS.BMP

It reads this way: C: means drive C; WINDOWS is the Windows folder; RED BLOCKS.BMP is the filename; and backslashes are used to separate things.

A pathname can tell you right where the file is. Occasionally you find pathnames referenced in user manuals or in Windows itself. Suppose, for example, that you're told to go out and hunt down the file represented by this pathname:

    C:\MyDocuments\Personal\Letters
        \Family\Zack.doc

You look on drive C, open the My Documents folder, open the Personal folder, open Letters, open Family, and then look for the file named Zack.doc.

Chapter 7

Messin' with Files

· ·

· ·

*W*indows stores information on disk in the form of files. Whether it's a word-processing document, a picture, an e-mail message, or a doodle, it's really a file on disk. The Save command puts the file there. The Open command opens the file up for more editing or wanton whatnot. And to all the files on disk, you are their lord and master.

As file lord of your PC, it's your job to keep the lot of them in line and obedient. Windows gives you various tools to do that: the Copy command, the Cut command (for moving files), and the Rename command. Then you have tools for finding lost files, making you their gentle shepherd. And if a file gets out of line, you can rub it out of existence, sending it to its doom like a ruthless judge or gravel-voiced bad guy from a Saturday morning cartoon show. Such is the life of a file lord, which I describe thoroughly in this chapter.

✔ Windows displays files as icons. The *icon* is really the picture you see, representing the file on disk.

✔ Everything on disk is a *file*. Some files are *programs,* and some files are *documents* or stuff you create.

File-Naming Rules and Regulations

One thing mankind is good at is giving things names. Find a new bug, planet, beast, comet, or disease, and you get to name it. Files are the same way, but without the fame — or infamy if they name a new disease after you.

You name a file when saving the file to disk, which happens in the Save As dialog box (see Chapter 6). When naming a file, keep the following ideas in mind:

Be brief. The best filenames are brief yet descriptive, like in the following examples:

```
Stocks
Outline
Chapter 1
Itinerary
Sinister Plot
```

Technically you can give a file a name that's up to 255 characters long. Don't. Long filenames may be *very* descriptive, but Windows displays them funny or not at all in many situations. Better to keep things short than to take advantage of a long filename size.

Use only letters, numbers, and spaces. Filenames can contain just about any key you press on the keyboard. Even so, it's best to stick with letters, numbers, and spaces. (See the next section, "Don't name a file this way!" for the handful of characters you cannot use to name a file.)

Upper- and lowercase don't matter to a computer. Although capitalizing Finland is proper, for example, a computer matches that to finland, Finland, FINLAND, or any combination of upper- and lowercase letters.

- ✔ The file's name reminds you of what's in the file, of what it's all about (just like naming the dog Downstoppit tells everyone what the dog is all about).

- ✔ If you give a file too long of a name, it's easier to make a single typo and confuse Windows when you try to open the file.

- ✔ Another long filename snafu: The rows of files listed in the Open or Save dialog box get farther and farther apart if a long filename is in the list. Shorter filenames mean shorter columns in a list.

- ✔ Also, if you give a file a long, long name, only the first part of that long filename appears below the icon.

- ✔ All the rules for naming files in the following sections also apply to naming folders.

- ✔ See Chapter 6 for more information about the Open dialog box.

What the heck is a filename extension?

The last part of a filename is typically a period followed by one to three characters. Known as the *filename extension,* Windows uses it to identify the type of file. For example, a .BMP extension tags a Paint graphics image, and .DOC indicates a document created by WordPad or Microsoft Word.

You don't want to mess with these extensions when you name or rename a file, because Windows *needs* those filename extensions. If Windows doesn't have the filename extension (or has the wrong one), it screws up when you try to open the file for editing.

To avoid inadvertently changing a filename extension, follow these steps:

1. **Start Windows Explorer (Win+E) or open the My Computer icon on the desktop.**

2. **Choose View➪Folder Options.**

   This command displays the Folder Options dialog box.

3. **Make sure that the Hide Files Extensions for Known File Types check box has a check mark in it.**

   If it doesn't, click in the check box so that it does. This step effectively turns off the display of filename extensions so that they can't get goofed up.

4. **Click OK to exit the Folder Options dialog box.**

Don't name a file this way!

Windows gets mad if you use any of these characters to name a file:

```
* / : < > ? \ |
```

Each of the preceding symbols holds a special meaning to Windows (or DOS). Nothing bad happens if you attempt to use these characters; Windows just refuses to save the file or to change the file's name. (A warning dialog box may glow in your face if you make the attempt.)

Another point to ponder: Although you can use any number of periods in a filename, you cannot name a file with all periods. I know that it's strange, and I'm probably the only one on the planet to have tried it, but it still won't work.

Renaming a file

If you think that the name you just gave a file isn't exotic enough, you can easily change it:

1. **Locate the file.**

   Use the My Computer or Explorer program to find your program, or it may be stuck right on the desktop.

2. **Select the file.**

   When you find the file, click it once with the mouse. This step selects the file, highlighting it on-screen.

3. **Press the F2 key.**

   F2 is the shortcut key for the Rename command. You can also choose File➪Rename from the menu, though F2 is handier because your fingers need to be on the keyboard to type in the new name anyway.

4. **Type a new name.**

   Press the Backspace key to back up and erase if you need to.

   Notice that the text for the old name is selected. If you're familiar with using the Windows text-editing keys, you can use them to edit the old name. (See the section in Chapter 14 about common Windows editing keys for more information.)

5. **Press the Enter key.**

   Doing so locks in the new name.

Note that all files *must* have a name. If you don't give the file a name (you try to leave it blank), Windows complains. Other than that, here are some file-naming points to ponder:

- ✔ You can press the Esc key at any time before pressing Enter to undo the damage and return to the file's original name.

- ✔ Windows doesn't let you rename a file with the name of an existing file; no two files in the same folder can share the same name.

- ✔ You can't rename a group of files at the same time. Rename files one at a time.

- ✔ You can also rename a file by right-clicking its icon with the mouse and choosing Rename from the shortcut menu that appears. Or you can click the file's icon once and choose File➪Rename from the menu.

Files Hither, Thither, and Yon

Files just don't stand still. You always find yourself moving them, copying them, and killing them off. If you don't do that, your hard drive gets all junky, and out of embarrassment, you're forced to turn off the computer when friends come over.

You mess with files primarily in the My Computer or Explorer programs. My Computer is friendlier and makes more sense if you're just starting out. After a time, you may prefer Explorer because it doesn't litter the screen with windows, one for every folder.

Selecting one or more files

Before you can mess with any file, you must select it. Like log rolling, you can select files individually or in groups.

 To select a single file, locate its icon in My Computer or Explorer. Click that icon once with the mouse. This step selects the file, which appears highlighted (blue, possibly) on-screen, similar to what's shown in the margin. The file is now ready for action.

You can select a group of files in a number of ways. The easiest way is to press and hold down the Ctrl (control) key on your keyboard. Then click each file you want to add to the group, one after the other. This method is known as *control-clicking* files.

Figure 7-1 illustrates a window in which several files have been selected by control-clicking them with the mouse. Each highlighted file is now part of a group, available for manipulation or death via one of the many file commands.

Another way to select files as a group — especially when the files appear together in the Icon view — is to lasso them. Figure 7-2 illustrates how you do this by dragging over the files with the mouse.

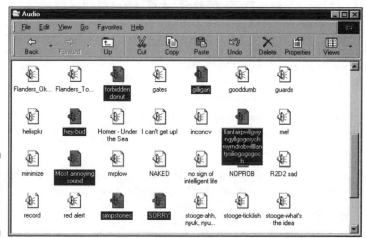

Figure 7-1: Select files by control-clicking.

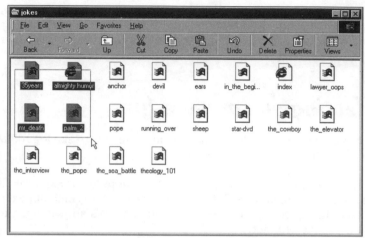

Figure 7-2:
Lasso a
group of
files with
the mouse.

To lasso the files, start in the upper-left corner above the file group; then click and hold the mouse button and drag down and to the right to create a rectangle surrounding the file icons you want to select, as shown in Figure 7-2. Release the mouse button, and all the files you've lassoed are selected as a group.

✔ To select all the files in a folder, choose Edit⇔Select All. The handy keyboard shortcut key for this procedure is Ctrl+A.

✔ To deselect a file from a group, just Ctrl+click it again.

Cutting and pasting (moving files)

In the old days, you didn't cut and paste a file — you *moved* it. In Windows, where everything is like kindergarten anyway, you cut and paste. To cut and paste (move) a file, follow these steps:

1. **Locate the file(s) you want to move.**

   Hunker down in the Explorer or My Computer program, looking for the file or files you want to move.

2. **Select the file(s).**

   Click the file once to select it. Or you can select a group of files by using the techniques described in the preceding section.

3. **Choose Edit⇔Cut.**

   You can also click the Cut button (if it's visible) or use the handy keyboard shortcut: Ctrl+X.

After cutting, the file appears dimmed in the window. It means that the file has been *cut* and is ready to be pasted. Nothing is wrong; keep moving on with the next step.

4. Open the folder where you want the file pasted (moved to).

Again, use the Explorer or My Computer program to hunt down the proper destination folder.

5. Choose Edit⇨Paste.

Or you can use the Paste button on the toolbar or the Paste command keyboard shortcut, Ctrl+V.

The file is deeply moved. (Don't eat the paste.)

You can also cut and paste folders; however, it's a Big Deal because you're also cutting and pasting the folder's contents — which can be massive. Don't do this casually; cut and paste a folder only when you're up for major disk reorganization.

Copying and pasting (copying files)

Copying and pasting a file works just like cutting and pasting, but the file is copied instead of moved. The original file remains where it was and fully intact. So after copying, you have two copies of the same file (or group of files if you're copying a whole hoard of them).

To copy a file, follow the same steps outlined in the preceding section for cutting and pasting a file (moving). In Step 3 (after finding and selecting the file), choose the Edit⇨Copy command.

Or you can use the Copy button on the toolbar (if visible).

Or you can use the Ctrl+C keyboard shortcut.

When you paste the file, you're pasting a full-on copy. The original file remains untouched.

- Oftentimes, you don't really need to copy a file anywhere on your hard drive. Instead, create a shortcut to that file. See the next section "Creating shortcuts."

- For copying a file to a floppy disk, refer to Chapter 5. But keep in mind that you can still copy and paste to move files to a floppy disk (or Zip disk for that matter).

- You can also copy or cut files from a floppy disk to your hard drive. The process works the same way no matter which type of disk you're working with.

Creating shortcuts

When you copy a file, you're copying *all* of the file. Sometimes copying all of it is unnecessary, especially for large files that swallow disk space like hungry bears eating endangered salmon. Sometimes instead of making a full copy, you can instead create a file *shortcut.*

A file shortcut is a 99-percent fat-free copy of a file. It enables you to access the original file from anywhere on your computer but without the extra baggage required to copy the file all over creation. For example, you can drop a shortcut to WordPerfect on the desktop, where you can always get to it — much quicker than using the Start menu.

Making a shortcut is a cinch: Just follow the same steps for copying a file, as detailed in the previous sections about cutting, copying, and pasting files. The only exception is that you choose Edit⇨Paste Shortcut from the menu rather than the standard Paste command.

To paste a shortcut on the desktop, right-click on the desktop. Up pops a shortcut menu, from which you can choose the Paste Shortcut command.

Shortcut to the old graveyard

✔ A shortcut icon has a little arrow in a white box nestled into its lower-left corner (see the figure in the margin). This icon tells you that the file is a shortcut and not the real McCoy.

✔ Shortcuts are also named *Shortcut to* followed by the original file's name. You can edit the *Shortcut to* part out if you like. See the section on renaming files, earlier in this chapter.

✔ You can make shortcuts for popular folders and stick them on the desktop for easy access.

✔ You can open a shortcut just like any other icon: Double-click to open a document, run an application, or open a folder.

✔ Have no fear when you're deleting shortcuts; removing a shortcut icon does not remove the original file.

Deleting files

Unlike credit cards and driver's licenses, files don't simply expire. You must make an effort to rid yourself of old or temporary files you don't need. Otherwise, files collect like lint balls outside a dryer vent.

To kill a file, select it and choose File⇨Delete. This process doesn't truly remove the file; it merely moves the thing over to the Recycle Bin. From there, you can easily undelete the file later.

You can also delete a selected file by pressing the Delete key on the keyboard.

Or you can click the Delete button on the toolbar (if you can see the toolbar).

Or even this: You can delete files by dragging them with the mouse. Drag the file from its window into the Recycle Bin icon on the desktop.

If you want a sensitive file utterly crushed, click it once with the mouse and press Shift+Delete. Windows displays a warning dialog box, explaining that the file will be utterly crushed (or something to that effect). Click Yes to zap it off to eternity.

✔ Windows may warn you about deleting a file. Are you *really* sure? You probably are, so click Yes to delete the file. (Windows is just being utterly cautious.)

✔ You can delete folders just like files, but keep in mind that you delete the folder's contents — which can be dozens of icons, files, folders, jewelry, small children, and food for the homeless. Better be careful with that one.

✔ Never delete any file in the Windows folder or any of the folders in the Windows folder.

✔ Never delete any file in the root folder of a hard drive.

✔ In fact, never delete any file unless you created it yourself.

✔ Don't delete programs! Instead, you can use a special tool in the Windows Control Panel for removing old applications you no longer need. See Chapter 19 for more information.

Undeleting files

Because you probably want your file back in a hurry, here it goes:

1. **Open the Recycle Bin on the desktop.**

   Double-click the Recycle Bin icon. It looks like a little trash can, as pictured in the margin, though it may look like something else depending on how you have Windows configured. (But it always says *Recycle Bin* beneath the icon.)

2. **Select the file you want recovered.**

   Click the file to begin its resurrection.

   Choose <u>V</u>iew⇨Arrange <u>I</u>cons⇨by <u>D</u>elete Date from the menu to display files in the order they were deleted (by date). That way, it's cinchy to find any recently departed files you may want back.

3. **Choose <u>F</u>ile⇨<u>R</u>estore.**

   The file is magically removed from the Recycle Bin and restored to the folder and disk from which it was so brutally seized.

4. Close the Recycle Bin window.

Click the window's X (close) button in the upper-right corner.

Windows has no time limit on when you can restore files; they're available in the Recycle Bin for quite some time. Even so: Don't let the convenience of the Recycle Bin lead you down the path of sloppiness. Never delete a file unless you're certain that you want it gone, gone, gone.

Working with Files Can Be a Drag

When you feel bold enough, you can copy and move files using your mouse only — no keyboard or menus. This is a skill honed by the *masters:* Grab files with the mouse and drag them where you want them.

The advantage to this trick is that it makes copying or moving files as easy as rolling the mouse around. The disadvantage is that you must have *two* or more folders open on your desktop at one time to make it work. As an example, Figure 7-3 shows two windows representing two folders.

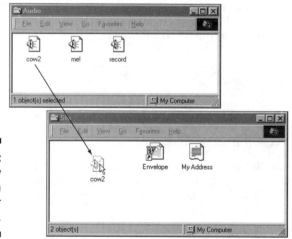

Figure 7-3:
Files fly between two folder windows.

Moving files: To move a file from one folder to another, drag it with the mouse from one window to another, which is sort of shown in Figure 7-4 (envision the dragging action in your head). The mouse is dragging the file cow2 from the Audio folder into the Sto folder.

Copying files: To copy a file from one folder's window to another, press and hold the Ctrl key, and drag the file. This process is known as a *control-drag.*

red butto⊞

You can confirm whether you're moving or copying a file by looking at the icon that you're dragging with the mouse: If the icon has a plus (+) by it (see the margin), you're copying it. No plus means you're moving it.

  ✔ Windows automatically moves files when you drag them between two folders on the same disk drive.

  ✔ Windows automatically copies files when you drag them from one disk drive to another; you have no need to press the Ctrl key in this situation.

  ✔ To move a file from one disk drive to another, press and hold the Shift key before you click the file to drag it.

And vice versa. To copy a file from one folder to another on the same disk drive, you hold down the Shift key (which acts like a toggle between copy and move).

Finding Wayward Files (And Programs)

That files disappear is no big deal. The fact that Windows has a nifty Find command is a big deal. It's a blessing. If only such a command existed for your car keys or glasses, the world would truly be a better place.

To find a wayward file in Windows, you need to know something about the file. Knowing one or more of the following tidbits will help you quickly and easily find any file on your computer:

  ✔ The file's name or at least part of it

  ✔ Any text in the file, words or part of sentences you remember

  ✔ The date the file was created, last saved to disk, or modified

  ✔ The file's type (or which program created it)

  ✔ The size of the file

The more information you can supply, the better Windows is at finding your file. Still, even with vague information, Windows displays a list of files — a longer list but a list nonetheless.

The following steps help you to find your file, no matter how much you know or can't remember about it:

1. **From the Start menu, choose Find⇨Files or Folders.**

   This action summons the Find command.

   If your keyboard has a Windows key, you can press Win+F, where the F means Find.

The cinchy way to copy and move files

Copying. Moving. Dragging. Control-dragging. It's a mess! The way I remember the difference between copying and moving files is not to memorize the techniques. Instead, I use the right mouse button to drag any file or group of files I want moved, copied, or shortcutted.

When you drag file icons around by using the right mouse button and then release the right

mouse button, a pop-up menu appears. That menu has four items on it:

✔ Move Here

✔ Copy Here

✔ Create Shortcut(s) Here

✔ Cancel

Select one of these options to move, copy, or paste a shortcut of the file (or files) you're dragging. Click Cancel to chicken out.

If you're using Explorer or My Computer or staring at the desktop, press the F3 key to summon the Find command.

In all instances, the Find dialog box appears, as shown in Figure 7-4.

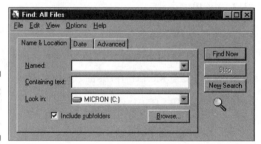

Figure 7-4:
The Find
dialog box.

2. **Describe the lost file.**

Your job is to fill in as much information about the lost file as you can.

If you know the file's name, put it in the Named text box, as shown in Figure 7-4. Type the full name. If you don't know the entire name, use asterisks (*) to replace the parts you don't know.

For example, if you know the file contains the word *report,* you can type ***report*** in the Named box. If you know the file starts with the letters *NU,* you can type **NU*** into the Named box.

(I describe other searching options at the end of this section.)

3. **Select the proper hard drive.**

   In Figure 7-4, drive C is chosen. If you're not sure which hard drive the file is on, select the Local Hard Drives option. Otherwise, drive C is best.

4. **Click in the Include Subfolders check box (if this option is not already selected).**

   You always want Windows to search the *entire* hard drive.

5. **Click the Find Now button.**

   This action sends Windows off on a merry chase to locate the file you've requested. One of two things happens when it's done:

   No dice. If the file isn't found, you see the text `There are no items to show in this view` displayed, along with the dismal counter (in the lower-left part of the dialog box) that says `0 file(s) found`. Oh well. Try again.

   Eureka! Any files matching your specifications are displayed in the (new) bottom part of the Find dialog box, shown in Figure 7-5. This list is similar to what the My Computer window shows in the Details view.

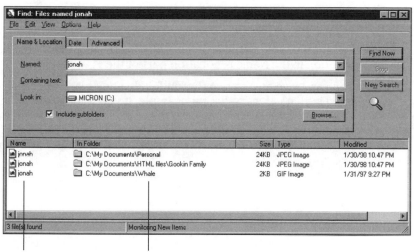

Figure 7-5:
Find has
found.

Name of files found   Location of files

6. **Do something with the file.**

   After finding the file, you can do whatever you want to with it. Double-clicking the file, for example, opens it. Or you can cut the file directly from the Find window and paste it back where you want it.

7. **Close the Find dialog box.**

You're done.

The list of files displayed when Find successfully finds something can get quite long. The list's length depends on how specific you are when you tell Windows what to find.

Here are some additional Find command tips and tricks:

✔ The titles in the found part of the dialog box (refer to Figure 7-5) can be used to sort the files in the list. For example, clicking the Size title sorts the files by their size. Click again to sort in reverse order.

✔ To find a file by its date, click the Date tab in the Find dialog box. There you can search for files created, modified, or saved on a specific date; between two dates; or a given number of months or days past.

✔ To find files of a specific type, click the Advanced tab in the Find dialog box. The Of Type drop-down list displays applications and file types for files on your computer. For example, to find all the sound files on your computer, just select Wave Sound from that list. Leave the Named text box blank (in the Name & Location panel), click Find Now, and Windows displays all the sound files on your PC.

✔ To find files of a specific size, click the Advanced tab and play with the Size Is and KB boxes.

✔ To find files containing a specific bit of text, fill in the Containing Text text box in the Name & Location part of the Find dialog box.

✔ You can leave any item in the Find dialog box blank to search for *any-thing* in that category. So, for example, if you want to find all files larger than 5,000 kilobits on your hard drive, click the New Search button, and then in the Advanced panel, select At Least and 5000 for the Size and KB boxes. Click Find Now, and you'll see a list of hefty files displayed.

Part III

The Non-Nerd's Guide to Computer Hardware

The 5th Wave — By Rich Tennant

GLOVES

And, of course, we have a version for Windows.

In this part . . .

Too bad the hardware-software thing can't be elevated to a classic conflict. You know: good versus evil, man versus woman, the rebels versus the empire, you versus the idiot driving the pickup truck. Unfortunately, there exists only harmony between hardware and software.

Between hardware and software, however, it's hardware that gets all the press. A new Pentium chip gets a mention on the nightly news, while a new version of some software program — the real brains of the operation — maybe gets a mention in a computer magazine, but that's it!

To keep the scales out of balance, I hereby present the hardware part of the book first. Face it: Hardware *is* more interesting. Software may control it, but there's just more to hardware — and such a variety — that it deserves to come first. So the chapters in this part of the book dwell on hardware.

Chapter 8

Just Your Basic Computer Guts

*Y*our PC may have a sleek, aerodynamic case, but beneath all that serious-colored plastic is a mess of ugly, naked electronics. It's an electronic sushi bar of diodes, resistors, chips, and chunks of technology. This scientific salad of stuff should be interesting only to the folks in the white lab coats. Alas, you too may be assaulted with the various terms as you use your PC: *motherboard, microprocessor, BIOS, ports, power supplies,* and *expansion slots.*

This chapter covers many things you can and cannot see inside your PC's console. Some of the things I discuss are important, yet buried deep in your computer's bosom. Other things are important because you can see them dotting the backside of your PC like barnacles on a whale. What these things are, what they do, and why you should care is all covered here.

- ✔ Your PC also houses various connectors, which I cover in Chapter 9.

- ✔ Chapter 11 details computer memory, which is inside your PC but deserves its own chapter.

- ✔ Disk drives, also located inside the PC, are covered in Chapter 10.

The Mother of All Boards

The *motherboard* is the main piece of circuitry inside your PC. Like the downtown of a big city, it's where everything happens.

The motherboard is important because the most important things inside your PC cling to it. In fact, for the most part, the console is simply a housing for the motherboard. (Disk drives used to be separate on some early systems.)

Figure 8-1 illustrates a typical PC motherboard. The interesting things to locate on it are in the following list. You don't need to memorize this list.

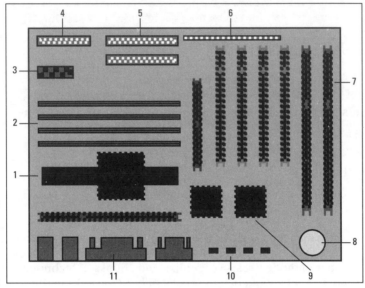

Figure 8-1:
The mother-
board
illustration.

1. The microprocessor — the computer's main chip

2. The computer's memory

3. Power supply connector

4. Floppy drive connector

5. Hard drive/CD-ROM connectors

6. Front panel connectors (blinking lights, speakers, other stuff)

7. Expansion slots and the special expansion cards that plug into them

8. Clock battery

9. The BIOS and various ROM chips

10. Sharp pointy things

11. External connectors (ports)

Although the motherboard contains a lot of items, it's essentially one unit and is referred to as such — just like the mall has many stores but everyone calls it *the mall*. The sections that follow highlight the things you should care about on the motherboard.

- ✔ IBM calls the motherboard in its computers the *planar* board. Ugh.

- ✔ You can add or remove only two things on the motherboard: extra memory and expansion cards (which plug into the expansion slots). This chore, referred to as upgrading, is best left to the gurus.

- ✔ Memory is covered in Chapter 11.

- ✔ Oh, some motherboards allow you to remove and add a microprocessor. I recommend against this, however. I tell you why later.

The Microprocessor

At the heart of every computer beats the *microprocessor*. That's the computer's main chip. No, it's not the computer's *brain*. (Software is the brain.) Instead, the microprocessor acts like a tiny, fast calculator. It just adds and subtracts (and does the tango and the jitterbug).

The microprocessor itself deals with other elements in the computer. Primarily these elements provide either *input* or *output,* which compujockeys call *I/O. Input* is information flowing into the microprocessor. *Output* is information the microprocessor generates and spits out.

Pretty much the whole computer obsesses over this input and output stuff.

- ✔ The main chip inside the computer is the *microprocessor,* which is essentially a tiny calculator with a BIG price tag.

- ✔ The microprocessor is also called the CPU, which stands for Central Processing Unit. Military types like the term.

- ✔ When your jaw is tired, you can refer to the microprocessor as the *processor.*

- ✔ Most microprocessors resemble large, flat, after-dinner mints — with hundreds of legs. The Pentium III microprocessor, however, is a large black box — about the size of an instant camera (but thinner).

Naming a microprocessor

In the old days, microprocessors were named after famous numbers: 8088, 8086, 80286, 80386, 80486, and on and on. Today, microprocessors are given proper and more powerful names, but not like Hercules or Samson or Larry. Instead, they're called Pentium and AMD and Cyrix.

Intel, the microprocessor's manufacturer, called its next-generation microprocessor the *Pentium*. (Using the number scheme, it would have been the 586.) The Pentium beget the Pentium Pro, then the Pentium with MMX, then Pentium II, and lately the Pentium III. (So they're turning back to numbers again.)

Other manufacturers make other microprocessors similar to the Intel Pentium but cheaper! These microprocessors have names like AMD and Cyrix and numbers like P5 and P6. Basically they're the same as the Pentium-whatever, but less expensive.

Intel itself has its own cheaper version of the Pentium called the Celeron, which has nothing to do with celery. It's just a cheapie Pentium.

- ✔ Intel is the world's leading manufacturer of computer microprocessors. The company developed the original 8088 that lived in the first IBM PC.

- ✔ The Pentium name actually came about because Intel was told it couldn't copyright a number like 586. So it wanted a unique name to separate its microprocessors from the competition.

- ✔ Little difference exists between a true Intel and non-Intel microprocessor. As far as your PC's software is concerned, the microprocessor is the same no matter who made it.

- ✔ The latest microprocessor as this book goes to press is the Pentium III (which is pronounced *pen-tee-um three*).

The measure of a microprocessor

Microprocessors are gauged by how fast they are. The speed could be miles per hour (mph), but unfortunately microprocessors have no wheels and cannot travel distances in any measurable amount of time. Therefore, the speed measured is how fast the microprocessor thinks.

Thinking speed is measured in megahertz (MHz). The higher the megahertz number, the faster the microprocessor. An old Pentium Pro running at 133MHz is much slower than a Pentium III running at 500MHz.

A microprocessor's power is also measured in how many bits it can chew up at once. All Pentium microprocessors can work with 32 bits of information at a time, which makes them very fast. (Older PC microprocessors worked with 16 or 8 bits at once.) A good analogy with bits in a microprocessor is cylinders in a car engine: The more cylinders, the more powerful the engine. A future microprocessor may be able to handle 64 bits. That would be very, very powerful.

"OK, wise guy, so which microprocessor lives in my PC?"

Who knows which microprocessor lurks in the heart of your PC? Better get a big wrench. Better still, right-click on the My Computer icon in the upper-left corner of the desktop. This action brings up a shortcut menu for your computer. Choose the last item, Properties. The System Properties dialog box appears, looking something like Figure 8-2.

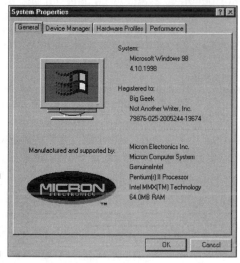

Figure 8-2:
The System
Properties
dialog box.

Details! Details! The first panel of the System Properties dialog box (General) contains information about Windows, you, and your computer. It says what type of microprocessor lives in your PC and the total amount of memory (RAM) your system has.

- ✔ In Figure 8-2, the computer has a Pentium II microprocessor and 64MB of memory.

- ✔ If you have a 486 system, then your microprocessor's number appears where you see `Pentium Pro(r)` in Figure 8-1. For a 486 microprocessor, it would probably just say 80486. This number is the microprocessor you have in your PC, not some secret code.

- ✔ Figure 8-2 also boasts that Micron Electronics, Inc., manufactured the computer. I am not an employee of Micron; I just bought my computer from the company. (It's an Idaho thing.) Your computer manufacturer may have its name displayed there as well. Ain't no way to get rid of it, either.

Upgrading your microprocessor

Just about every PC sold today has a special doojobbie on the motherboard that allows you to replace your PC's microprocessor. You just lift out the old, pokey one and replace it with a faster, newer one. Simple. Elegant. And expensive!

In my travels, I know of few people who actually upgrade their microprocessors. Only if you've made the wrong microprocessor decision when you first bought your PC is it necessary. Normally, after two or three years (when a newer, faster microprocessor becomes available), going out and buying a whole new computer makes more sense. After all, other things would need updating inside the PC as well: the hard drive, ports, and other technology. And often the reasons for needing a new microprocessor imply that you need more memory, so why not replace everything at once?

- ✔ If you really want to replace your microprocessor, have someone else do it for you. Often the places that sell the upgrades include installation with the microprocessor price.

- ✔ Remember that PC manufacturers and dealers buy their microprocessors in bulk. Their new computers are sometimes cheaper than an upgrade.

Connectors for Things Various and Sundry

Every gizmo in the computer connects to the motherboard. Some of the connectors are external, such as the ports covered in Chapter 9 (item 11 in Figure 8-1). You plug things into those connectors yourself. Other connectors are internal, which connect various goodies inside the computer case to the motherboard.

I need more power!

Inside your PC's case, next to the motherboard, is the *power supply.* The power supply does three things: It brings in power from the wall socket, it supplies power to the motherboard and disk drives, and it contains the on/off switch.

To supply power to the motherboard, the power supply uses a power connection on the motherboard (item 3 in Figure 8-1). You rarely unplug this connection. Only if the power supply blows up (I should really say *fail* instead of *blow up*) do you need to replace it.

Don't panic! Power supplies are designed to fail. Sometimes they really do blow up, but they don't explode. They merely die and emit a puff of smoke. The power supply is designed to protect the delicate electronics inside your PC. It would rather die than fry your system. And power supplies are easy to replace, so popping them in is really no big deal (and rarely do they pop).

- The power supply makes most of the noise when your PC runs. It contains a fan that regulates the temperature inside the console, keeping everything nice and cool. (Electronic components get hot when electricity races through them — just like you would! This heat has the ugly consequence of making them misbehave, which is why cooling is needed.)

- Power supplies are rated in watts. The more stuff your computer has — the more disk drives, memory, expansion cards, and so on — the greater the number of watts the power supply should provide. The typical PC has a power supply rated at 150 or 200 watts. More powerful systems may require a power supply of 220 or 250 watts.

- One way to keep your power supply — and your computer — from potentially going poof (even in a lightning strike) is to invest in a surge protector or UPS. See Chapter 2 for details.

Disk drive connectors

Your PC's motherboard also has connectors for the floppy drives (remember there can be two) and two hard drives, or a hard drive and a CD-ROM drive.

If you ever add a tape backup drive to your PC, it's often placed in the position of floppy drive B, using the same connector floppy drive A uses to connect to the motherboard.

Hard drives and CD-ROM drives can also be connected to the motherboard via an expansion card plugged into one of the expansion slots (item 7 in Figure 8-1). More about this in a few pages.

Oh, and DVD drives generally plug into a special expansion card that sits in an expansion slot.

Sharp pointy things and other electronic salad

Finally, lots of other miscellaneous things may be lurking on your PC's motherboard. Most of them are just chips or diodes or resistors or whatever.

Some sharp pointy things that you may have to deal with someday are called *jumpers.* A jumper is a connector that works like a switch. You put a small black box over two pointy wires to connect them, or turn on the switch. Remove the black box to un-jump the switch.

Figure 8-3 illustrates the three ways you can fix a jumper. The little black jumper box is usually on or off (to the side).

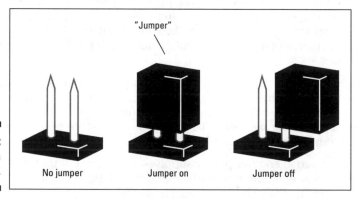

"Jumper"

No jumper   Jumper on   Jumper off

Figure 8-3:
We have a
jumper.

You may have to set or remove jumpers when you upgrade memory or (heaven forbid!) upgrade your PC's microprocessor. If so, your computer's manual tells you what to do. Or — better still — have the dealer do it all for you!

- ✔ It's best to have the experts worry about jumpers.

- ✔ Never move a jumper — or even open your PC — with the power on.

- ✔ Jumpers are all labeled, usually with a stencil on the motherboard. For example, jumper W2 has a W2 by it on the motherboard.

Expansion Slots

To add more goodies and expand your PC's abilities, the motherboard sports special long, thin slots. These are *expansion slots,* into which you can plug special *expansion cards.* The idea is that you can expand your system by adding options not included with the basic PC.

Your PC can have anywhere from zero to a dozen expansion slots. Some home systems have none — which keeps the price low — and most of the options are built-in with the home system. But most typical PCs have three to eight, depending on the size of the console.

Figure 8-4 shows an enlargement of the expansion slot area on the motherboard shown in Figure 8-1 (which is just an example, though it's based on my latest computer). Note that three types of expansion slots exist: ISA, PCI, and AGP.

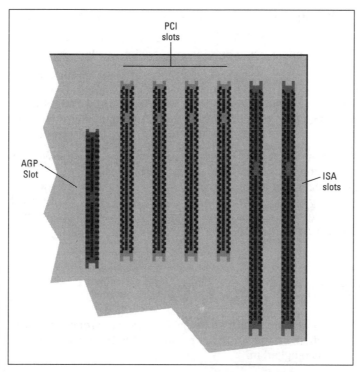

Figure 8-4:
Various
types of
expansion
slots.

ISA. The oldest type of slot is the ISA, which stands for (get this) Industry Standard Architecture. That's because it never really had a name until another, better type of expansion slot came along. ISA slots hang around because a lot of older hardware still comes on that type of expansion card. This format, however, is fading fast, and not every new PC sold has ISA expansion slots on the motherboard.

PCI. The PCI slot is the most common form of internal expansion for a PC (for a Macintosh, too, but that's not the subject here). PCI slots are very fast and sport flashier and better devices than the older ISA slots. Chances are good that if you buy an expansion card, it will be a PCI card.

AGP. The AGP slot is the Accelerated Graphics Port connector. It's a special type of slot that takes only video expansion cards, usually the spendy nice ones that do all sorts of amazing graphics. Not every PC has this type of slot.

Expansion slots and the cards that plug into them make it tinker-toy simple to add new features and power to your PC. And although anyone can plug in a card and expand a computer system, this job is best left to those experts who enjoy such things.

- ✔ Small footprint PCs have the fewest expansion slots. Tower computer models have the most.

- ✔ For more information on video expansion cards, see Chapter 12.

- ✔ The salespeople never tell you this one: Most expansion cards come squirming with cables. This mess of cables makes the seemingly sleek motherboard look more like an electronic pasta dish. Some cables are threaded inside the PC; others are left hanging limply out the back. The cables are what make the upgrading and installation process so difficult.

- ✔ After you add a new expansion card, you need to tell Windows about it. On a good day (sunshine, hot coffee, birds chirping, like that), Windows recognizes and automatically configures the new hardware when you restart your PC. Otherwise, you need to open up the Control Panel and start the Add New Hardware icon. The details of this procedure are far too boring to list here.

Tick Tock Goes the Clock

Most computers come with an internal clock. Tick-tock. The clock is battery operated, which enables it to keep track of the time, day or night, whether or not the PC is plugged in.

To check the current time, gander at the far-right side of the Windows taskbar. Living in the system tray is the current time, as shown in Figure 8-5.

Figure 8-5:
The current
date and
time (more
or less).

✔ If you point the mouse at the time, Windows displays the current date and time in a long format. This format is shown in Figure 8-5.

✔ If you don't see the time, click the Start button to pop up its menu and choose Settings⇨Taskbar & Start Menu. In the Taskbar Options panel in the Taskbar Properties dialog box, look for the Show Clock check box on the bottom. Click in that check box to select that option. Click the OK button, and Windows shows you the time on the taskbar.

✔ The format for the date and time varies depending on how your computer is set up. Windows displays a date and time format based on your country or region. This book assumes the typical (and I agree, backward) U.S. method of listing the date.

✔ Who cares if the computer knows what time of day it is? Well, because your files are time- and date-stamped, you can figure things out, like which is a later version of two similar files or two files with the same name on different disks.

Computers make lousy clocks. That's why you don't see them keeping time at the end of the pool during the Olympic games. Why do computers seem to lose track of the time a few minutes every day? Who knows! But you can always reset the time, which is nice.

To set or change the date and time on your PC, double-click the time in the taskbar: Point the mouse at the time on the right end of the taskbar and double-click. Click-click. This action displays the Date/Time Properties dialog box, as shown in Figure 8-6.

Manipulate the controls in the Date/Time Properties dialog box to change or set the date or time.

To set the time, type in the new time. For example, type **10:00** if it's 9:58 or so. Then when the time lady (or whoever) says it's 10:00, click the Apply button in the Date/Time Properties dialog box. That action sets the time instantly. Click OK when you're done.

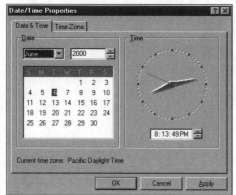

Figure 8-6:
The
Date/Time
Properties
dialog box.

The BIOS

The BIOS is a special chip on the motherboard that contains your PC's personality. BIOS stands for Basic Input/Output System. Encoded on that chip are the simple instructions for the computer to communicate with its various pieces and parts.

For example, the BIOS contains software to talk to the keyboard, monitor, and expansion slots; display the manufacturer's logo; and do other simple activities. It's not as complex as the operating system, but it's necessary to get the PC going in the morning.

✔ BIOS is pronounced *Bye-Oss*.

✔ BIOS is also known as ROM. Refer to Chapter 11 for information on what a ROM chip is.

✔ In addition to the main BIOS, your computer may have other BIOSes. For example, the video BIOS controls your system's graphics display, the hard drive BIOS controls the hard disk, and so on. Your network adapter may have its own BIOS. Normally, when you see the term BIOS by itself, it refers to the PC's main BIOS.

Chapter 9

Ports, Jacks, and Holes

● ●

In This Chapter

▶ Why you need jacks or ports

▶ Keyboard and mouse ports

▶ USB ports and devices

▶ Serial ports

▶ Printer ports and nonprinter devices

▶ Joystick ports

▶ Audio jacks (not ports)

▶ SCSI ports and their devices

● ●

Right around back, on your PC console's rump, is a host of holes and plug-in places. They're ugly. That's probably why that side of your PC faces the wall — or at least faces away from you. Yet, like expansion slots inside the console (see Chapter 8), these holes help you expand your PC system, as well as connect various important items to the main console unit.

This chapter is about the holes in your PC's backside. Officially they're known as *jacks,* probably because some guy named Jack discovered the first hole on the back of an ancient Egyptian computer. Another term, equally official, is *port.* It means the same thing as jack, which is just another term for hole. As with most things in a computer, keeping the air clear with a single, well-defined and descriptive term is not the top priority.

Holes for Every Occasion

A hole is really a *jack* or connector on the back of your PC. Into the jack, you can plug any one of a variety of external devices with which your computer can communicate.

Some jacks are dedicated to certain devices. Other jacks, known as *ports,* can connect to a variety of different and weird things.

Figure 9-1 illustrates a panel typical to the backs of many PCs. That's where you find common jacks clustered. You may find more jacks on the various expansion cards, but the bulk of them will be in one place, as shown in Figure 9-1. Here's the list:

1. Keyboard connector
2. Mouse connector
3. USB connector (usually two of them)
4. Serial port connector (usually two of them)
5. Printer (parallel) port connector
6. Joystick port connector
7. Audio connectors (three of them)

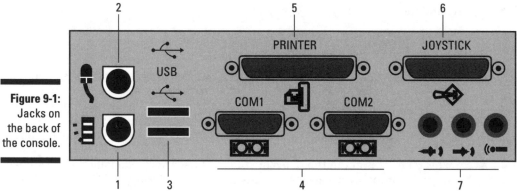

Figure 9-1:
Jacks on the back of the console.

The following sections describe the different devices that can plug into these various ports.

✔ More ports can be added to any PC through an expansion card. For example, you can add a USB port to your computer with a $60 expansion card. (I did.)

✔ Your PC may or may not have a second serial port or a USB port. These are things you should have known about *before* you bought your PC, which is why I'll push another of my books here, *Buying a Computer For Dummies,* also available from IDG Books Worldwide, Inc.

✔ The USB (Universal Serial Bus) port — the latest addition to the PC's host of ports — has the power and versatility to eventually replace just about every other port on the PC.

✔ Your PC may also sport a video port for the monitor. You may find it with the other ports or on an expansion card. Chapter 12 covers all things video.

✔ Another popular type of port is the SCSI port, though it tends to be a technical thing. See the section "The Scuzziest Port of All: SCSI," later in this chapter.

In Plugs the Keyboard and the Mouse

The keyboard and mouse connectors look the same on most PCs. That's because they are! Although one is labeled for the keyboard and another for the mouse, they're really the same type of port; the computer is smart enough to figure out which is the keyboard and which is the mouse.

✔ Although both keyboard and mouse ports are identical, just for luck's sake plug the keyboard into the port with the keyboard label and the mouse into the port with the mouse label.

✔ Older (and I mean *way* older) PCs had a larger keyboard connector. If you ever use one of these keyboards, you can buy a special adapter to allow it to plug into the newer, smaller keyboard connectors.

✔ Some computer mice plug into the serial port instead of the special mouse port. If so, plug the mouse into serial port 1. Chapter 13 discusses why using this port is better than using serial port 2.

✔ Some keyboards and mice may plug into the USB port instead of their own custom connectors. See? It's taking over. . . .

USB Is Da Bomb

The most versatile jack on the back of your PC is the USB port. Unlike most other ports, USB was designed to host a number of different and interesting devices, making it replace just about every other connector on the PC's rump.

✔ USB stands for Universal Serial Bus. It's pronounced *yoo-es-bee*, not *uss-ub*.

✔ Unlike your printer or various other jacks, USB devices all come with their own cables. Yee-ha!

Doing the USB thing

 To use the USB port, you must first ensure that your PC has one or more USB connectors. You must look behind your PC and check for the dime-sized USB connector, which usually appears next to the USB symbol (shown in the margin). If you're lucky, you also see the letters USB, as shown in Figure 9-1.

The second thing you need are USB devices. These external devices plug into the USB port. A lot of them exist: monitors, speakers, joysticks, scanners, digital cameras, floppy drives and other storage devices, modems, and electroshock therapy devices, and the list goes on. More and more USB devices are appearing every day.

- Don't worry if your PC lacks a USB port. You can always add one via an expansion card.

- Windows 98 works best with USB devices. If you have Windows 95, you need to get special software, which often comes with the USB card or with your PC when you buy it.

Connecting a USB device

One reason the USB port is poised to take over the world is that it's smart. Unlike other connectors on a PC, when you plug a USB device into a USB port, Windows 98 instantly recognizes it and configures the device for you. You don't even need to turn off or reset your computer. Amazing.

For example, I bought one of those monitor-top video cameras for my PC. After plugging the thing into the USB port (with the computer on), Windows instantly recognized the camera, installed the proper software, and let me use it right way. (I still had to install the camera software, but the whole process was a heck of a lot easier than unscrewing the case.)

- You can plug in USB devices as you need them. So if you have a scanner and joystick hooked up, unplug one and plug in your PC's camera instead. No penalty or glitch occurs when you make this change.

- Some USB devices don't even need an extra power cord; the USB device uses the power from the console. For example, my USB scanner just plugs into the computer — that's all! Other USB devices, such as monitors, may require a separate power cable.

- The USB is not a total solution. The port's speed is too slow to make it possible for fast hard disk drives to be connected. This problem may be solved in the future, however.

Expanding the USB universe

Most PCs have two USB connectors. Into them you can plug two USB devices. If you have more USB devices, you can unplug and replug devices as you see necessary.

If you want to use more than two USB devices on your PC at a time, you have several options. One is to get a USB expansion card and add more USB connectors to your PC. The second and more likely option is to buy a USB *hub*. That's a device that plugs into your PC's USB port and gives you more USB ports, as illustrated in Figure 9-2.

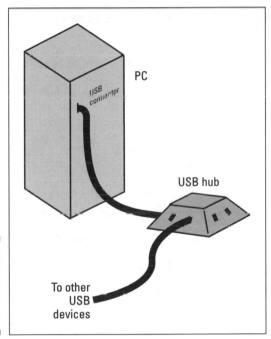

PC

USB connector

USB hub

Figure 9-2:
Add more
USB ports
with a USB
hub.

To other
USB
devices

Using hubs, you can expand your PC's USB universe out to the maximum 127 USB devices. Hopefully you'll run out of desk space before that.

- A USB hub can be powered by the USB cable or, more often, plugged into the wall.

- The maximum number of USB devices is 127, and USB cables can be no more than 3 meters in length. That means, if this were a math question, your computer could theoretically control a USB device sitting some 381 meters away! (That's over 1,200 feet for you Americans.)

✔ Some USB hubs are built into USB devices. A few USB monitors, for example, have USB hubs that add two or four more USB ports. Some USB keyboards have an extra port on them for connecting a USB mouse.

✔ The first hub (actually your PC) is the *root* hub. Beyond that you can connect only a certain number of hubs to the computer, depending on your PC's hardware. This maximum number will, most likely, never be known because the cost of the USB devices required to reach that limit would bankrupt most small countries.

Serial or COM Ports

Cereal ports are named after Ceres, the Roman goddess of agriculture. Wait. Wrong type of cereal.

Serial ports are, next to the USB port, the most versatile type of connector on your PC. The serial port can have a variety of interesting items plugged into it, which is why it's generically called a serial port instead of a this-or-that port.

You can often plug the following items into a serial port: a modem, a serial printer, a mouse, some types of scanners, digital cameras, or just about anything that requires two-way communications.

The most common device plugged into the serial port is an external modem. For this reason, serial ports are also called COM ports, for communication.

Most computers come with two serial ports, dubbed COM1 and COM2.

✔ A serial port can also be called a modem port.

✔ Serial ports are also called RS-232 ports.

✔ If the serial port connected to a popular trash-can-shaped robot, it would be called the R2-D2 port.

✔ Unlike USB ports, you can plug only one item into a serial port at a time. That's okay because most of the serial port's devices are those that are consistently connected to the PC: modem, scanner, mouse, and so on.

✔ You can plug a computer mouse into a serial port. In that case, the mouse is called a serial mouse. Refer to your local pet store for more information on mice or turn to Chapter 13.

The Ever-Versatile Printer Port

Mysteriously enough, the printer port is where you plug in your printer. The printer cable has one connector that plugs into the printer and a second that plugs into the computer. Both connectors are different, so plugging a printer cable in backward is impossible.

You can also use the printer port as a high-speed link to certain external devices. It's speed and design make it possible to connect external disk drives — such as CD-ROMs, CD-Rs, DVDs, Zip drives, and Jaz drives — and external tape drives to your PC using the printer port.

When used to connect an external device, the printer port cable *passes through* the device to be used with the printer. In Figure 9-3, the printer cable is connected to the PC and the external device, and then a second printer cable connects the external device to the printer.

Using the printer port is one of the least expensive ways to add an external device to your PC.

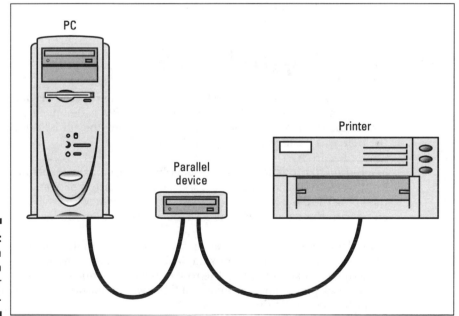

Figure 9-3:
Sticking a
device on
the printer
port.

- ✔ Plugging an external device into the printer port does not interfere with printing. It seems like it should, but it doesn't.

- ✔ You can put only one device between the printer and your PC. You cannot, say, add a second external CD-ROM on a printer port that already has an external device between the PC and printer.

- ✔ If you need to put more than one device on the printer port, then you need a printer port *gang* box, also known as an A-B switch. This device allows you to hook up more than one doojobbie to the printer port and manually switch between them. Be wary that it may not work properly with all devices, but it is a way around the one-item-per-printer-port limitation.

- ✔ For the printer port to work with an external device, you must configure your PC so that the printer port operates in *bidirectional* mode. Have your guru or dealer configure the PC's setup program so that the port is configured as bidirectional (either EPP or ECP, depending on the device's requirements).

- ✔ For more information on printers, refer to Chapter 15.

- ✔ Printer ports are also called *parallel ports,* or to old-time nerds, they're known as *Centronics* ports. People who refer to ports in this manner should be slapped.

The Joy of Joystick Jacks

Believe it or not, one of the first expansion options for the original IBM PC was a joystick port. IBM didn't call it that. No, IBM called it the A-to-D port, for Analog-to-Digital. That sounds very scientific, doesn't it? But the truth is, the hole was designed for plugging in a joystick.

In addition to a joystick, you can also plug a MIDI musical instrument into the joystick (A-to-D) port. You plug a special gadget into the joystick port and then plug the 5-pin MIDI cable into the gadget. Most MIDI keyboard starter kits come with this gadget (which has a real name, but I'm too lazy to look it up).

Also, if you're a closet Mr. Science type, then you can use the joystick port for "scientific applications." For example, I have an anemometer (one of those wind things) that mounts on the roof of my office and connects to the PC via the joystick port. That way I can tell if the wind is blowing even without looking at the trees outside.

Audio Connectors

Since about 1995 or so, most PCs are sold with audio jacks. These jacks allow you to connect an external speaker, microphone, or other sound-producing device to your PC.

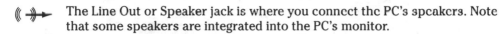 The Line Out or Speaker jack is where you connect the PC's speakers. Note that some speakers are integrated into the PC's monitor.

The Microphone jack is where you plug in a microphone, which allows you to record your own voice or the lovely ambient noises of your computer room.

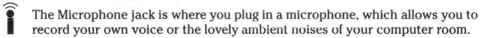 The Line In jack is for connecting some other external sound-producing device to your PC. For example, using the proper audio cables available at Radio Shack, you can hook up your VCR to the PC and hear a movie through your PC's speakers. Invite the neighbors!

The Scuzziest Port of All: SCSI

A mad scientist once crossed the plain serial port with a USB port. The result was the SCSI port. Like a serial port, it's very fast — the fastest port on any PC (for now). And like the USB port, you can connect device after device to the SCSI port.

Because the SCSI port is faster than USB, you can use it to connect the following types of devices:

- Hard drives, up to 14 of them
- A scanner
- A tape backup drive
- A CD-ROM drive, CD-R, CD-RW, and on and on
- A removable hard drive or magneto-optical drive

Oh, I could name more, but them's the basic bones.

Unique to the SCSI port is the way its devices are *daisy-chained* to the PC. Figure 9-4 illustrates this setup. You can chain together up to 15 devices on an Ultra Wide SCSI port. Thirteen of those devices can live outside the PC; two on the inside.

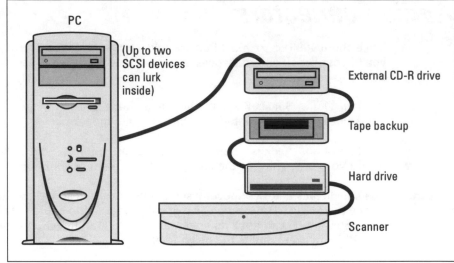

Figure 9-4:
Daisy-
chaining
SCSI
devices to
the PC.

The biggest drawback to the SCSI port is that it's a bear to configure. Each SCSI device must have its own ID number. And the last device on the cable must have a gizmo called a *terminator* (not Arnold Schwarzenegger) attached. So I recommend SCSI ports only to those PC users who can tolerate the extra fuss.

Oh, I should add that SCSI devices use thick obnoxious cables that tend to mess up the back of your PC. (Add in the power cords for the external devices, and you create a land into which no man dares venture.)

- ✔ SCSI is pronounced *scuzzy.*

- ✔ My spell checker thinks *scuzziest* should really be *Sucrets.*

- ✔ SCSI stands for Small Computer Serial Interface, or Small Computer System Interface, depending on which PC dictionary you buy.

- ✔ The Ultra Wide SCSI format can support up to 15 devices; 2 inside the PC and 13 outside. Older SCSI formats supported only 7 devices.

- ✔ You probably don't need a SCSI port inside your PC. However, if you notice your PC has limited expansion slots and space inside the console, adding a SCSI expansion card and external devices is often the only way to go.

- ✔ Next to the printer port, the SCSI port is the only way to add more external disk storage to your PC. And SCSI can add more hard drives and devices than the silly printer port.

- ✔ Supposedly a new standard called *FireWire* (a scary name, if there ever was one) will supplant SCSI in the future.

Chapter 10

All About Disks and Drives

In This Chapter

▶ The different types of disks

▶ How hard drives work

▶ Information on CD-ROM, CD-R, DVD, and so on

▶ Floppy disk information

▶ Zip and Jaz drives

▶ The amazing SuperDisk

*M*adly spinning in your PC's bosom is a wonderful device called a disk drive. Actually, your PC probably has several of them: hard drive, CD-ROM, and floppy. These sisters three make up your PC's long-term storage bins. No PC is complete without at least one of each. And then there are variations on a theme: CD-Rs, DVDs, SuperDisk drives, and so on. All that's missing are those refrigerator-sized things with reel-to-reel tapes on them, like in the movies.

Disk drives are important to your PC because that's where the computer's operating system, your software, and all the lovely things you create reside. This chapter is about disks and drives and all the madness that comes with them. I provide hardware information here; for using your disk drives with Windows, refer to Chapter 5.

Different Types of Disk Drives for Different Needs

In the beginning was the floppy disk. And it was good.

Actually, when the microcomputer first dawned in the late 1970s, the main storage medium was a cassette recorder with a special cassette tape. Then came the floppy drive, which was faster and more reliable.

Eventually the hard drive (always on the scene) came down in price until it was a standard fixture on all PCs. Then came the CD-ROM drive, first a novelty for a multimedia computer and now standard fare on all PCs.

Beyond the CD-ROM, many other interesting flavors of disk drives are available. The following list summarizes the most common types and how they're used.

Floppy drives. A floppy drive eats floppy disks, which typically store 1.44MB of information. That's enough storage to make backup copies of your documents for transportation between two computers, but that's about it. About ten years ago, all PC software came on floppy disks. Today some software still comes on floppies, but in most cases, a CD-ROM disc is used instead.

Hard drives. The PC's main long-term storage device is the hard drive. The hard drive's disk stores gigabytes of information, more then enough for Windows, your software, and all the data you can create. Unlike with floppy disks, you cannot remove a hard disk.

CD-ROM drives. A CD-ROM drive eats CD-ROM discs, which look just like music CDs. Computer CDs can store hundreds of megabytes of information, and most new computer software comes on a CD. Unlike hard drives and floppy disks, you cannot write information to a CD-ROM disc. The *RO* in CD-ROM means read-only. But the read-only nature is typically not a problem, and special types of CD-ROM drives allow you to write information.

Beyond these basic types of disk drives, you may find other drives, common or not, spinning and humming inside your PC. Here's the lot:

DVD-ROM drives. A DVD-ROM drive eats DVD-ROM discs, which look just like regular CD-ROM discs but store lots more information. DVD-ROM discs can store as much information as 20 CDs, or about enough space to store a full-length movie or a copy of every promise ever made by all American politicians. (Well, maybe not.)

Zip drives. A special type of disk drive on many computers sold today is the Zip drive. Zip drives eat Zip disks, which work much like floppy disks, although they can store 100MB of information — more than 75 floppy disks at about half the cost. Newer Zip models can store up to 250MB on a single disk.

Jaz drives. A bigger brother to the Zip drive is the Jaz drive, which can store 1GB or 2GB on a single disk, depending on the drive. These massive disks are ideal for exchanging large files between PCs or just for use as an extra storage device or for backup.

LS-120 SuperDisk drives. These floppy disk replacements both read and write to standard floppy disks but also accept large-capacity 120K *super* disks. The disks come standard on some computers but can be added to others. They may eventually replace the standard floppy drive.

Specialty drives. Many, many different types of disk drives are available, depending on your long-term storage needs. In addition to the more popular types just mentioned, you can also find MO or magneto-optical disks, floptical disks, and other strange and wondrous formats. It's enough to drive you batty.

Here are some general disk drive thoughts for you to ruminate:

- ✔ The drive is the device that reads the disk.

- ✔ The disk is the thing that contains the data — the media inside the drive.

- ✔ The information is stored on the disk, similar to the way a movie is stored on a videocassette.

- ✔ All disks are *hardware*. The information stored on them is software, just as your videocassette of *The Ten Commandments* isn't the movie itself; the movie is recorded on the cassette. (The movie is like software, and the cassette is hardware.)

- ✔ The terms hard disk and hard drive are often used interchangeably, although incorrectly so.

- ✔ IBM, always proving that it's different, calls the hard drive a *fixed disk*. No, it does not mean that the disk was once broken. (It's fixed, as in immovable.)

- ✔ Zip drives are not related to the ZIP file format, which is used to compress files downloaded from the Internet or from other users.

Driving a Hard Disk

Hard drives are the main storage place for most PCs. They're internal units, mounted inside the PC's console case. On some PCs, you can see the front of the hard drive on the case. On other PCs, all you see is a tiny light that blinks every time the hard drive is accessed.

The hard drive itself is a hermetically sealed unit. No air can get in or out. Therefore, the mechanism that reads and writes information can be very precise, and lots of information can be written to and read from the disk reliably. (This is why hard drives are nonremovable.)

Inside the hard drive are the hard disks. Most hard drives have two or more disks, each of which are stacked on a spindle. A device called a *read-write head* is mounted on an actuator arm that allows it to access both sides of all the disks in the hard drive at once. Figure 10-1 attempts to illustrate this concept.

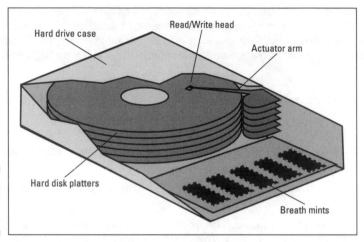

Figure 10-1:
The guts of
a hard drive.

Read/Write head
Hard drive case
Actuator arm
Hard disk platters
Breath mints

> ✔ Some types of removable hard drives exist, though the CD-R drive is quickly making the need for such drives obsolete. Read more about CD-R later in this chapter.
>
> ✔ You may have only one hard drive in your PC, but Windows may show it to you as drives C and D or even C, D, and E. This is because of an old limitation on disk size. With Windows 98, this limitation has been eliminated.
>
> ✔ A second hard drive can be added to most PCs, which is the best way to increase disk storage. Hard drives are cheap!

The hard drive connection

Hard drives connect to your PC's motherboard in one of two ways: directly or via an expansion card.

Most hard drives are connected directly, using something called IDE or *Integrated Drive Electronics*. This special feature allows hard drives and CD-ROMs to be directly attached to the motherboard.

Another way to attach hard drives is through a SCSI port. The SCSI port is usually added via a SCSI adapter card plugged into one of the motherboard's expansion slots. From there, you can add SCSI hard drives and CD-ROM drives either internally or externally.

> ✔ Only IDE hard drives can be plugged into IDE motherboards. SCSI hard drives must be plugged into SCSI expansion cards.
>
> ✔ If you have SCSI on your PC, make sure you buy SCSI hard drives for it.

> ✔ A great debate is raging over which type of hard drive standard is best: IDE or SCSI. For general use, IDE is best. But if you really want to expand your PC, I would recommend SCSI. Honestly, whichever hard drive came in your PC is what you're stuck with.

Saving disk space

The biggest problem with hard drives is that they eventually run out of room. There's no way to avoid your hard drive filling up, but you can delay the eventuality. Here are my thoughts:

> ✔ Run the Disk Cleanup utility at least once a month. From the Start menu in Windows 98, choose Programs➪Accessories➪System Tools➪ Disk Cleanup.
>
> ✔ Consider copying games to Zip or Jaz disks.
>
> ✔ Consider buying a CD-R and copying old files there for archival purposes.

> ✔ Don't use DriveSpace or any other disk-doubling program. These programs are really software alchemy that makes a crowded disk situation worse in my opinion. Installing a second hard drive is much better than putting up with the mental anguish of a disk doubling program.
>
> ✔ Buy a second, larger disk drive. Most PCs can squeeze two hard drives into their console. Have your dealer or guru add the second hard drive. Don't forget to use it!

The Shiny Media

CD-ROM drives became popular on computers starting in the mid 1990s. These drives can store and access megabytes of information, which make them ideal for installing new software or for accessing information such as fonts, graphics, or other types of handy references.

Several different types of CD-ROM disks and drives are available for every PC. The following list details them all:

CD-ROM. The traditional CD drive. These drives eat computer CDs that can store up to 600MB of information. Alas, the information can only be read; you cannot add new information to a CD-ROM.

CD-R. The R stands for *recordable*. Unlike a traditional CD-ROM, with a CD-R you can record information to a CD, making your own computer or music CDs in the process. The drives can read traditional CDs as well. However, once the CD is written to, information there cannot be erased or changed.

CD-RW. To solve the problem of being able to write information once to a CD-R, the CD-RW was developed. These disks work similar to hard drives and floppy disks; you can both read and write to them, adding information a bit at time. The disk can also be erased and used again.

DVD. If your PC doesn't have a DVD drive now, your next PC probably will. This drive is the next-generation CD-ROM drive, with DVD discs capable of storing up to 17GB of information on a two-sided disc. Just like computer CDs, however, you can only read from the DVD discs.

DVD-RAM. The latest craze is the DVD-RAM, which is a DVD disk that can be read from and written to. These babies are really expensive, however, making them a luxury for DVD developers only.

The following sections elaborate on these various types of shiny media drives.

- The speed of a CD-ROM drive is measured in X. The number before X indicates how much faster that drive is than the original PC CD-ROM drive (which plays as fast as a musical CD player). So a 32X drive reads information from the disc 32 times faster than the original PC CD-ROM drive.

- The CD-R drive is a specialty device not usually offered as a basic PC option. You can add one at any time, usually as an external model that attaches to the printer port.

- CD-R drives require special CD-R disks. The disks are written to just like any other disk drive in your PC. However, if you want to read the disk in another computer's CD-ROM drive, the CD must be *burned*. From that point on, it can no longer be written to.

- You can use CD-R drives to create musical CDs as well. A special program that comes with the drive allows you to set things up — even to print a CD disk label!

- CD-R drives usually have two speeds: a reading speed and a writing speed, both measured in X. The writing speed is generally slower than the reading speed.

- Special CD-RW disks are required for CD-RW drives. These disks can be repeatedly written to, modified, erased, and read from.

- Beware of low-cost, cheapie CD-R disks! The best ones to get are the green and gold (the color of the disk). Other, inexpensive disks may not be readable in all CD players.

- DVD is an acronym for Digital Versatile Disk.

- DVD drives look just like CD-ROM drives, although they have the DVD logo on them, plus a special DVD light that flashes when a DVD disk is being read.

✔ Although the DVD discs look just like computer CDs, they're capable of storing more than 4GB of information on a disk (compared with 600MB for a typical computer CD). Some future versions of DVD discs are rumored to be able to hold more than 17GB of information (barely enough for Excel 2010, most likely).

✔ Unfortunately, not much (if any) software is available on DVD discs. Sure, you can view movies on your PC. But beyond that, little software has appeared. (DVD's other acronym spells out as Digital *Video* Disk, designed to eventually replace the VCR in most homes.) Someday this may change, but DVD drives will have to be fairly standard before that happens.

Land of the Floppies

Floppy drives eat floppy disks. And between the two, the disks are more interesting. Floppy drives? Boring as a toaster. An unplugged toaster.

The amazing floppy disk itself

Allow me to be boring: The floppy disk is a 3½-inch, high-density diskette. The diskette may also be referred to as *IBM formatted* or *DS, HD*. It's all the same type of disk, the only one you can buy in most places. The only one your PC's floppy drive will eat.

Figure 10-2 shows what a typical 3½-inch floppy disk looks like, top and bottom. Here are some floppy disk points to ponder:

✔ It's tempting to use these disks as beverage coasters. Don't. Moisture can seep underneath the sliding metal thing and freak out the disk inside.

✔ Nothing is wrong with buying discount disks in bulk. I just did and saved enough for me to get my teeth capped and begin my singing career.

✔ Pay a little extra and buy preformatted disks. Look for a box that says *IBM Formatted* or *Formatted for IBM and Compatibles*. This effort saves you some time later because unformatted disks must be formatted before you can use them. (I cover the subject of formatting in Chapter 5.)

✔ No, the *IBM* on the label of a preformatted box of disks does not mean that they're only for IBM-brand computers. If you have a PC, you can use an IBM disk.

✔ Most 3½-inch disks come in little plastic sleeves. You can throw away the sleeves.

Write-protect
notches

Figure 10-2:
The
standard
3½-inch
floppy disk.

✔ Keep floppy disks away from magnets, including telephone handsets, speakers on radios and TVs, executive-style paper-clip holders, desk fans, photocopiers, 1.21-gigawatt power amplifiers, and the planet Jupiter.

✔ Don't set books or heavy items on top of disks. The pressure can push dust granules into the disk.

✔ Avoid extreme temperatures. Don't leave a disk sitting on the dash of your car or even on a window sill. And, even if the novel thought occurs to you, don't store your disks in the freezer.

✔ Don't touch the disk surface; touch only its protective cover. Don't spray WD-40 inside, even if the disk makes a noise as it spins. (Your disk drive is probably making the noise, anyway. Keep the WD-40 out of there, too.)

✔ Never remove a disk from a floppy drive when the drive light is on. Wait.

✔ When you're mailing a disk, don't use a floppy disk mailer from the drugstore. Don't fold the disk in half and mail it in a standard-size envelope. Instead, buy a photo mailer, which is the same as a floppy disk mailer but doesn't cost as much.

Write-protecting a floppy disk

You can protect floppy disks in such a way as to prevent yourself or anyone else from modifying or deleting anything on the disk.

To *write-protect* a 3½-inch disk, locate the little sliding tile on the lower-left side of the disk as you slide it into the drive. If the tile covers the hole, the disk can be written to. If you slide the tile off the hole (so that you can see through it), the disk is write-protected (refer to Figure 10-2).

When a disk is write-protected, you cannot alter, modify, change, or delete anything on that disk. You cannot accidentally reformat it. You can read from the disk and copy files from it. But changing the disk's contents — forget it!

Non-Floppy Removable Disk Solutions

Floppy disks used to come in several sizes and capacities. Back when IBM was leading the PC hardware market, a new disk size and format were introduced with just about every new-generation PC. That stopped in 1987 with the introduction of the PC's 1.44MB floppy disk — which is still used today.

Since floppy development stagnated, several competing disks have emerged to supplement removable storage on a PC. These include the Zip, Jaz, LS-120, and other types of disk drives, all covered in their own little neat sections.

- ✔ Actually, floppy development has proceeded since 1987. One such disk was the ill-fated ED floppy disk, which stored 2.88MB on a disk. It never caught on (like, duh!).

- ✔ Several different disk formats have come and gone, each trying to replace the floppy. The following sections deal with only the most popular and widely available formats. New formats or standards that appear will be added to future editions of this book.

- ✔ The original floppy disk? It was 8-inches square! Very popular in the mid-1970s. Early PCs used the 5¼-inch square floppy until the 3½-inch *microfloppy* took over in '87.

- ✔ Most large-format, nonfloppy disk solutions (magneto-optical disks, for example) have been replaced by the CD-R.

Zippity do dah

For the past several years or so, Zip disks have been all the rage. Zip drives are offered as an option on many new PCs, and you can add a Zip drive internally or externally to just about any PC.

Zip disks store 100MB or 250MB per disk, depending on which Zip drive you have. That's a whole lotta floppies. The disks are great for backing up files, storing files long term, or transporting large files between two computers. Figure 10-3 illustrates a typical Zip disk. It's about 4-inches square, only slightly larger than a floppy disk.

The Zip disk has only a couple of drawbacks. First, the drives are only made by one company (Iomega), unlike floppy drives which are made by several companies as a standard.

The second drawback is that Zip disks are expensive, typically $10 or more for a single disk when you buy them in bulk. Still, the cost is less than an equivalent stack of floppies and more convenient.

See Chapter 5 for more information on Zip drives.

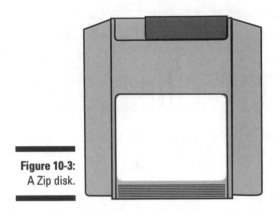

Figure 10-3:
A Zip disk.

All that Jaz

Jaz disks are like a big brother to the Zip disks. The Jaz disks are made by the same company as Zip disks, but they store lots more information: either 1GB or 2GB per disk, depending on the Jaz drive. This storage capacity makes Jaz work almost like a removable hard drive — and it stores much more information and is easier to deal with than either a CD-R or CD-RW drive.

After inserting a Jaz disk into the Jaz drive, the disk is accessed just like any other disk on your PC. You can use them one after another to increase your total disk storage space without buying new hardware.

Like Zip disks, Jaz disks are pricey: $100 for a 1GB disk or $120 for a 2GB disk. That compares with about $200 for a typical 2GB hard drive.

Look! Up in the sky! It's SuperDisk!

SuperDisk is really a brand name for what the geeks call an LS-120 floppy drive. It's a special type of floppy drive that eats both standard 3½-inch floppies as well as 120MB disks. So this floppy drive makes an ideal replacement for your PC's floppy drive (and comes standard on some PCs).

The 120MB disks themselves look just like regular floppy disks, but the drive recognizes the difference and lets you store up to 120MB worth of junk on each disk. The drive does that through special metallic magic that you need not concern yourself with — but it works!

- ✔ SuperDisks themselves cost about $8 each in bulk.
- ✔ You can add a SuperDisk to any PC by replacing the existing floppy drive.
- ✔ Someday the LS-120 SuperDisk may replace the standard PC floppy drive.

Chapter 11

Memory (RAM-a-lama ding-dong)

· ·

· ·

*D*o you know if you have enough memory? How could you remember something like that? No matter how old people get, they never run out of memory. It's a limitless resource, though remembering certain dates seems to elude various male members of the species. Too bad it's not the same for your computer, where memory is gobbled up quicker than a stray Snickers bar at a fat camp.

Memory, or random-access memory (RAM), is a storage place in a computer, just like disk space. Unlike disk storage, memory is the only place inside the computer where real work gets done. Obviously, the more memory you have, the more work you can do. But not only that, having more memory means the computer is capable of grander tasks, such as working with graphics, animation, sound, and music — and your PC remembers everyone it meets without ever having to look twice at a name tag.

What Is Memory?

All computers need memory. That's where the work gets done. The microprocessor is capable of storing information inside itself, but only so much. It needs extra memory just like humans need notepads and libraries.

For example, when you create a document with your word processor, each character you type is placed into a specific location in memory. Once there, the microprocessor doesn't need to access it again unless you're editing, searching or replacing, or doing something active to the text.

After something is created in memory — a document, spreadsheet, or graphic — you save it to disk. Your disk drives provide long-term storage for information. Then, when you need to access the information again, you open it back into memory from disk. After it's there, the microprocessor can again work over the information.

The only nasty thing about memory is that it's volatile. When you turn off the power, the contents of memory go *poof!* This is okay if you've saved to disk, but if you haven't, everything is lost. Even resetting your computer zaps the contents of memory. So always save (if you can) before you reset or turn off your PC.

- ✔ The more memory you have, the better. With more memory, you can work on larger documents and spreadsheets, enjoy applications that use graphics and sound, and boast about it to your friends.

- ✔ All computers have a limited amount of memory, which means that someday you may run short. When that happens, you see an error message shouting, "Out of memory!" Don't panic. The computer can handle the situation. You can add more memory to your system if you like. Consult your favorite computer guru for help.

- ✔ One of the sure signs that your PC needs more memory: It slows to a crawl. I have a laptop with only (only!) 8MB of memory. Under Windows 98 that's just not enough memory, and though it gets work done, I spend a lot of time waiting for the computer to catch up. (I think I'll steal a few memory chips from my wife's laptop. Shhh! Don't tell!)

- ✔ Turning off the power makes the *contents* of memory go bye-bye. It doesn't destroy the memory chips themselves.

- ✔ When you open a file on disk, the computer copies that information from disk into the computer's memory. Only in memory can that information be examined or changed. When you save information back to disk, the computer copies it from memory to the disk.

- ✔ The term RAM is used interchangeably with the word memory. They're the same thing. (In fact, RAM stands for random-access memory, in case you've been working any crossword puzzles lately.)

Common memory questions

How much memory do I need?

Your brain has all the storage you'll need for a lifetime.

No, I mean how much memory does my computer need?

The amount of memory your PC needs depends on two things. The first, and most important, is the memory requirement of your software. Some programs, such as spreadsheets and graphics applications, require lots of memory. For example, Adobe Photoshop (a graphics package) says — right on the box — that it needs 16MB of RAM. Yowie!

The second and more limiting factor is cost. Memory costs money. It's not as expensive as it was back in the old stone-tablet days of computing, but it still costs something.

Generally speaking, all computers should have at least 16MB of RAM, preferably 32MB. You're screaming with 64MB of RAM, and 128MB may seem outrageous now, but it will probably be the minimum when Windows 2010 comes out.

Can I add more memory to my PC?

Yes. You typically add it because your applications need more memory. The programs just won't run (or will run sluggishly) without more memory. (Refer to "Adding more memory to your PC," later in this chapter.)

Can I lose computer memory?

No. Your computer has only a finite amount of memory, but it cannot be lost to anything. Programs use memory when you run them. For example, when you run WordPerfect, it eats up a specific amount of memory. But when you quit WordPerfect, all that memory is made available to the next program. So while a program runs, it grabs memory for its own uses. When the program is done, it reluctantly lets the memory go.

What about copying programs?

Copying a program or file uses some memory, but don't confuse disk memory with computer memory or RAM. You can copy a huge file from one disk to another without worrying about running out of memory. The operating system (Windows) handles the details. (Now, you may run out of disk space, but that's another problem.)

What's a *memory leak?*

It's a bad term that describes what happens when a dead program just sits in memory taking up space. Say, for example, Netscape Navigator crashes (which seems to happen a lot). Windows survives that crash, but a dead copy of Netscape may still lurk in memory, taking up space. That's what they mean by memory leak. Or any time memory is used for something but not given up afterward, that's also a memory leak. It's nothing for you to worry about. Shutting down and restarting the computer fixes it.

How much memory is in my PC right now?

This information may be a mystery to you, but it isn't a secret to your computer. The System Properties dialog box shows you how much memory lives inside the beast: Right-click on the My Computer icon on the desktop. Choose Properties from the shortcut menu that appears. You'll see a dialog box similar to the one shown in Figure 11-1.

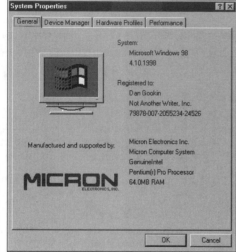

Figure 11-1:
How much
memory is in
this PC?

The amount of memory (shown as RAM) appears right beneath the type of microprocessor that lives in your PC. In Figure 11-1, it says the computer has 64.0MB of RAM. That's adequate.

Memory in your PC

Memory is a component of the motherboard, sitting very close to the microprocessor. It exists as a series of tiny chips called DRAM chips.

The DRAM chips typically come as groups soldered together on a thin strip of fiberglass. The whole shebang is referred to as a SIMM or DIMM. It's about the size of a pocket comb, as shown in Figure 11-2.

Each SIMM or DIMM card contains 4, 8, 16, or 32 megabytes of memory. These cards are plugged into memory slots on the motherboard, each slot being a *bank* of memory. So a PC with 64MB of RAM may have four banks of 16MB SIMMs installed.

Figure 11-2:
A typical
SIMM.

- DRAM stands for dynamic random-access memory. It's pronounced *dee-ram,* and it's the most common type of memory chip installed in a PC.

- SIMM stands for single in-line memory module.

- DIMM stands for dual in-line memory module.

- Memory bank slots on the motherboard are shown in Figure 11-1.

- Whether your PC needs SIMM or DIMM memory depends on the design of the motherboard.

- DIMMs and SIMMs are similar in appearance, though DIMMs allow memory to be accessed more efficiently. Eventually, DIMMs will replace SIMMs as the best way to upgrade memory in a PC.

Adding more memory to your PC

There is no electronic equivalent of Geritol for your computer. If you think your PC has tired RAM or maybe it didn't have enough memory in the first place, you can always add more.

Adding memory to your computer is Lego-block simple. The only difference is that the typical Lego block set, say the cool Space Station or Rescue Helicopter set, costs under $20. Your computer, on the other hand, may cost 100 times that much. Adding memory is not something to be taken lightly.

Upgrading memory involves five complex and boring steps:

1. **Figure out how much memory you need to add.**

   For example, suppose your PC has 16MB of RAM and you need 32MB to run that program that lets you talk to your PC. You need another 16MB — or more if you can afford it.

2. **Figure out how much memory you can install.**

   This is a technical step. It involves knowing how memory is added to your computer and in what increments. If you have an empty bank of memory, then this step is actually quite simple. But if your PC doesn't have any empty memory banks, then it can be complex — and expensive. Better leave this task to your dealer or computer guru.

3. **Buy something.**

   In this case, you buy the memory chips themselves, or you buy the expansion card into which the memory chips are installed.

4. **Pay someone else to plug in the chips and do the upgrade.**

   Oh, you can do it yourself, but I'd pay someone else to do it.

5. **Gloat.**

After you have the memory, brag to your friends about it. Heck, it used to be impressive to say you had 640K of RAM. Then came the "I have 4 megabytes of memory in my 386 or 8 megabytes of memory in my 486." Today? Anything less than 128 megabytes and your kids will roll their eyes at you.

✔ PC memory usually comes in given sizes: 4MB, 8MB, 16MB, and then in multiples of 16MB after that. Yeah, oddball sizes are available, but just about everything can be divided evenly by two.

✔ Another shocker: You may think that moving from 16MB in your system to 64MB requires that you buy 48MB of memory chips. Wrong! It may mean you have to buy the full 64MB and then toss out your original 16MB. It all has to do with how memory physically fits in the PC, which is something even the gods themselves don't fully understand.

Boring technical details on RAM, ROM, and Flash Memory

RAM stands for random-access memory. It refers to memory that the microprocessor can read from and write to. When you create something in memory, it's done in RAM. RAM is memory and vice versa.

ROM stands for read-only memory. The microprocessor can read from ROM, but it cannot write to it or modify it. ROM is permanent. Often, ROM chips contain special instructions for the computer — important stuff that never changes. Because that information is stored on a memory chip, the microprocessor can access it. The instructions are always there because they're unerasable.

Flash Memory is a special type of memory that works like both RAM and ROM. Information can be written to Flash Memory like RAM, but it doesn't erase when the power is off like RAM. By using Flash Memory, manufacturers can update and upgrade your PC's BIOS or other components by running a special program. Otherwise, you would need to replace the chips — which is more work.

✓ If you want to try upgrading memory yourself, go ahead. Plenty of easy books on the subject of upgrading memory are available, as well as how-to articles in some of the popular magazines. I still recommend having someone else do it, however.

Measuring Memory

Many interesting terms orbit the planet memory. The most basic of these terms refer to the quantity of memory (see Table 11-1).

Table 11-1		Memory Quantities	
Term	*Abbreviation*	*About*	*Actual*
Byte		1 byte	1 byte
Kilobyte	K or KB	1,000 bytes	1,024 bytes
Megabyte	M or MB	1,000,000 bytes	1,048,576 bytes
Gigabyte	G or GB	1,000,000,000 bytes	1,073,741,824 bytes
Terabyte	T or TB	1,000,000,000,000 bytes	1,099,511,627,776 bytes

Memory is measured by the *byte*. Think of a byte as a single character, a letter in the middle of a word. For example, the word *spatula* is 7 bytes long and would require 7 bytes of computer memory storage.

A half page of text is about 1,000 bytes. To make this a handy figure to know, computer nerds refer to 1,000 bytes as a *kilobyte,* or 1K or KB.

The term *megabyte* refers to 1,000K, or 1 million bytes. The abbreviation MB (or M) indicates megabyte, so 16MB means 16 megabytes of memory.

Further than the megabyte is the *gigabyte*. That is 1 billion bytes or about 1,000 megabytes.

The *terabyte* is 1 trillion bytes, or enough RAM to dim the lights when you start the PC.

Other trivia:

✓ The term *giga* is actually Greek, and it means giant.

✓ The term *tera* is also Greek. It means monster!

- ✔ You have no reason to worry about how much ROM (read-only memory) you have in your computer.

- ✔ A specific location in memory is called an *address*.

- ✔ Bytes are composed of eight bits. The word *bit* is a contraction of binary digit. Binary is base two, or a counting system that uses only ones and zeros. Computers count in binary, and we group their bits into clusters of eight for convenient consumption as bytes.

And just what the heck is *extended memory?*

Back in the old days, several dozen terms were used to describe memory in a PC: conventional memory, DOS memory, upper memory, high memory, HMA memory, expanded memory, DMPI memory, extended memory, and on and on.

The only memory term you see used any more is *extended memory*. All the memory in your PC is extended memory, which is a holdover term from the ancient days where memory terms were important.

What does this mean to you?

If you see software that says it requires 16MB of extended memory, then know that they merely mean 16MB of memory. All the memory in your PC is extended already.

Chapter 12

Amazing Monitors and Glorious Graphics

- -

In This Chapter

▶ Understanding PC monitors and graphics

▶ Adjusting your monitor

▶ Using an LCD monitor

▶ PC graphic adapter information

▶ Changing the desktop background (wallpaper)

▶ Adjusting the graphics resolution and colors

▶ Adding a screen saver to Windows

▶ Using two monitors in Windows

- -

*T*he PC's monitor is the first thing you notice on a PC. It's what you look at when you use the computer. And the monitor is what makes the best target should you ever decide to shoot your computer. (But keep in mind that the monitor is only the messenger; what you really want to destroy is the console.)

If your computer were a person, then the monitor would be its face. This chapter is about your PC's face, both the hardware part and how Windows can manipulate that face to make it more pleasing for you.

What's in a Name?

Is it a monitor? Is it the screen? Whatever *it* is, it looks like a TV set sitting on or nearby your computer.

The monitor is the box. It contains a picture tube, like a TV. So if the whole thing fell on the floor, you could say, "The monitor fell on the floor. It was an accident."

The screen is the image that appears on the monitor. It appears on the glass part. This is confusing because you could say, "My screen says the computer doesn't like me," and it means the same thing as, "My monitor says the computer doesn't like me." Either way, the computer doesn't like you.

Figure 12-1 illustrates this monitor/screen concept, mostly because I need another figure in this chapter.

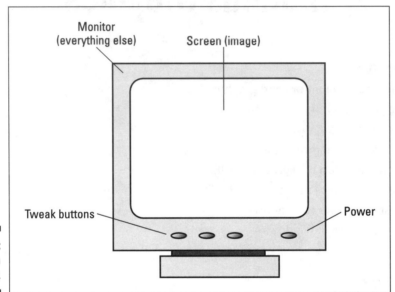

Monitor
(everything else)

Screen (image)

Tweak buttons

Power

Figure 12-1:
Parts of a
monitor.

Nerds refer to the entire monitor/screen thing as a CRT, which stands for cathode ray tube. And note that it's *cathode* ray tube, not *catheter* ray tube.

Monitors and Adapters

The monitor is only half of the video system in your PC. The other half is known as the *display adapter.* It's the circuitry that runs the monitor, controlling the image that the monitor displays.

Figure 12-2 illustrates the monitor/adapter relationship. The display adapter exists either as part of the motherboard or on an expansion card plugged into the motherboard. A cable then connects the monitor to the console. And, of course, the monitor plugs into the wall.

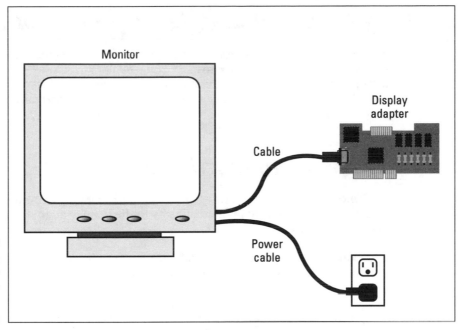

Figure 12-2:
The monitor
and display
adapter.

The monitor itself is rather dumb. It's really the display adapter that makes things happen on the monitor. Between the two, the display adapter is what determines your PC's graphics potential.

- You need both a monitor and display adapter.

- In some PCs, especially laptops, the display adapter is built into the motherboard.

- Most laptops will let you add an external monitor using an external graphics port.

- USB monitors connect to the PC through the USB port.

- If your PC has more than one monitor (and they can, you know), then it must have one video adapter for each monitor or a special video adapter that supports dual monitors. See the section "Dueling Monitors," later in this chapter, for more information.

- The display adapter may also be called the display adapter card, video adapter, video hardware, video system, or jangawangawaawaaboo.

Getting to Know and Love Your Monitor

A PC's monitor is really a *peripheral*. It's a separate device that need not be sold with the computer (the console). Some dealers even offer a range of different monitors for sale with a computer. Each brand offers different features, but all monitors serve the same function — displaying information the computer coughs up.

The physical description

Each monitor has two tails. One is a power cord that plugs into the wall. The second tail is a video cable that connects to the display adapter port on the back of the console.

You usually find the monitor's on-off button on the front of the monitor, near the bottom right. (It's a total bias against left-handed people, part of the larger adroit conspiracy.)

Additional buttons adorn the front of the monitor, which you use to control the monitor's display. These buttons may be visible like a row of ugly teeth, or they may be hidden behind a panel. The next section discusses what they do.

Some monitors display a message when the monitor is turned on but the PC is not (or the monitor is not receiving a signal from the PC). The message may read `Invalid Sync` or `No Signal`, or it may urge you to check the connection. That's okay. The monitor pops to life properly when you turn the console on.

All the technical information you need to know

A lot of technical nonsense is used to describe a monitor's abilities. Out of that pile of jargon, only two terms are really necessary: size and dot pitch.

Size. Monitors are judged by the picture tube size, just like TVs. The size is measured on a diagonal, so beware that it's not a width or height thing. Common sizes for PC monitors are 15, 17, 19, and 21 inches. The most popular size is 17 inches, though personally I love the 19-inch monitors and absolutely swoon over the 21-inch monsters! Oooooooo!

How big is big?

Q: You state that a monitor's diagonal measurement may not be the same as its viewing area; the size of the screen is occasionally a few inches smaller than the glass. Don't you mean that the size of the screen is occasionally a few inches smaller than the entire front of the monitor (including the plastic border)? I consider the glass to be the screen. Most PC's have a screen (or glass area) that is smaller than the entire front of the monitor.

A: The diagonal measurement *is* the glass area. The screen displayed on that area is even smaller. My best advice is usually to view the monitor with your own eyes to see how big it really is.

Dot pitch. This refers to the distance between each dot, or pixel, on the screen (as measured from the center of each pixel). The closer the dots, the better the image is. A dot pitch of 0.28 mm (millimeters) is really good, with smaller values being even better.

Beyond these two terms are a whole grab bag of technical terms used to describe a monitor. The best judge, really, is your own eyeballs. If the monitor looks good, buy it!

- ✔ Other aspects of the display — such as resolution, colors, and video memory — are all part of the display adapter hardware, not the monitor.

- ✔ I'm a big fan of flat-screen monitors. These are monitors with special picture tubes that are flatter than traditional tubes. (Don't confuse these with LCD monitors, often called flat *panel*.)

Adjusting the monitor's display

In the early days, you were lucky if your monitor had contrast and brightness knobs. Today, the adjustments you can make to your monitor are endless. Sometimes you make adjustments using a row of buttons that adorn the front of your monitor, looking almost like a second keyboard. Other times you use an annoying combination of buttons like for setting the time on a digital clock.

If your monitor has a row of buttons, then each one adjusts a certain aspect of the display. Often plus (+) and minus (-) buttons are used to adjust each aspect. So, for example, to adjust contrast, you press the contrast button and then the plus or minus button. An on-screen display gives you feedback.

Figure 12-3 shows some common symbols used to adjust many PC monitors.

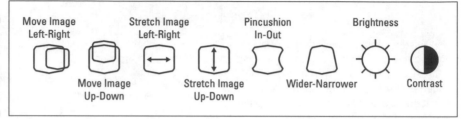

Figure 12-3:
Icons found on the typical PC monitor.

Some monitors have only a few buttons on them but use an on-screen display to select options. Figure 12-4 shows a typical on-screen display. You use one set of buttons on the monitor to select an item and then use plus (+) and minus (-) buttons to adjust each aspect of the display. Note the icons similar to those shown in Figure 12-3 are used to indicate various settings.

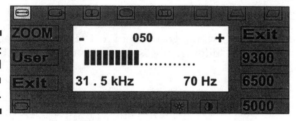

Figure 12-4:
A typical on-screen display.

✔ The on-screen information appears over any other image displayed on the monitor. Don't let it freak you out.

✔ Older monitors may not have as many adjustments as are shown in Figure 12-3. They may also lack on-screen displays.

✔ By pressing the Left-Right, Up-Down, and then the stretch buttons, you can adjust the monitor's image to fill the screen. This makes the most efficient use of your monitor.

✔ Monitors may also display frequency information, such as 31KHz/60Hz, when they change screen modes, such as when you play a game and the screen changes to another resolution.

✔ Most monitors also have a Save or Store button, which remembers the settings you've entered, making them permanent.

Fancy LCD displays

Eventually, your computer will be connected to a flat-panel LCD monitor, similar to the screens used on PC laptops. Not only are these monitors lightweight, thin, and beautiful to look at, but they'll also induce envy into anyone who sees them. The bad news? They're very expensive.

- ✔ If you want to go LCD monitor shopping, forget the graphics! The best judge of an LCD screen is text. Fire up a word processor in the store and see how the text looks. Some LCD monitors display glorious graphics but tepid text.

- ✔ The best LCD monitors to get are those that come with their own digital display adapter. They typically plug into the AGP (Accelerated Graphics Port) slot on your PC's motherboard, so make sure your PC has an AGP slot before buying one.

- ✔ Quite a few LCD monitors also plug into standard VGA ports. No problem there.

- ✔ A 15-inch LCD monitor has approximately the same viewing area as a standard 17-inch monitor, which is due to the LCD monitors being wider than most CRT monitors.

- ✔ LCD monitors are available in just about every size, from 14 inches diagonally up to 21 inches. Those 21-inch monsters are beautiful but very expensive.

- ✔ Be sure to check the viewing angle on an LCD monitor, which is the number of degrees to the left or right of the monitor at which the image fades. Monitors with a 160-degree or wider viewing angle are best.

Cleaning your monitor

Computer monitors grow dust like a five o'clock shadow. And, in addition to the dust, you always find fingerprints and sneeze globs on your screen. Monitors are messy.

To clean your monitor, spray some window cleaner on a soft towel or tissue. Then gently rub the screen. You also can use vinegar if you want your computer to have that tossed-salad smell. You can spray some electronics spray cleaners right on the screen; be sure the cleaner is specially made for that use.

Never spray window cleaner directly on the screen. It may dribble down into the monitor itself and wreak electronic terror. And never clean an LCD monitor; rubbing an LCD monitor with anything other than a dry towel can severely damage it.

All About Display Adapters

The secretive, internal part of a PC's video system is the display adapter. It's an expansion card that plugs into your PC's motherboard and gives your computer the ability to display lovely text and graphics on the monitor.

Display adapters come in various price ranges and have features for artists, game players, computer designers, and regular Joes like you and me and guys named Joe. Here's the quick roundup:

✔ The measure of a display adapter is how much memory (video RAM) it has. Most adapters come with at least 1 to 4MB of memory. The more expensive, fancier models can have up to 16MB. Wow.

✔ The more memory the display adapter has, the higher the resolutions it can support and the more colors it can display at those higher resolutions.

✔ Many display adapters are advertised as supporting 3-D graphics. That's okay, but they only work if your software supports the particular 3-D graphics offered by that display adapter. (If so, the side of the software box should say so.)

✔ If your PC has a DVD drive, you need a display adapter capable of producing the DVD image on the monitor. The display adapters typically have an S-Video Out port on them, which lets you connect a TV to the computer for watching things on a larger screen.

✔ Some high-resolution graphics systems are only applicable to certain kinds of software. Computer graphics, CAD, and animation and design are all areas where paying top dollar for your display is worth it. If you're using only basic applications, such as a word processor, you don't need top-dollar displays.

Tweaking the Display in Windows

The knobs on your monitor control the monitor. To control the display adapter — which really does all the work, you need to use Windows. Specifically, you use the Display icon in the Control Panel to tweak various aspects of your monitor's display.

The following sections discuss various strange and wondrous things you can do in the Display Properties dialog box, summoned by the Display icon in the Control Panel. But first, here's how you display the Display Properties dialog box:

1. **From the Start menu, choose Settings⇨Control Panel.**

   The Control Panel's main window appears.

Display

2. **Double-click the Display icon.**

   This action conjures up the Display Properties dialog box, similar to what's shown in Figure 12-5.

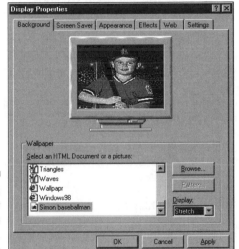

Figure 12-5:
The Display
Properties
dialog box.

3. **Mess with the Display Properties dialog box.**

   You can change the desktop's background, add a screen saver, and change the system colors or screen resolution using the Display Properties dialog box. The sections that follow outline how to perform these miracles.

4. **Close the Display Properties dialog box.**

   When you're done, you can click the OK button to keep your changes, or click Cancel to go back to the way things were.

ASK DAN

Monitoring your monitor

Q: After having my computer for only five months, I got a fatal exception error one day while the screen saver was on. Could the monitor be causing the problem?

A: No, it's not your monitor. The monitor cannot cause the computer to crash. When it breaks, you just can't see anything.

You can also instantly summon the Display Properties dialog box by right-clicking anywhere on the desktop. From the shortcut menu, choose Properties, and lo, there you are!

Changing the background (wallpaper)

The background, or *wallpaper,* is what you see when you look at the desktop. You can see a pattern or a pretty picture or just about anything other than the dingy gray that Windows really wants to display.

Summon the Display Properties dialog box, as described in the preceding section. Make sure the Background panel is forward, as shown in Figure 12-5.

You can put an image up on the desktop two ways. The first is with a pattern, and the second is with a graphical image or wallpaper.

The patterns are listed when you click the Pattern button in the Display Properties dialog box. A bunch of them are displayed, each of them equally boring.

The Wallpaper area lists a bunch of graphics files you can apply to the desktop. If the image is large enough, it can cover the entire screen. If it's small, you may want to tile it on the screen, in which case you'd click in the radio button by the word Tile if you have Windows 95. In Windows 98, you would select Tile from a drop-down list.

Anytime you select a new pattern or wallpaper, it appears in the mini-monitor preview window. It's rather small, so the effect isn't stunning. If you want to see a true preview, click the Apply button.

If you created your own graphics file, you can use it as the wallpaper. First, the graphics must be a bitmapped image or BMP file. You can also use GIF files, but you have to use the Browse button to locate and select them. (See Chapter 22 for information on scanning in images to be used as wallpaper.)

Click OK to keep your new desktop wallpaper.

Adjusting the resolution and colors

Muster the Display Properties dialog box, as foretold earlier in this chapter in "Tweaking the Display in Windows." Click the Settings tab to bring that panel forward. What you see will look something like Figure 12-6.

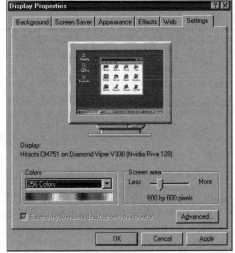

Figure 12-6:
The Display
Properties
dialog box,
Settings
panel.

The Settings panel in the Display Properties dialog box is where you tweak your monitor's color and resolution. You can have only so much of both, and this part of the dialog box lets you see just how much you can get away with.

I'm not going to go through all the details here. Basically, you select your colors first, from 16 colors on up to 16 bit or 32 bit or whatever huge value Windows gives you.

Next, select a resolution. You notice that the mini-monitor preview window changes to reflect your choice. And if you select a higher resolution, don't be surprised if the number of colors decreases. These two things are linked, in case you haven't guessed.

✔ If you're fortunate enough to have a 21-inch or larger monitor, run Windows at the 1024 x 768 resolution at minimum. This setting displays a ton of information on the screen at once and uses 256 or more colors. You can adjust most of your software (typically through some sort of *Zoom* command) to display text larger on the screen, making it an even trade-off.

✔ Some computer games change the monitor's resolution to allow the games to be played. This is okay, and the resolution should return to normal after playing the game.

✔ If you have trouble seeing tiny images on the screen, consider the 640 x 480 resolution.

- Some kids' games demand that resolution be set to exactly 256 colors. It will say so when you install the program.

- The number of colors and resolution depends on your graphics adapter's abilities. Don't blame me if it isn't that high.

Adding a screen saver

A long, long time ago, PC monitors were susceptible to the dreaded *phosphor burn-in*. After time, the same image became *etched* on your screen. Visions of 1-2-3 or WordPerfect would haunt PC users, even with the monitor turned off!

One of the preventative measures against phosphor burn-in was to run a screen-saver program. That program would blank the monitor. So after several minutes of inactivity — no typing or moving the mouse — the screen went blank. Touching the mouse or pressing any key resumed computer operation, but the screen saver saved the monitor from phosphor burn-in.

Fortunately, today's monitors are less likely to suffer from phosphor burn-in. Still, the screen saver remains, mostly as a toy. (Though in Windows, using a screen saver is the best way to password-protect your PC. More on that in a moment.)

Bring up the Display Properties dialog box, as discussed in "Tweaking the Display in Windows." Click the Screen Saver tab to bring that panel forward. The dialog box should look something like Figure 12-7.

Easing monitor sickness

Q: I wrote to you awhile back about how to deal with motion sickness while on the computer. You wrote back with the good idea of an anti-glare screen, which does help, but I had already purchased one, and I was still getting sick.

I wanted to share with you a suggestion that my sister-in-law gave me. She needed to find some motion sickness bracelets for her car travel. Well, I thought, if they work for cars why not computers? They definitely help! They are called Travel-Eze wristbands, and I bought them at Walgreens. I doubt that they are strong enough for a person like me to play games on the computer, but they really seem to be helping me with just normal stuff.

A: Your suggestion is passed on, and thank you! Also, the reader points out that you can *tap* on certain pressure points on the wrist and behind the ear to alleviate some forms of motion sickness.

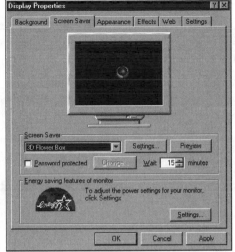

Figure 12-7:
Select a
screen
saver here.

You select a screen saver from the Screen Saver drop-down list. The preview window (screen) in the dialog box shows you what you're getting yourself into.

Click the Settings button to make adjustments for your chosen screen saver.

Click the Preview button to see what the screen saver does in full-size mode. (Move the mouse a tad to turn the screen saver off.)

In the Wait box, enter the number of idle minutes after which you want the screen saver to kick in.

- ✔ A safe key to press for switching off the screen saver is Ctrl. Unlike other keys on your keyboard, this key doesn't mess with any application that appears after the screen saver vanishes.

- ✔ No, pressing Ctrl doesn't switch off the screen saver; it merely hides it so you can see the desktop again.

- ✔ A cool way to switch off the screen saver is to pound your desk with your fist. That jostles the mouse and deactivates the screen saver.

- ✔ The Password Protected check box allows you to put a password on your screen saver (set with the Change button). This is a great way to protect your PC when you're away; only by knowing the password (or resetting the PC) can you stop the screen saver and use the computer.

- ✔ If you forget the password, you have to reset the computer to regain control. There's no other way around it.

Conjuring a screen saver

Q: I just downloaded a screen saver from the Internet. How do I get it to work in Windows? It doesn't show up in the Screen Saver dialog box?

A: You must save the screen saver file in the System folder in the Windows folder

(C:\Windows\System). Once there, you can summon the Display Properties dialog box, and you'll see the custom screen saver there in the list.

Dueling Monitors

With Windows 98 and the proper hardware installed, your PC can handle two or more monitors. Notice I said *proper hardware.* You can't just go out and buy a second video adapter and have everything work. It must be one of the handful recognized by Windows as dual-monitor happy. When you meet that weird requirement, you can have two (or more) monitors on one PC.

You adjust the two monitors in the Display Properties dialog box. Right-click on the desktop and select Properties from the shortcut menu. In the Display Properties dialog box, click the Settings tab to bring that panel forward. You'll see your two monitors displayed, as shown in Figure 12-8.

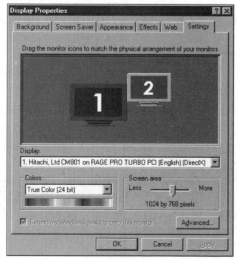

Figure 12-8:
Dueling monitors.

You can drag the monitors' images inside the dialog box to position them left, right, or on top of each other. The numbers on each monitor correspond to the monitors listed in the drop-down Display list.

Now what's the point? Obviously, more monitors give you more screen acreage. You can read e-mail on one monitor and browse the Web on another. Whatever. It's all greed, you know.

- ✔ The WINDOWS folder on drive C contains a file called DISPLAY.TXT. Open that file and read the information there about which video adapters are supported for dual monitors.

- ✔ If the second monitor is recognized, Windows displays a text message on it when your PC starts. That's your "Yippee! It worked!" signal that everything's okay.

- ✔ To activate a monitor, click its icon in the Display Properties dialog box. Click Yes if you're asked to enable the monitor.

- ✔ Each monitor can have its own resolution and settings. Just select the monitor from the Display drop-down list and select the necessary settings.

- ✔ The desktop image appears on both monitors.

- ✔ You can drag windows from one monitor to the other. It's really kind of neat to see.

- ✔ Games run only on your main monitor (the one that's active when the PC first starts). DOS programs also run on the main monitor only. In the future, some games may take advantage of multiple monitors, but I wouldn't count on it. (Two monitors are just too weird.)

- ✔ Maximizing a window enlarges it to fill the entire screen of one monitor only. You can, however, stretch a window across several monitors.

- ✔ If you're going to add the second monitor yourself, do this: Remove your PC's first adapter and then add the second adapter. Configure the second adapter and then reinstall the first adapter. That approach avoids the biggest problem installing the second monitor, which is finding the proper driver (software). For some reason, Windows finds the drivers best when working one at a time.

What's a screen dump?

No, a screen dump is not a pile of old monitors somewhere in the desert.

A *screen dump* is the process of taking the information on your computer screen and sending it off to the printer or to a file. Under DOS, the magic Print Screen key on the keyboard initiated this procedure. In Windows, the Print Screen key does kind of the same thing, but nothing is printed.

In Windows, when you press the Print Screen key, you take a snapshot of the desktop. All that graphical information is saved like a photograph in the Clipboard. You can then paste the information into any program that can swallow graphical images. So even though nothing prints, you still get a dump of what was on the screen.

Chapter 13

Eeek! (The Mouse Chapter)

. . . .

In This Chapter

▶ Recognizing your PC's mouse

▶ Reviewing various types of mice

▶ Hooking a mouse up to your PC

▶ Using the mouse

▶ Pointing, clicking, double-clicking, dragging

▶ Cleaning your mouse

▶ Adjusting the mouse in Windows

▶ Using a left-handed mouse

▶ Dealing with mouse woes

. . . .

*T*he Macintosh may have been the first personal computer to come with a mouse, but today it's hard to find any PC that's sold without its own mouse. Some mice are fun, like the wacky models Logitech sells. Other mice, like the IBM computer mouse (which has the serious IBM letters etched into its case), are meant strictly for business. Regardless, a mouse is a necessary thing to have, especially when you're using a graphically drunk operating system like Windows.

✔ Doug Englebart invented the computer mouse at the Stanford Research Institute in the 1960s. He received only $10,000 for his invention, but in 1997, he won the $500,000 Lemelson-MIT Prize for American Innovation.

✔ The plural of computer mouse is *mice.* One computer has a mouse. Two computers have mice.

✔ And just why isn't one lice a louse?

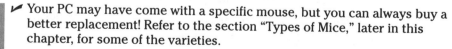

Correction!

Q: Lice *is* plural for louse. Hence the terms lousy and delouse.   **A:** I stand corrected!

Say "Hello" to the Mouse

A computer mouse is a little plastic rodent running around on your desk. It looks like a bar of soap with a large, rolling ball embedded in its belly. On the top, you find at least two push buttons. A tail, or cord, runs from the mouse into the back of your PC. Figure 13-1 shows a typical mouse.

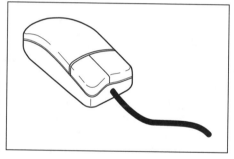

Figure 13-1:
Typical computer mouse.

You need a mouse, especially in an operating system like Windows, to control graphics and graphical whatnots on the screen. The mouse makes an ideal companion to the keyboard, helping you get work done in a graphical madhouse like Windows.

TIP

✔ Your PC may have come with a specific mouse, but you can always buy a better replacement! Refer to the section "Types of Mice," later in this chapter, for some of the varieties.

✔ Designate a special mouse area on your desk and keep it clear of desk debris so that you have room to move the mouse around. An area about the size of this book is typically all you need to roll the mouse around.

✔ A mouse works best when moved across a *mouse pad,* which is a small piece of plastic or rubber that sits on your desk. The mouse pad provides more traction than your slippery desktop. Also, it reminds you to keep that area of your desk clean.

✔ The best mouse pads have rough surfaces, which the mouse can really grip. Poorly designed mouse pads are slick and should be avoided. Also, having an image on your mouse pad is a status symbol. Kinkos and other places even let you create your own mouse pad image using any photograph.

Types of Mice

There are many species of computer mice. Beyond the common bar-of-soap model are upside-down mice, mice with too many buttons, radio mice, pen mice, and on and on. The sections that follow describe various types of computer mice you can buy.

✔ I once did a magazine review of computer mice. The magazine sent me 30 different mice to evaluate. I wrote about the most interesting 12, none of which resembled the traditional computer mouse.

✔ I even saw a mouse with 52 buttons on it, allowing you to use it as a keyboard. (I wonder why the thing never caught on?)

✔ Another type of mouse is the USB mouse. Though it's not different-looking, it does connect to the PC via the USB port. See Chapter 9 for more information on the USB port.

The wheel mouse

The wheel mouse, shown in Figure 13-2, has an extra button between the two standard buttons. That button is a wheel, which you can spin up or down to scroll a document in those few Windows programs that obey the wheel mouse. Or you can press and hold the wheel button to *pan* the document up or down or left or right.

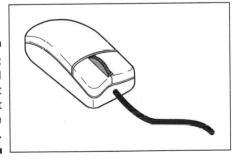

Figure 13-2: The wheel mouse that Microsoft calls the IntelliMouse.

After using the Microsoft IntelliMouse for a while, I can say that I've come to like it. I use the wheel all the time to scroll documents — typically by pressing and holding the wheel button instead of spinning the wheel. It's nifty. And this opinion has nothing to do with the fact that Microsoft gave me the mouse free. Nothing whatsoever.

- ✔ Other than the wheel and its extra scrolling abilities it gives you in some programs, a wheel mouse offers no advantage over the standard two-button mouse.

- ✔ Only specific applications bother with the wheel. They include all the Microsoft Office programs (Office 97 and later), plus all of Windows' own programs if you install the wheel mouse diskettes.

- ✔ No, your finger turns the wheel. You don't have to turn the mouse upside down or slap it with your palm like the old Atari Football game.

The upside-down mouse (the trackball)

A trackball mouse looks like a regular mouse turned upside down, as shown in Figure 13-3. Instead of rolling the mouse around, you use your thumb or index finger to roll the ball itself. The whole contraption stays stationary, so it doesn't need nearly as much room, and the cord never gets tangled.

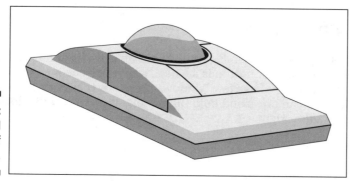

Figure 13-3:
A trackball
type of
mouse.

Trackballs aren't for everyone. The only crowd that really loves them are the artist types, who prefer the precise movements the trackball gives you. Are you wearing all black? Have on a beret? If so, you'll probably love a trackball mouse.

Connecting the Mouse

The computer's mouse plugs into the mouse connector on the back of the console. Simple.

Serial mice plug into the computer's serial port. If you have a serial mouse, plug it into COM1, because COM2 is often used as the modem port and plugging the mouse into COM2 can cause problems.

If your PC uses a USB mouse, plug it into the USB port. There is usually a spare USB port on the keyboard, if your PC is so equipped.

- ✔ If your PC has a COM3 port, you may plug the mouse into it instead of COM1.

- ✔ It's a good idea to turn your computer off before you connect or disconnect the mouse.

- ✔ You don't need to turn the computer off before connecting a USB mouse; USB is designed that way.

- ✔ USB and other PC ports are covered in Chapter 9.

- ✔ The mouse may come with its own software, which you install by using the Windows handy install program thingy. See Chapter 19.

- ✔ The tail points *away* from you when you use the mouse. (Oh, I could tell a story here about a former boss, but I won't.)

Using Your Computer Mouse

The computer's mouse controls a pointer or mouse cursor on the screen. When you move the mouse around, rolling it on your desktop, the pointer on the screen moves in a similar manner. Roll the mouse left, and the pointer moves left; roll it in circles, and the pointer mimics that action; drop the mouse off the table, and your computer yells out, "Ouch!" (Just kidding.)

You don't need to squeeze the mouse; a gentle grip is all that's necessary.

- ✔ Most people hold the mouse in their palm with their thumb against the left edge and their ring finger against the right edge. The index finger and middle finger can then hover over the buttons along the top. (If this were medieval times, the mouse would be a fist weapon, not a finger weapon.)

- The first time you use a mouse, you want to move it in wild circles on your desk so that you can watch the pointer spiral on the screen. This urge takes a long time to wear off (if it ever does).

- When the mouse cord becomes tangled, raise the mouse in your hand and whip it about violently.

Point the mouse

When you're told to *point the mouse,* it means you move the mouse on the desktop, which moves the mouse pointer on the screen to point at something interesting (or not).

Try not to pick the mouse up and point it at something like a TV remote control. It just doesn't work that way.

Click the mouse

A click is a press of the mouse button.

Often you read *click the mouse on the OK button.* This instruction means a graphic or something-or-other is on the screen with the word OK on it. Using the mouse, you move the pointer over the word OK. Then, with your index finger, click the mouse button. This action is referred to as *clicking the mouse on something* (though you could roll the mouse around on your forehead and click it there if you like — just make sure no one's looking).

- The button to click is the *left* mouse button, the one under your index finger. That's the main mouse button.

- If you need to click the right button, the instructions will tell you to *right-click* or to *click the right mouse button.* Same for the wheel button, should your mouse have one of those.

- When you push the button on your mouse, it makes a clicking noise. So most programs tell you to *click* your mouse button when they really mean for you to *press* the mouse button.

- When clicking the button, push it down once and release it. Don't hold it down continuously. (Actually, it makes two clicks — one when pushed and another when released. Is your hearing that good?)

- Sometimes you may be asked to press a key combination along with clicking the mouse. A popular combo is Ctrl+click, which means to press and hold down the Ctrl (control) key on your keyboard before you click the mouse button.

Double-clicking the mouse

A double-click is two rapid clicks in a row. You do this in Windows to open something.

✔ The time between clicks varies, but it doesn't have to be that quick.

✔ Try not to move the mouse around between the clicks; both clicks have to be on the same spot.

✔ Clicking and double-clicking are two different activities. When the manual says to click, click the mouse's left button once. Double-clicking is clicking the left button twice.

✔ If you double-click your mouse and nothing happens, you may not be clicking fast enough. Try clicking it as fast as you can. If this speed is too quick for you, you can adjust it. See the section 'Double-clicking doesn't work!' later in this chapter.

Dragging the mouse

You drag with the mouse to select a group of items on the screen or to pick up and move something.

To drag with the mouse, follow these steps:

1. **Point the mouse cursor at the something you want to drag.**

2. **Press and hold the mouse's button.**

   That's the left button. Press and hold the button down — don't click it! This action has the effect of picking up whatever the mouse is pointing at on the screen.

   If it's not picking something up, a drag also selects objects by drawing a rubber-band-like rectangle around them.

3. **Move the mouse to a new location.**

   The drag operation is really a *move;* you start at one point on the screen and move (drag) the whatever to another location.

4. **Release the mouse button.**

   Lift your finger off the left mouse button. You're done dragging.

When you release the mouse button, you let go of whatever it was you were dragging.

- You can also drag to select a group of items. In this case, dragging draws a rectangle around the items you want to select.

- Dragging is used in many drawing and painting programs to create an image on the screen. In this sense, dragging is like pressing a pen tip or paintbrush to paper.

- You can also drag using the right mouse button instead of the left. This action is usually called a right-drag.

- Sometimes you may be asked to press and hold a key while dragging, referred to as a Ctrl+drag (Control+drag) or Shift+drag or some other key combination. If so, press that key — Ctrl, Shift, Alt, or whatever — *before* you first click the mouse to drag something.

Selecting with the mouse

Selecting is the same as clicking. When the manual says to select that doohickey over there, you move the mouse pointer and click the doohickey. Simple.

To deselect something, such as when you click the wrong thing or change your mind, just click elsewhere, on the desktop for instance. That action deselects whatever object you've clicked, rendering it free to escape.

Mouse hygiene: Cleaning your mouse ball

Your desk constantly collects a layer of dust and hair, especially if you have a cat around or a picture of a cat on your mouse pad. If your mouse isn't behaving the way it used to, you may need to clean its ball. It's easy; there's no need for the repair shop or a guy in a van.

Turn the mouse upside down, and you see a little round plate holding the ball in place. Push or twist the plate in the direction of the arrow that says *open*. The plate should come off, and the ball will fall out, roll off the desk, and under your chair.

Pull out any hair or debris from the mouse-ball hole and brush any stray offal off the ball itself. Put the ball back inside and reattach the plate, and you're on your way.

Try to keep the mouse pad clean as well: Brush it off occasionally to clear away the potato chips, drool, and other detritus that accumulates there.

Tweaking the Mouse in Windows

Lurking in the Control Panel is the Mouse icon, which opens up the Mouse Properties dialog box, which is where you can tweak your mouse. The following sections describe a few handy things you can do there. Here are the general steps you take to open the Mouse icon up for business:

1. **Open the Control Panel.**

   From the Start menu, choose Settings⇨Control Panel. The Control Panel's main window appears.

2. **Open the Mouse icon.**

Mouse

   Funny how that mouse icon looks like the type of mouse Microsoft is currently selling. Oh, whatever. Double-click the Mouse icon. This action brings forth the Mouse Properties dialog box, as shown in Figure 13-4.

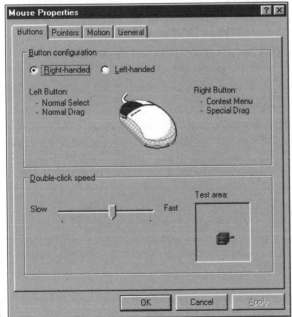

Figure 13-4: The Mouse Properties dialog box.

If you have the Microsoft IntelliMouse (the wheel mouse) installed on your PC, then you see a different dialog box, one with even more goodies and things to do than the boring old "I'm a stupid two-button mouse" dialog box. A sample is shown in Figure 13-5.

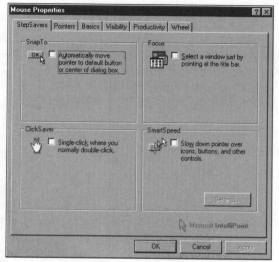

3. **Goof around in the Mouse Properties dialog box.**

Several subtle things are permissible in the Mouse Properties dialog box. A few of the more popular tasks are discussed in the sections that follow.

4. **Close the dialog box.**

When you're done messing around, you have two choices: Click the OK button to keep your changes, or click Cancel to return to the way things were before.

"Double-clicking doesn't work!"

If you can't seem to double-click, one of two things is happening: Either you're moving the mouse pointer a little bit between clicks, or the double-click *rate* is set too fast for human fingers to manage.

Bring forth the Mouse Properties dialog box, as discussed in the preceding section.

For normal, nonwheel mice: Click the Buttons tab to bring that panel forward. (It should look something like Figure 13-4.)

In the Double-Click Speed area is a slider. Drag the slider to the right to make double-clicking easier. Drag the slider to the left if you keep accidentally moving the mouse between clicks.

To test this setting, first click the Apply button. This action resets Windows to your new mouse specifications. Then double-click the jack-in-the-box in the Test area. If you double-click the box and the stupid clown pops up, you have a proper double-click speed set.

If you have the wheel mouse: Click the Basics tab (see Figure 13-6). Double-click in the Set box (on the clouds) to set your double-click speed. Then test your speed by clicking the umbrella in the Test box. Keep trying until you find your speed; both the double-clicks in the Set and Test boxes must match.

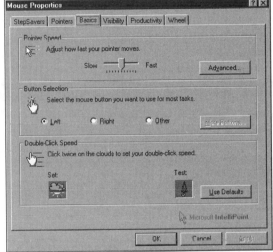

Figure 13-6:
The wheel
mouse's
Basics tab
in the
Mouse
Properties
dialog box.

Click OK to close the Mouse Properties dialog box.

"My buddy has an animated mouse pointer. How do I get one?"

Animated cursors are set up in the Pointers tab in the Mouse Properties dialog box. Follow these steps:

1. **Open the Mouse Properties dialog box and gander at the Pointers page.**

   Opening the Mouse Properties dialog box is described earlier, in "Tweaking the Mouse in Windows."

2. **Select the pointer you want to change.**

   That hourglass pointer sure looks dull.

3. **Click the Browse button.**

   A Browse dialog box opens. See Chapter 6 for more information on the Browse dialog box (which works like an Open dialog box).

   The Browse dialog box should be set to the folder where Windows stores all its mouse pointer things. If not, change to the \WINDOWS\ CURSORS folder on your C drive.

4. **Click a new cursor in the dialog box.**

   Some of the cursors are shown as icons. Others are just shown using the dull "I am a file" icon Windows loves so much.

5. **Preview that cursor.**

   After clicking the cursor, look in the Preview box to see if it's an animated cursor or not. Animated cursors move. (Did I need to say that?)

6. **If you don't like the cursor, repeat Steps 4 and 5.**

7. **Click Open.**

   The cursor you select replaces the one Windows stupidly has suggested in the Pointers page of the Mouse Properties dialog box.

8. **Click OK.**

   Your change is locked in.

If you download animated cursor files or get a disk full of them from a friend, you should save them in the Cursors folder in the Windows main folder. (The pathname is C:\WINDOWS\CURSORS.) That way they show up in the list when you select a new pointer in the Browse dialog box.

"I'm a southpaw, and the buttons are backward!"

Hey, Lefty, if you just can't stand the idea of using a mouse in the right-hand/left-brain dominated world, you can switch things over — even putting the mouse on the nontraditional left-hand side of your PC keyboard. (Oh, brother. . . .)

Summon the Mouse Properties dialog box using the instructions offered in "Tweaking the Mouse in Windows," earlier in this chapter. In the Buttons or

Basics panel, click the proper button to select a left-handed mouse. This action mentally switches the buttons in the Windows head: The right button takes on left-button tasks and vice versa.

✔ This book and all manuals and computer books assume that the left mouse button is the main button. Right-clicks are clicks of the right mouse button. If you tell Windows to use the left-handed mouse, these buttons are reversed. Keep in mind that your documentation will not reflect that.

✔ There is no setting for ambidextrous people, wise guy!

Mouse Woes

Mice are just the most innocent of things when it comes to terror in your computer. They really can be reliable and trustworthy, but every so often, they annoy you by not working properly. The following are some common mouse-related ailments and how to fix them.

The mouse is a slug

Slow mice happen over time. Why? Who knows. Personally, I think gunk gets inside the mouse and slows it down. Not even removing the mouse ball and cleaning it up helps. It's just gunk.

The solution here is drastic: Buy another mouse. Computer mice typically work well for two to three years. After that, for some reason, they get sluggish and jerky. Rather than pound your mouse into your desktop, just break down and buy a new one. You'll be amazed at how much better it works and how much more calmly you use the PC.

The vanishing or stuck mouse

After a terrifically productive session of managing your files, you may suddenly notice that your mouse is gone.

No! Wait, there it is!

But then it's gone again, vanishing in and out like a Cheshire cat. I have no idea why this is so.

Or the mouse pointer may just sit there dead on the screen. You move the mouse. Nothing. You motivate the mouse with your handy repertoire of nasty epitaphs. Nothing. You slam the mouse into your desktop. Nothing. Nothing. Nothing.

The solution: Reset your computer. See Chapter 2.

Chapter 14

The Keyboard Chapter

*Y*ou probably have keys, a whole ring full of them. I used to think the more important you were, the more keys you had. That still may be true.

Pianos have 88 keys, 55 white and 33 black. They can take years to master.

Your computer has a keyboard with over 100 keys on it. Often you're expected to master it in less than a week. Egads! Then what are you wasting time for? Hurry up and read this, the keyboard chapter!

Know Thy Keyboard

Your keyboard is the direct line of communication between you and the computer. The computer has no ears. You can try yelling. You can wave your arms. But the computer hears nothing unless you type something to it on the keyboard.

Your typical PC keyboard

The typical PC keyboard is shown in Figure 14-1. The nerds call it the *enhanced 104-key keyboard*. Yes, it has 104 keys on it. You can count them yourself, if you have the time.

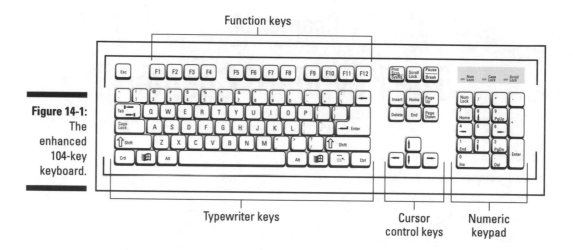

Figure 14-1:
The
enhanced
104-key
keyboard.

In the olden days, this keyboard was known as the *enhanced 101-key keyboard.* That's before Microsoft added the three extra *Windows* keys clustered around the spacebar. Older keyboards (and some new models) lack these extra keys.

See the section, "What are those weird Windows keys?" later in this chapter, for more information on the Windows keys.

Basic keyboard layout

Four main areas are mapped out on your PC's keyboard, as shown in Figure 14-1:

Function keys: These keys are positioned on the top row of the keyboard. They are labeled F1, F2, F3, and on up to F11 and F12.

Typewriter keys: These keys are the same type of keys you'd find on an old typewriter: letters, numbers, and punctuation symbols.

Cursor-control keys: Often called *arrow keys,* these four keys move the text cursor in the direction of their arrows. Above them are more cursor control keys — the six pack of Insert, Delete, Home, End, PgUp, and PgDn.

Numeric keypad: Popular among bank tellers with zippy fingers, the numeric keypad contains the calculator-like keys.

✔ The numeric keypad has a split personality. Sometimes it's used to generate numbers, other times it duplicates the cursor keys. See the section "Keys to change the keyboard's mood," later in this chapter, for more information on this duplicity.

✔ The keys labeled F1, F2, and so on, are called *function keys*.

✔ The cursor-control keys are used to move the text cursor around, which typically looks like a blinking toothpick when you type or edit text in Windows. The mouse pointer is often called the cursor, though the cursor keys don't move it around.

✔ The PgUp and PgDn keys stand for Page Up and Page Down. The labels on the key caps may be fully spelled out or abbreviated.

✔ Insert and Delete are editing keys, often used with the cursor keys.

✔ The Print Screen key may also be labeled PrtScr or Print Scrn.

So where is the Any key?

Nothing is more frustrating than hunting down that elusive *Any* key. After all, the screen says, `Press any key to continue`. So where is it?

Any key refers to, literally, any key on your keyboard. But why beat around the bush: When it says to press the Any key, press the spacebar.

✔ If you can't find the spacebar, or you think it's the place where you order drinks on the Starship Enterprise, press the Enter key.

✔ So why do they say "Press any key" instead of saying "Press the spacebar to continue"? I guess it's because they want to make things *easy* for you by giving you the whole keyboard to choose from. And if that's really the case, why not just break down and say, "Slap your keyboard a few times with your open palms to continue"?

Know your ones and zeros

On a typewriter, the lowercase letter *L* and the number 1 are often the same. In fact, I remember my old Royal upright lacked a 1 key altogether. Unfortunately, on a computer there is a big difference between a one and a little *L*.

If you're typing 1,001, for example, don't type l,00l by mistake — especially when working with a spreadsheet. The computer will gag.

The same holds true for the uppercase letter *O* and the number 0. They're different. Use a zero for numbers and a big *O* for big O things.

Sometimes zero is displayed with a slash through it, like this: Ø. That's one way to tell the difference between O and 0, but it's not used that often.

Where is the Help key?

Whenever you need help in Windows, whack the F1 key. F1 equals help — no way to commit that to memory. However, I've included a little fake key cap cover on this book's Cheat Sheet. Clip it out and paste it over the F1 key on your keyboard.

What are those weird Windows keys?

Most PC keyboards today sport three new keys: the Windows key, the Shortcut Menu key, and another Windows key. They sit between the Alt and Ctrl keys on either side of the spacebar (refer to Figure 14-1).

 The Windows key serves the same purpose as pressing Ctrl+Esc: It pops up the Start menu thing. You can also use it for a few quick shortcuts, as shown in Table 14-1.

Table 14-1	Win Key Shortcuts
Key Combo	**Function**
Win+D	Displays the desktop (minimizes all Windows)
Win+E	Starts Windows Explorer
Win+F	Displays the Find Files dialog box
Win+P	Displays the Printers window
Win+R	Displays the Run dialog box

 The Shortcut Menu key displays the shortcut menu for whatever item is currently selected on the screen. This is the same as right-clicking the mouse when something is selected.

Keys to change the keyboard's mood

Several keys affect the way the keyboard behaves. The first three of these keys are the Lock sisters:

Caps Lock: This key works like holding down the Shift key, but it only produces capital letters; it does not shift the other keys as a typewriter's Shift Lock key would do. Press Caps Lock again, and the letters return to their normal lowercase state.

Num Lock: Pressing this key makes the numeric keypad on the right side of the keyboard produce numbers. Press this key again, and you can use the numeric keypad for moving the text cursor around on the screen.

Scroll Lock: This key has no purpose in life. Some spreadsheets use it to reverse the function of the cursor keys (which move the spreadsheet instead of moving the cell highlight). Scroll Lock does little else important or famous.

Other keys that affect the way the keyboard behaves are the modifier keys. These keys work in combination with other keys to do various interesting and unbelievable things:

Shift: Hold down the Shift key to make capital letters. By pressing the Shift key, you also can create the %@#^ characters that come in handy for cussing in comic strips. When you release the Shift key, everything returns to normal, just like a typewriter.

Ctrl: The Control key, abbreviated as Ctrl, is also used like the Shift key; you press it in combination with another key. In most Windows programs, the Ctrl key is used with various letter keys to carry out specific commands. For example, if you hold down the Ctrl key and press S (Ctrl+S), you save something. Likewise, in most programs, you press Ctrl+P to print, and so on for each clever letter of the alphabet.

Alt: Like the Shift and Ctrl keys, the Alt key is used in combination with other keys to carry out commands. For example, holding down the Alt key and pressing the F4 key (Alt+F4) closes a window on the desktop. You press and hold the Alt key, tap the F4 key, and then release both keys.

Here are more thoughts on these, the moody keys on your keyboard:

- ✔ The Caps Lock, Num Lock, and Scroll Lock keys have lights. When the light is on, the key's feature is turned on.

- ✔ On some computers the Num Lock is already on when the computer starts. Annoying, huh?

- ✔ When Num Lock is on, the numeric keypad produces numbers. Remember that fact when you use your spreadsheet. Otherwise, those numbers you thought you just typed in actually move the cell highlighter all over creation.

- ✔ The Caps Lock key is not the same as a typewriter's Shift Lock key. Caps Lock affects only letters, not every key on the keyboard.

- ✔ If you type **This Text Looks Like A Ransom Note** and it looks like tHIS tEXT lOOKS lIKE a rANSOM nOTE, the Caps Lock key is inadvertently turned on. Press it once to return everything to normal.

- ✔ If you press the Shift key while Caps Lock is on, the letter keys return to normal. (Shift kind of cancels out Caps Lock.)

✔ Even though you may see Ctrl+S or Alt+S with a capital *S,* this doesn't mean you must type Ctrl+Shift+S or Alt+Shift+S. The *S* is simply written in uppercase because Ctrl+s looks like a typesetting error.

✔ Don't be surprised if these shift keys are used in combination with each other. I've seen Shift+Ctrl+C and Ctrl+Alt. You use Ctrl+Esc to pop up the Start menu. Just remember to press and hold the Shift keys first, and then tap the letter key. Release all the keys together.

✔ Some manuals use the term ^Y rather than Ctrl+Y. This term means the same thing: Hold down the Ctrl key, press Y, and release the Ctrl key.

✔ With some programs, you do press the Alt or Ctrl keys by themselves. For example, you can press the Alt key to activate the menu bar in a Windows program. You can also press the Ctrl key by itself to switch off the Windows screen saver.

The all-powerful Enter key

Nearly all PC computer keyboards have two keys labeled Enter. Both keys work identically, with the second Enter key placed by the numeric keypad to facilitate rapid entry of numbers.

So what is the Return key? Many early computers sported a Return key. Essentially, it's the same thing as the Enter key. I bring this up because I just saw a manual the other day that said to *press Return.*

There is no Return key!

Press the Enter key when some dopey manual suggests that you press Return.

✔ Pressing the Enter key is the same as clicking OK in a dialog box.

✔ In your word processor, only press Enter at the end of a paragraph.

✔ In a Web browser, you press the Enter key after typing a Web page address to view that page (well, eventually).

✔ Don't press Enter after filling in a text box inside a dialog box. Use the Tab key to move from text box to text box. This rule also applies when using some database programs; use the Tab key to skip merrily between the fields. La, la, la.

✔ The difference between Enter and Return is only semantic. Enter has its roots in the electronic calculator industry. You pressed Enter to enter numbers or a formula. Return, on the other hand, comes from the electronic typewriter. Pressing Return on a typewriter caused the carriage to return to the left margin. It also advanced the paper one line.

The Tab key

The Tab key is used two different ways on your computer.

In a word processor, you use the Tab key to indent paragraphs — just like the old typewriter's Tab key.

In a dialog box, you use the Tab key to move between the gizmos in the dialog box. Use Tab instead of Enter, for example, to hop between the First Name and Last Name fields. This also holds true for filling in a form on the Internet: Use the Tab key, not Enter, to fill in the blanks.

> ✔ The Tab key often has two arrows on it — one pointing left and the other right. These arrows may be in addition to the word *Tab,* or they may be on there by themselves to confuse you.

> ✔ The computer treats a tab as a single, separate character. When you backspace over a tab in a word processing program, the tab disappears completely in one chunk — not space by space.

Slashing about

Two slash keys are on your keyboard, and you can easily be confused.

The forward slash (/) leans forward (duh!), like it's falling to the right. You use this slash primarily to denote division, such as 52/13 (52 divided by 13).

The backslash (\) leans to the left. You use this character in *pathnames,* which are complex and discussed only near the end of Chapter 6, where no one can find them.

Escape from Windows!

The one key that says "Hey! Stop it!" to Windows is the Escape key, labeled Esc on your keyboard.

Pressing the Esc key is the same as clicking Cancel or "No Way" in a dialog box. And it closes most windows, but not all, just to keep you guessing.

> ✔ Esc can be a good pinch hitter to try first when something goes awry.

> ✔ To close any window or quit any program, use the mysterious Alt+F4 key combination.

Don't bother with these keys

Some keys on the keyboard meant something to some old program, now long forgotten. I'm wishing this on the Windows and Shortcut Menu keys myself. But until they become useless, the following keys no longer hold any meaning for Windows:

Pause. Honestly, the Pause key doesn't work in Windows. In DOS, it would pause output. So if you were displaying a long file on the screen, you could press the Pause key, and everything would stop. In Windows, the Pause key does nothing. And Windows is so slow anyway, who would want to pause it?

SysRq. The System Request (Ah! That's what it means!) key was supposed to be used for the next version of DOS. But a next version of DOS never came about, nor was a use ever found for the SysRq key. Though it lingers on the keyboard's face like an ugly mole.

Break: By itself, the Break key does nothing. When used in combination with the Ctrl key (Ctrl+Break), the Break key could be used to stop old DOS programs. In Windows, though, Break does nothing.

Other strange and useless key thoughts:

- ✔ The Pause key may also be labeled Hold on some keyboards.

- ✔ If you ever do use the DOS window and need to stop a program, then you can use either Ctrl+Break or Ctrl+C — assuming you can remember either one.

- ✔ Why is the key called Break? Why not call it the Brake key? Wouldn't that make sense? Who wants a computer to break, anyway? Golly.

"Must I learn to type to use a computer?"

No one needs to learn to type to use a computer. Plenty of computer users hunt and peck. In fact, most programmers don't know how to type; they sit all hunched over the keyboard and punch in enigmatic computer languages using greasy, garlic-and-herb potato chip-smeared fingers. But that's not being very productive.

As a bonus to owning a computer, you can have it teach you how to type. The Mavis Beacon Teaches Typing software package does just that. Other packages are available, but I personally love the name "Mavis Beacon."

Trivia: A computer software developer once halted all development and had his programmers sit down and learn how to touch type. It took two whole weeks, but afterward, they all got their work done a lot faster and had more time available to break away and play games.

For math whizzes only (like any would be reading this book)

Clustered around the numeric keypad, like campers roasting marshmallows around a fire, are various keys to help you work with numbers. Especially if you're dabbling with a spreadsheet or other number-crunching software, you'll find these keys come in handy. Take a look at your keyboard's numeric keypad right now just to reassure yourself.

What? You were expecting a × or ÷ key? Forget it! This is a computer. It uses special oddball symbols for mathematical operations:

- + is for addition.
- - is for subtraction.
- * is for multiplication.
- / is for division.

The only strange symbol here is the asterisk for multiplication. Don't use the little *X!* It's not the same thing. The / (slash) is okay for division, but don't waste your time hunting for the ÷ symbol. It's not there.

The Keyboard Follies

Keyboards aren't without their sticking points — and I don't mean what happens when you spill a cola in there. The following sections mull over some of the more trying times you may have with your PC keyboard.

"My keyboard beeps at me!"

Common problem. Many potential causes and cures.

Reason 1: You can't type anything! Whatever program you're using doesn't want you to type or expects you to be pressing some other key. Remember that in Windows you can only use one window at a time — even if you're looking at another window.

Reason 2: You're typing too fast. The PC's keyboard can only swallow so many keys at once. When its li'l stomach is full, it starts beeping at you until it can digest.

Reason 3: You have a keyboard beep feature turned on. Have your guru run your PC's Setup program to eliminate the beep. Or have him or her discover which program produces the beep and eliminate it.

Reason 4: The computer is dead! Refer to Chapter 2 for information on resetting.

"Oops! I just spilled java into the keyboard!"

Sooner or later, you'll spill something gross into the keyboard. The grossest liquids are thick or sugary: soft drinks, fruit juice, cheap sherry, or St. Bernard drool (not sugary, but thick). These things can seriously damage the keyboard. Here's what to do:

1. **Pick up the glass or push the St. Bernard out of the way.**

2. **Save your work (if the keyboard is still functional), turn off the computer, and unplug the keyboard.**

3. **Turn the keyboard upside down and give it a few good shakes (away from your coworkers' keyboards, if possible).**

4. **Use a sponge to sop up as much stuff as possible and then just let the keyboard dry out.**

   It usually takes about 24 hours.

Surprisingly enough, the keyboard will probably still work, especially if the beverage didn't contain much sugar. Unfortunately, it may not work. The keyboard contains special circuitry, and if that circuitry is damaged, you may need to buy yourself another keyboard. (At least that's cheaper than buying a whole new PC.)

Some companies sell plastic keyboard covers. These covers are custom fitted to the keyboard and work well. Smokers, especially, should consider purchasing one.

"Ouch! My wrists hurt!"

Repetitive anything can be bad: smoking, eating, drinking, running for Congress, and typing on your computer keyboard. This can be a serious problem, especially if you rely on your computer for your job.

Many typists suffer from something called Carpal Tunnel Syndrome, also called Repetitive Stress Injury (RSI).

RSI is a soreness caused when muscles rub against each other in a small wrist passage called the carpal tunnel (the names Lincoln Tunnel and Holland Tunnel are already copyrighted by the State of New York). The carpal tunnel collapses, changes from a horseshoe shape into something narrower that causes the muscles (tendons, actually) to rub.

Various solutions are available for this problem. Some sufferers wear expensive, reinforced gloves that, if they don't actually help alleviate the pain, at least draw sympathetic stares from onlookers. And crunching your wrist by squeezing your palm below the thumb and little finger can help. But the best thing to do is to avoid the problem in the first place.

Here are several things you can do to avoid RSI:

Get an ergonomic keyboard. Even if your wrists are as limber as rubber tree plants, you may want to consider an *ergonomic* keyboard. That type of keyboard is specially designed at an angle to relieve the stress of typing for long — or short — periods of time.

Use a wrist pad. Wrist pads elevate your wrists so that you type in a proper position, with your palms *above* the keyboard, not wresting below the space-bar. Remember Sister Mary Paul and how she whacked your slouching wrists? She was right!

Adjust your chair. You should sit at the computer with your elbows level with your wrists — just like your typing teacher used to beg.

Adjust your monitor. Your head should not tilt down or up when you view the computer screen. It should be straight ahead, which doesn't help your wrists as much as it helps your neck.

- ✔ Ergonomic keyboards cost a little more than standard keyboards, but they are well worth the investment if you type for long hours, or at least want to look like you type for long hours.

- ✔ Some mouse pads have built-in wrist elevators. These are great for folks who use mouse-intensive applications.

- ✔ Many keyboards come with adjustable legs underneath for positioning the keys to a comfortable angle.

- ✔ If you can't adjust your desk or keyboard to the right height, buy a chair that can be adjusted up or down, or have your building supervisor install hydraulic lifts in the basement.

Chapter 15

Welcome to Printerland

· ·

· ·

*I*n the happy computer family, printers are often orphans. Even though they're as necessary as monitors and keyboards, printers aren't sold with the computer. They're an afterthought. They're ugly stepchildren, poised to go berserk at the next big family function, making a scene and causing Grandma to grab her chest and wince, "Oh, my!"

Your computer needs a printer almost as much as it needs a monitor and keyboard. Printers are necessary. And they're cheap and rather good at producing something on paper — that elusive *hard copy* that's often the end result of your hours of PC toil. Welcome to Printerland.

Hello! I'm Steve, and I'll Be Your Printer

Printers are devices that produce an image on paper. The image can be text or graphics, in color or in black ink. Using the printer is often the last step in creating something on the PC. It's the end result of your labors. Therefore, the image produced must be as good as possible.

Two major types of printers are popular today: *inkjet* and *laser.* The following sections discuss the merits of each and how they work.

- ✔ Printers are judged by the quality of image they produce.

- ✔ Printers are also judged by their price. Generally speaking, you can pay anywhere from just over $100 to thousands of dollars for a printer.

- ✔ Printers were once judged by their speed, but printer speed just isn't a big issue anymore.

- ✔ The printer produces *hard copy,* which is anything you do on your computer screen that eventually winds up on paper.

The Ever-Popular Inkjet Printer

Inkjet printers are the most popular type of computer printer sold today. They're primarily color printers, and they produce high-quality text or graphics on just about any type of paper. Some higher-end inkjet printers are even capable of photographic quality output.

Figure 15-1 illustrates a typical inkjet printer, which looks a lot like the author's inkjet printer. I've flagged important things to see in the illustration.

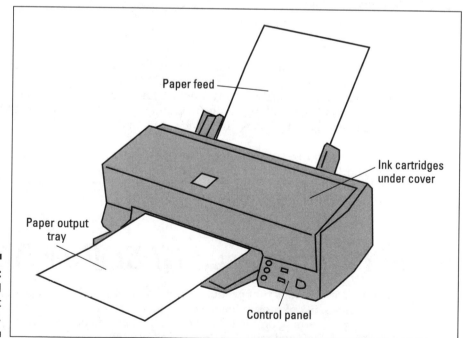

Figure 15-1:
A typical inkjet printer.

Inkjet printers work by literally lobbing tiny balls of ink on paper. The teensy tiny ink balls stick to the paper, so this type of printer needs no ribbon or toner cartridge; the ink is jetted out directly, which is how the printer gets its name.

Most inkjet printers print with both color and black inks. The ink is stored in tiny cartridges, typically one cartridge contains black ink and another contains colored inks.

These printers are also inexpensive. Some of the low-end models run only a couple of hundred dollars. The higher-end models produce a better image faster but can cost from $800 to over $1,000. This variety in price makes the inkjet printer one of the best suited for any PC.

- Inkjet printers are by no means messy. The ink is dry on the paper by the time the paper comes flopping out of the printer.

- Low-end inkjet printers cost less because they're dumb; they contain no internal electronics to help create the image. Instead, the computer is required to do the thinking, which slows things down a tad. When you pay more for an inkjet printer, the smarts are usually included with the printer (and the price).

- A special type of inkjet printer is the all-in-one, such as the OfficeJet by Hewlett-Packard. This printer is a standard color inkjet printer, but you can also use it as a fax machine and a scanner. Obviously all-in-one printers cost more than a typical inkjet, but they do *three* common things that most offices require. Check into such a printer if you need faxing, printing, and scanning abilities.

Going broke buying ink cartridges

With an inkjet printer, you get an inexpensive printer that prints very well and prints in color. Computer users would have *killed* for such a dream years go. So what's the catch?

The catch is that inkjet ink cartridges cost a ton! In fact, if you print a lot, you'll probably spend twice as much a year on ink cartridges than you did on the printer to begin with.

Cartridges run dry. For example, printing a very large blue poster utterly drained the color ink cartridge on my printer. Replacement cost: $25. Ouch! And the printer demanded that I change the cartridge, even though the red and yellow inks were still full.

- If possible, try to buy inkjet cartridges in bulk.

- Several online and mail order dealers offer cheap prices on ink cartridges, better than you'll find locally or in an office supply superstore.

✔ Make a note of what type of inkjet cartridges your printer uses. Keep the catalog number somewhere handy so you can always reorder the proper cartridge.

✔ If the ink cartridge has nozzles, then you can refill it on your own. Refill kits are sold everywhere, and they're cheaper than continually buying new cartridges. However, they work best if the cartridge has nozzles. If the cartridge is just a storage bin, then you're better off buying new ones.

✔ Always follow the instructions for changing cartridges carefully. Old cartridges can leak and get messy ink all over. I suggest having a paper towel handy and putting the used cartridge in a paper towel while you walk to the trash can.

✔ You don't always have to print in color with an inkjet printer! You can also just print in black ink, which saves the (often spendy) color cartridge from running low. The Print dialog box (covered later in this chapter) often has an option that lets you choose whether you want to print with color or black ink.

Buying special paper

Don't let the expensive paper ads fool you; your inkjet printer can print on just about any type of paper. Even so, the spendy paper *does* produce a better image.

My favorite type of inkjet paper is called *laser paper*. It has a polished look to it and a subtle waxy feel. Colors look better on this paper, and black-ink text documents have a much nicer feel than printing on regular photocopier paper.

The best (and most outrageously expensive) paper to buy is special photographic paper. Using this paper with your printer's high-quality mode prints color images that look just like photographs. But at $1 per sheet, this is the kind of paper that's best used for special occasions.

Another fun paper: iron-on transfer paper. With this paper, you can print an image (reversed) and then use an iron to *weld* that image to a T-shirt.

Laser Printers from Beyond Infinity

If inkjet printers are for fun, laser printers are for work. Used primarily in the office place, laser printers are great for producing both text and graphics, but usually only in black and white. Color laser printers are available, but they're outrageously expensive, especially when a low-cost inkjet printer can do most color jobs.

Figure 15-2 illustrates a typical laser printer, which usually resembles a squat copy machine. Paper is fed into the printer via a tray. The paper scrolls through the printer, and the final result appears on top.

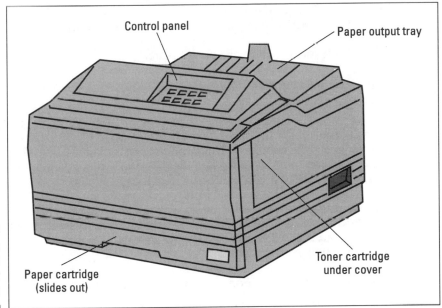

Control panel

Paper output tray

Toner cartridge under cover

Paper cartridge (slides out)

Figure 15-2: A typical laser printer.

Laser printers work like photocopiers. The difference is that the computer creates the image and etches it using a laser beam instead of a reflected image.

Laser printers are generally more expensive than inkjet printers and a wee bit faster. The color laser printers are outrageously expensive, but their color quality is usually better than that of inkjets.

✔ Laser printers make their images using heat. The laser beam etches an image on a *drum*. That drum is then dusted with something called *toner*. The toner sticks to the drum where the laser beam etched the image. The drum then rolls over the paper where a heated roller literally welds the image to the paper. The process is so ingenious you'd think aliens thought of it first, but they didn't.

✔ Be careful when changing toner cartridges! They're not as potentially messy as ink cartridges (which can leak), but if dropped or damaged, the toner cartridges can leak dusty toner. The toner gets everywhere, and it's not the most healthy substance.

Examining Your Printer's Control Panel

Every printer has a control panel. The fancy models have LCD screens that display lots of text: `Printer jammed`; `I'm out of paper`; `That's plagiarism`; and so on. Other printers, less fancy, may just have an on-off button and a page eject button. Whatever, look at your printer's panel now.

You should locate two things on the panel:

- ✔ The on-line or select button
- ✔ The form feed button

The purpose of the on-line or select button is to tell your printer whether or not to ignore the computer. When the printer is off-line or deselected, the computer can't print. You would take the printer off-line if, for example, you had to un-jam it or if you wanted to eject a page of paper.

The form feed button is often necessary to eject a page of paper from the printer. Right now I can't think of any specific instances when you'd need to do that, but I know I've had to write about it enough that it's not a blue-moon type of activity.

- ✔ The computer can print only when the printer is on-line or selected.

- ✔ My inkjet printer has only two buttons, on-line and form feed. You can carry out other printer functions by using a special dialog box in Windows.

- ✔ Some laser printers may have an on-line button but no form feed button. In that case, you need to refer to your printer's manual for information on doing a form feed, which involves choosing a menu item or pressing a combination of keys somehow.

- ✔ Speaking of manuals, it's a good idea to keep your printer's manual handy. You may never read it, but if your printer suddenly pops up and displays `Error 34`, you can look up what Error 34 is in the manual and read how to fix it. (This is the voice of experience talking here.)

Setting Up Your Beloved Printer

This is the easy part: To set up your printer, you plug it into your PC. Simple enough.

Start by turning your computer off. Make sure the printer is off, too.

Plug one end of the printer cable into the printer port on the back of your PC's console. Specifically, you find a connection called the *printer port* on the rear of the PC's console. It may be labeled as such or dubbed *LPT1*. Plug the other end of the cable into the printer. (If you get good at this, you can charge your friends fifty bucks to perform the same feat for them.)

You also need to plug the printer into the proper power socket. Do not plug the printer into a UPS. And you should plug laser printers directly into the wall, not into a power strip or UPS.

There. You're done with hardware installation.

  ✔ Placing your printer somewhere within arm's reach of your PC helps.

  ✔ If your PC has more than one printer port, plug your printer into LPT1, the first printer port.

  ✔ A single computer is capable of handling two printers. You need a second printer port on your PC, but you must have a terribly big ego to be that possessive.

Loading it with paper

Your printer needs to be loaded with paper. The days of printing on thin air and magic tablets are still in the future.

Both inkjet and laser printers load up using sheets of paper, similar to photocopier paper. (The old impact printers used continuous fan-fold paper.)

For inkjet printers, load up the paper in the tray, either near the printer's bottom or sticking out the top.

Laser printers require you to fill a cartridge with paper, similar to the way a copy machine works. Slide the cartridge all the way into the printer after it's loaded up.

  ✔ Always make sure that you have enough printer paper.

  ✔ You can buy standard photocopier paper for your printer.

  ✔ Some printers are capable of handling larger-sized paper, legal or tabloid sizes. If so, make sure you load the paper properly and tell Windows or your application that you're using a different-sized sheet of paper.

  ✔ Check your printer to see how the paper goes in, either face down or face up. And note which side is the top. This info helps you when loading things such as checks for use with personal finance software. (See the section "Important Printer Points to Ponder" at the end of this chapter.)

✔ Avoid using erasable bond and other fancy dusted papers in your laser printer. These papers have talcum powder coatings that come off in your laser printer and gum up the works.

Loading it with ink (or the ink substance)

Before you can print, you need to infuse your printer with the inky substance.

Inkjet printers use little ink cartridges. Carefully unwrap the foil around the new cartridge. Remove any tape or covering, per the package's instructions. And insert the ink cartridge into the printer, again following the instructions for your specific ink printer.

Laser printers require drop-in toner cartridges. They're easy to install and come with their own handy instructions. Just don't breathe in the toner or you'll die. Some manufacturers sell their cartridges with return envelopes so you can send the old cartridge back to the factory for recycling or proper disposal.

✔ I suggest buying rubber gloves (or those cheap plastic gloves that make you look like Batman) and using them when changing a ribbon or toner cartridge.

✔ Another option for an old toner cartridge is recharging. You can take it to a special place that will clean the old cartridge and refill it with toner. This process actually works and is often cheaper than buying a whole new cartridge.

Telling Windows about Your Printer (Software Installation)

Most likely, you set up Windows to work with your printer when you first brought your PC home. One of the first setup questions Windows asks is, "Which printer are you using?" and you, or someone else, followed the steps and chose the proper printer. No sweat.

If you just bought a new printer, however, you need to set that one up manually. Connect your printer to the PC if you haven't already (see "Setting Up Your Beloved Printer," earlier in this chapter). Make sure that your printer is on, loaded with paper, and ready to print. Then tell Windows all about your printer by heeding these steps:

1. **Choose Settings➪Printers from the Start menu.**

   Pop up the Start menu, and from the Settings submenu, choose the Printers item. A window appears listing all the printers you may already have connected to your PC, network printers, plus a special Add Printer icon.

2. **Open the Add Printer icon.**

   Add Printer

   Double-click the Add Printer icon to open it.

   Look, Ma! It's the Add Printer Wizard!

3. **Click the Next button.**

4. **If you're not setting up a network printer, click the Next button.**

   If you're setting up a network printer, have someone else help you immediately!

5. **Describe your printer's make and model to Windows.**

   Using the dialog box (shown in Figure 15-3), click your printer's manufacturer and then pluck out the model number.

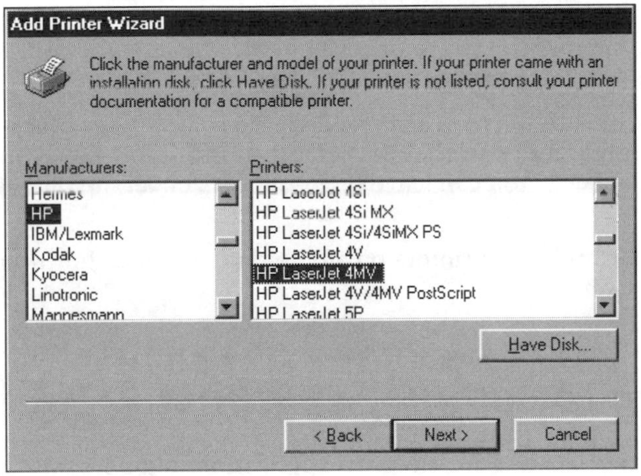

Figure 15-3:
Select your
printer's
make and
model from
this dialog
box.

> **Add Printer Wizard**
>
> Click the manufacturer and model of your printer. If your printer came with an installation disk, click Have Disk. If your printer is not listed, consult your printer documentation for a compatible printer.
>
> Manufacturers:
> - Hermes
> - HP
> - IBM/Lexmark
> - Kodak
> - Kyocera
> - Linotronic
> - Mannesmann
>
> Printers:
> - HP LaserJet 4Si
> - HP LaserJet 4Si MX
> - HP LaserJet 4Si/4SiMX PS
> - HP LaserJet 4V
> - HP LaserJet 4MV
> - HP LaserJet 4V/4MV PostScript
> - HP LaserJet 5P
>
> Have Disk...
>
> < Back   Next >   Cancel

If your printer isn't listed, you need a special installation disk that (hopefully) came with the printer. If so, click the Have Disk button and browse for the disk using the Open dialog box techniques described in Chapter 6.

6. **Click the Next button.**

7. **Pick the printer port from the list.**

   It will probably be LPT1, your first printer port.

8. **Click the Next button.**

9. **Click the Next button again.**

10. **Click Finish.**

    You're done.

You can print a test page on your printer if you like. Personally, I'm shocked that the test page isn't a catalog and order form for Microsoft products. But it ensures that your printer is connected properly and everything is up to snuff.

Basic Printer Operation

Here are the steps required to turn your printer on:

1. **Flip the switch.**

   ✔ Always make sure that your printer is on before you start printing. Like, duh.

   ✔ Your laser printer doesn't need to be on all the time. Laser printers draw lots of power when they're on, even more when they're printing. Only turn on your laser printer while you're printing

   ✔ An exception to the on-while-printing rule is for Energy Star laser printers. Energy Star means that the printer runs in a low-power mode while it's not working. You can leave those suckers on all the time if you like. I do.

   ✔ You can leave inkjet printers on all the time because they don't use much power.

Printing something, anything

Under Windows, printing is a snap. All applications support the same print command: Choose File⇨Print from the menu, click OK in the Print dialog box, and — zit-zit-zit — you soon have hard copy.

   ✔ The common keyboard shortcut for the print command is Ctrl+P.

   ✔ Always save your stuff before you print. Not that anything bad may happen; it's just a good reminder to save.

✔ Many applications sport a Print toolbar icon. If so, you can click that button to quickly print your document.

✔ It's usually a good idea to preview your printing before you condemn even more of our North American forests to death. Many Windows programs have a File➪Print Preview command that lets you pour over the page before it's splattered all over a tree slice. Save an owl. (Or something like that.)

I want to print sideways

Printing on a sheet of paper long-ways is called printing in the *landscape* mode. Almost all Windows programs have this option.

From the Print dialog box, click the Properties button. Click the Paper tab in your printer's Properties dialog box, as shown in Figure 15-4. Click the Landscape option. Click OK to close the dialog box, and then click OK in the Print dialog box to print in the landscape mode.

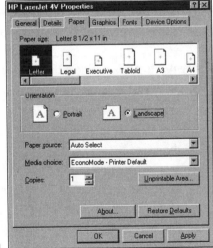

Figure 15-4: The Paper panel in the Properties dialog box.

Some programs may not use the Paper tab in the printer's Properties dialog box. For example, in Microsoft Word, it's the File➪Page Setup command, Paper Size panel. Whatever.

Once is not enough

Q: In your book you say that you should only recharge a used laser toner cartridge once. This isn't so. Today's modern toner recharging methods allow you to reuse one cartridge several times.

A: I stand corrected. At $120 for a new cartridge, recharging is a handy and inexpensive option.

Printing the screen

Even though the keyboard has a button named Print Screen, it won't send a copy of the screen to the printer. At least not directly. If you really need a printed copy of the Windows desktop or some window on the screen, follow these steps:

1. **Arrange the screen so that it looks the way you want it printed.**

2a. **If you want a snapshot of the whole screen, press the Print Screen key.**

2b. **If you want a snapshot of only the top window on the screen, press Alt+Print Screen.**

3. **Open the Paint program.**

   From the Start menu, choose Programs⇨Accessories⇨Paint.

   The Paint program appears on the screen.

4. **Choose Edit⇨Paste.**

   This action pastes the image into the Paint program.

   If a warning dialog box tells you the image is too big, click the Yes button.

5. **Print the image.**

   Choose File⇨Print.

   The Print dialog box appears.

6. **Click OK to start printing.**

If the image is very large, you might want to take advantage of the File⇨ Print Preview command. It shows you how the final image will look, as well as how many pages it will print on (if it's incredibly huge).

Feeding an envelope

To stick an envelope into your printer, just shove it into the special slot. Oftentimes you must open a hatch on the front of the computer to reveal the slot. A special illustration on the hatch tells you which way to place the envelope: face up or down, and top right or top left. Then you tell your software to print the envelope and — *thwoop!* — there it goes and comes back again, complete with a nifty address.

- ✔ Obviously, feeding an envelope to a printer is different for each type of printer.

- ✔ Also obviously: Each program has a different command for printing envelopes. Typically, you have to tell the program how the envelope goes into your printer so that it knows in which direction to print the address.

- ✔ Some printers require you to press the On-line or Select button to print the envelope. For example, on my printer I set everything up and stick the envelope in the hatch, and then I print with my software. After a few seconds, the printer's display says "Me feed!" which I properly interpret to mean "Press my On-line button, doofus!" which I do and then the thing prints.

Important Printer Points to Ponder

Printers don't come with cables! You must buy the cable separate from the printer.

The printer cable can be no more than 20-feet long. That length is ridiculous, of course, because the best place for your printer is within arm's reach.

Printers don't come with paper. Always buy the proper paper for your printer. And stock up on it, too; go to one of those discount paper warehouse places and buy a few boxes.

Never let your printer toner get low or ink cartridges go dry. You may think squeezing every last drop of ink saves you money, but it's not good for the printer.

Laser printers sometimes show a *toner low* light or warning message. When you first see it, you can take the toner out of the printer and rock it from side to side. Doing so redistributes the toner and gets more mileage from it. But you can do it only once! Replace the old toner as soon as you see the *toner low* light again.

Inkjet printers generally warn you that the ink cartridge is low, either on their panel or on your computer's screen. Change the ink cartridge at once! Some printers are really stubborn about this.

Most printers have little pictures on them that tell you how the paper goes into the printer. Here is how those symbols translate into English:

- ✔ The paper goes in face down, top side up.
- ✔ The paper goes in face down, top side down.
- ✔ The paper goes in face up, top side up.
- ✔ The paper goes in face up, top side down.

If one side of the paper has an arrow, it usually indicates whether the top side is up or down. Then again, this could all be wrong, and what they're telling us is that we need to start using stone tablets all over again.

Chapter 16

The Very Model of a Modern Modem

Computer communications has come a long way. Modems were once options and considered a pricey peripheral. Not any more! Recently I ordered a PC without a modem, and the dealer thought I was nuts. O, how times have changed!

This is your modem chapter. It's a hardware chapter, because the software side of using a modem is all Internet, Internet, Internet, which I cover in Part V of this book. This chapter explains modem mania without getting lost in the jumbled jungle of jargon that confounds computer communications.

What Does a Modem Do?

Poetically, a modem takes the rude ones and zeros of computer language and translates them into tones, literally singing binary information over the phone lines to other modems. The other modems then take the song and translate it back into ones and zeros for the other computers.

Scientifically, the modem takes digital information from your computer and translates it into analog signals (sounds) that can be sent over common phone lines.

Figure 16-1 shows a typical modem (an external model) though you can't discern the digital-to-analog translation part of the modem by examining the figure.

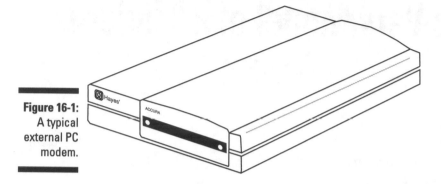

Figure 16-1:
A typical
external PC
modem.

✔ You (the human) don't actually use the modem directly. Instead, communications software is responsible for sending and receiving information using the modem.

✔ The communications software dials the modem, connects with another modem, and then gets the two computers to talk.

✔ Modems plug into serial ports. This is true even if you have an internal modem. Refer to Chapter 9 for the lowdown on ports.

✔ Modem is a contraction of *modulator-demodulator*. But instead of calling it a *lator-lator,* they chose *mo-dem*. Also, there are more modem jokes in the computer world than anything else, typically "How many *modem* do you want?"

Modem Features

A bazillion different types of modems are available — internal and external models, models with different speeds and features, different brand names, and prices from super cheap to down-payment-on-a-house expensive. It's modem madness!

Does it live inside or outside the computer?

Modems come in two main breeds:

Internal: This type of modem fits inside your computer console.

External: This type of modem lives in its own box that sits outside your computer console.

Both types work in exactly the same way; the external modem just has a little plastic box housing the mechanism, plus an extra power cord and cable connecting it to a serial port.

- ✔ Internal modems are cheaper. They plug into an expansion slot inside your computer. The back of the card is visible at the back of your computer; that's where its phone lines plug in and hang out.

- ✔ External modems cost more because you have to pay for their plastic box. You also have to buy a serial cable to connect it to your PC's serial port.

Although external modems cost a little more and take up shelf space near your computer, they have the following advantages:

- ✔ External modems have a little row of lights along the front that correspond to the online action. A light goes on when the modem is connected to another computer, for example. Other lights convey similar informational tidbits.

- ✔ Most external modems have better speakers. You can listen when the modem dials, and you can hear if you have a busy signal. (This feature comes in handy when using the modem on rapid redial to win radio station giveaways.)

- ✔ Because the external modem sits on a shelf, you can more easily reach its volume control knob. The internal modem's knob — if it even has a volume knob — is around back.

- ✔ External modems are transportable. They're easier to take to the repair shop. You can also use them with other computers or take them to a friend's house. (This is a serious step toward computer nerddom.)

- ✔ Because external modems plug into one of your PC's serial (COM) ports, you don't have any device drivers or interrupts to worry about. (Internal modems tend to be a real pain to install and set up properly.)

- ✔ Finally, anyone can install an external modem: Take it out of the box and peel back the Styrofoam and wrapping. Set it on your desktop. Plug the power cord into the wall. Plug the phone cord into the wall (and optionally plug the phone that was plugged into the wall into the modem). Plug one end of a modem cable into the modem. Plug the other end into your PC. *Plug, plug, plug your modem, gently into the wall; merrily, merrily, merrily, merrily, comm is such a ball!*

Internal modems have the following advantages:

- ✔ They don't junk up your desktop. Unlike outboard modems, internal models have only one cable: the one that goes into the wall (and maybe a second cable that goes to your phone). They don't have power cords or serial cables.

- ✔ Internal modems are always ready. You have to remember to turn on an external modem; internal modems are on all the time.

- ✔ Internal modems usually come with cool software, such as a communications program, faxing software, and maybe even some Internet stuff.

I feel the need for speed

Just as some computers are faster than others, some modems are faster than others. But all modems are relatively compatible: The fastest modems can still talk to the slower ones.

Modem speed is measured in bits per second (bps), or how many bits a modem can toss across the phone line in one second. You're probably reading this sentence at what would be equivalent to 300 bps. But at that slow speed, downloading a Web page would take several minutes.

Three common modem speeds are available today: 28.8 Kbps, 33.6 Kbps, and the fastest 56.6 Kbps, where Kbps is kilobits per second or 1000 bps.

28.8 Kbps. A minimum for the Internet. AOL's fastest speed (alas).

33.6 Kbps. The second-fastest speed.

56.6 Kbps. The fastest standard modem speed. A must for the Internet.

Faster speeds are available, but you need to use other, nonstandard modems to get there. See the section "The merry land of modems," later in this chapter, for the full details.

Some people use the word *baud* to describe modem speed. That's inaccurate. The correct term is bps. Correct them enthusiastically if you want to sound like a true computer geek.

"What is this fax-modem thing?"

Modem developers noticed the similarity between modem technology and fax machine technology several years back. They could easily combine the two, and the result was called a *fax modem*.

With the proper software, a fax modem can communicate not only with other PCs and modems, but also with fax machines. It was a glorious day for the computing masses back then.

Today, nearly all modems have the ability to send or receive a fax. It's like having automatic transmission in your car; it's just not a big enough deal to brag about any more.

To use your modem like a fax machine, you need special fax software. Windows uses a program called Microsoft Fax to do the job. Fortunately, your modem probably came with special fax software that's (I'll bet a billion dollars) much, much easier to understand and use than anything Microsoft could dream up.

The merry land of modems

Long ago there were only two kinds of modem: smart and dumb. I'm not making that up!

Modems were called *smart* if they could dial the phone and answer and if they could be controlled by software.

Dumb modems (and this term truly opens up a can of worms) were simple devices usually controlled by two or more switches. You would manually dial a phone number, and then turn the modem on or put the telephone handset into a cradle. Dumb. Dumb. Dumb.

Today, all modems are smart. But within the smart-modem world different types of modems are available. Some are designed to operate a certain way, and others require a special service to utilize their extra speed. Here's the short list, and a summary appears in Table 16-1:

Typical, standard modem. Standard, off-the-shelf modems can connect to your existing phone system. The price varies with the speed — the current top speed of 56 Kbps costs you anywhere from $50 to $150, depending on the modem's make and model.

Soft modem. This type of modem contains no real smarts. Instead, the computer does the processing. This may sound like a lot of overhead, but the advantage is that you can upgrade the modem's smarts using software. Buying a new modem is a thing of the past; just upgrade the soft-modem software, and you have a brand new modem. Or so they say.

Duo modem. This modem achieves its speed by cheating: It uses two phone lines at once. So you need two available phone lines, the modem, plus permission from your Internet service provider to login two times at once.

ISDN modem. The next step up from the traditional modem is the ISDN model. It requires that you have ISDN service, which your phone company can install (and gladly charge you for), and it's available almost everywhere. Beyond that you need an ISDN modem, which more than doubles the speed of your Internet connection.

xDSL modem. This type of modem gives you fast access by taking advantage of unused frequencies in the phone line, like those pauses when your teenager is saying, "I dunno, what do you want to do?" Aside from limited availability, the only drawback is that you must be within a few miles of the phone company's main office to get xDSL service. Oh, and it's expensive, too.

Satellite modem. For those who can't get xDSL, a similar service is available via satellite. You need a satellite, modem, and subscription to the service. The satellite then provides information to your computer at ultra-fast speeds. You do, however, still need a regular modem to *send* information to the Internet. (The satellite modem is receive-only.)

Cable modem. This type of modem is the fastest you can buy, often faster than the computer can keep up with! Two ugly downsides: You need to live in an area serviced by a cable company that offers cable-modem access, and when more of your neighbors begin using their cable modems, the overall speed decreases. But at 2:00 a.m., your cable modem *smokes!*

- ✔ ISDN stands for Integrated Services Digital Network.

- ✔ Another advantage of ISDN is that you can often receive faxes and use a standard telephone on the same line as your modem connection.

- ✔ xDSL stands for (something) Digital Subscriber Line. The most common variation is ADSL for Asymmetric Digital Subscriber Line, but other letters are available for *x*, depending on your phone company.

- ✔ ISDN, xDSL, satellite, and cable services charge you additional fees for connecting. So in addition to paying more for a fancy modem, plus paying for Internet access, you must pay for the connection.

Table 16-1	Comparison of Modems, Price, and Speed	
Modem Type	*Average Price*	*Speed (in bps)*
Standard	$80	56K
Soft modem	$140	56K
Duo modem	$250	112K

Modem Type	Average Price	Speed (in bps)
ISDN modem	$300	128K up to 512K
Satellite modem	$300	512K
xDSL modem	$400	8,000K
Cable modem	$180	30,000K

Connecting Your Modem

Setting up a modem is so easy a 65-year-old retired male doctor could do it. The following sections tell you how.

> ✔ The best way to use a modem is with its own phone line. Just about every house or apartment has the ability to have a second line added without paying for extra wiring. If so, have the phone company hook that line up and use it for your modem. Why? Because . . .

> ✔ You can't use your phone while your modem is talking. In fact, if somebody picks up another extension on that line, it garbles the signal, possibly losing your connection — not to mention that he or she hears a horrid screeching sound.

Hooking up an internal modem

Let someone else plug the internal modem into one of your PC's expansion slots; or maybe it just came that way from the factory. Your job is to connect only one thing: a phone cable from the modem into the phone wall socket or *phone jack.*

Figure 16-2 shows what the back of the internal modem may look like. Two phone jacks are there. Plug one end of the phone cable into the Line hole. Plug the other end of the phone cable into the wall jack.

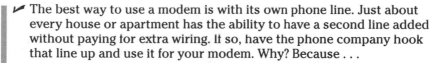

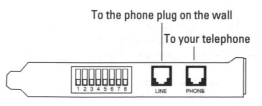

Figure 16-2: Important stuff on the back of an internal modem.

Phone connectors have a little release lever on them. When properly connected, they click into place. Ain't no way that sucker's falling out of there.

It doesn't matter which end of the phone cord goes into the wall or modem; plugging in a modem is just like plugging in a phone. If a phone is already plugged into the wall, unplug it. Then plug it into the Phone hole in the back of your modem.

Table 16-2 offers a quick summary of what plugs into what. Some modems use symbols instead of names for the various connectors on their rumps.

Table 16-2	Plugging What into What for Your Modem
Hole Name	*How It Goes*
Line	Plug a phone cable from this hole on your modem into the phone jack on the wall.
Line In	Same as the Line jack.
Phone	Plug your telephone into this jack on the modem.
Line Out	Same as the Phone jack.
DTE	Plug a serial cable into this connector on the back of your external modem; plug the other end into a serial port on the back of your PC. (External modems.)
Power	Plug the power cord into this hole on the external modem; plug the other end into a power strip or wall socket. (External modems.)

Hooking up an external modem

Unlike an internal modem, anyone can connect an external modem. You don't even need a screwdriver. You do have more cables to connect, but that's not a true bother. Besides, after it's all hooked up, you never have to mess with it again.

You connect four things to the back of an external modem. Figure 16-3 shows them all, though they may appear differently on the back of your modem.

Start by plugging one end of a serial cable into the rear of your PC. Plug it into either COM1 or COM2. Plug the other end of the cable into the back of your modem. The cables only go in one way. You can't screw it up.

Next, plug the modem into the phone jack on the wall. Stick one end of the phone cord into the wall jack; stick the other end into the Line hole on the back of the modem. Notice that the connector snaps into place so it won't accidentally fall out.

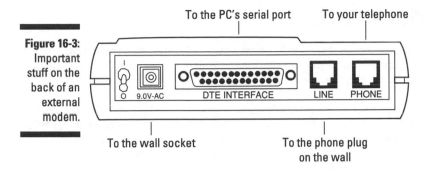

To the PC's serial port   To your telephone

Figure 16-3:
Important
stuff on the
back of an
external
modem.

To the wall socket   To the phone plug
on the wall

If you had a phone connected to the wall jack, plug it into the modem's Phone hole. If you're using only the modem on that line, you don't need to plug anything into the Phone hole.

Make sure that the modem is turned off. (The switch is either on the side or back.) Plug the power cord into the modem, and then plug the power cord into a wall socket or power strip.

- Refer to Table 16-2 for a quick summary of what plugs into what.

- Notice that the serial port on the rear of your PC uses 9 wires, but the plug on the rear of the modem uses 25. (Don't bother counting them; I did that for you.) The modem only needs 9 wires. It has a 25-wire connector for tradition.

- Some modems use symbols instead of names for the connector holes.

- Sometimes you may find the names or symbols on the bottom of the modem instead of the back.

- Familiarize yourself with the modem's on-off switch. Look for the volume control, which may be behind the modem or under one of the sides.

- It's okay to leave your external modem on all the time. You can turn it off to save power, but remember to turn it back on before you use it. If you don't, your communications software will become bewildered.

Installing your modem with Windows

After setting up your modem, you must tell Windows about it. This task isn't as painful as it used to be, thanks to the Windows hardware installation wizard.

Chapter 19 covers the hardware installation wizard. Skip up there for more information on what to do next.

Some Modem Hints

People who tell you that they don't have any problems with their modems are either lying or trying to sell you one (or both). There's probably a specific psychological term called *modem woe*. I'm certain of it.

Being a modem user since way, *way* back, I've collected a list of helpful hints and suggestions to make your modeming life easier. Better to read about this stuff here than suffer the consequences of being stuck in a hotel room in outer Wambooli, unable to deal with a phone jack that looks like a coin return on a slot machine.

Check out Chapter 30 for information on dealing with modem problems.

Making the modem appear even when Windows doesn't see it

For some annoying reason, Windows tends to lose track of the modem after you reset the computer. For example, having just reset or turned the PC on, you try to connect to another computer or the Internet. Windows bemoans that it cannot find the modem. Yeah. Right.

The solution? Just try again, and it should work.

- ✔ Don't blame yourself when this happens.

- ✔ If you have an external modem, double-check to make sure that it's turned on before you dial. (Sometimes this "modem's not there" problem happens when you turn an external modem off and on again.)

Dealing with "local" long distance

The phone companies seem to delight in forcing us to dial our own area codes for *local long distance*. This requirement goofs up some modem programs, which assume that because the number is in your area code, it's not long distance!

To get Windows to believe local long distance isn't local, you need to fool it into thinking you're dialing from someplace other than your local area code. To do so, pretend your computer is a laptop and create a new calling location for it. See the section "Changing your location for a laptop," later in this chapter.

It dials too fast!

Modems dial phone numbers all by themselves. They can dial slow. They can dial fast. But that's not a problem. What can be a problem is when you need to dial a 9 or an 8 before the phone number to get an outside line. That means Mr. Modem should wait after the 9 or 8 before dialing the number, or you end up connecting with the nice lady who tells you that if you can't use a phone, you may as well run away from civilization and start herding yaks.

To slow down your modem after it dials an 8 or 9 to get an outside line, add a comma after the 8 or 9 in the number you dial. For example:

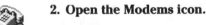

    8,11-202-555-7892

The preceding number is what I would dial to connect with the Pentagon's war room. But because my hotel in Budapest has a slow connection, I stuck a comma after the 8.

Changing your location for a laptop

If you use a laptop PC on the road, you need to tell Windows about your new location so that it can dial the modem properly from wherever you are.

1. **Open the Control Panel**

   Choose Settings➪Control Panel from the Start menu.

2. **Open the Modems icon.**

   Double-click the Modems icon to open it, which displays the Modems Properties dialog box. But don't tarry there.

3. **Click the Dialing Properties button.**

   The Dialing Properties dialog box appears, as shown in Figure 16-4.

4. **Click the New button.**

   The words New Location appear in the I Am Dialing From text box.

5. **Type in a name for wherever you are.**

   For example, when I visit San Diego, I have a separate entry for the Hilton (out by the beach) and my mom's house (in El Cajon).

Modems

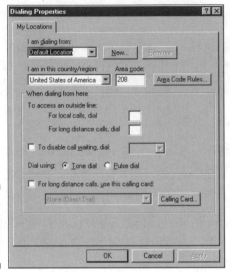

Figure 16-4:
The Dialing
Properties
dialog box.

6. **Type the area code, the country, and other vital stats for your remote location.**

   Here you're telling Windows just how to dial different phone numbers from that new location. (Windows is smart and knows about long distance and the like.)

7. **Click OK to save the information to disk.**

The next time you use the Dialing Properties dialog box, you can select any of your locations from the I Am Dialing From drop-down list. That way you don't have to reenter information every time you're on the road.

✔ If you don't have a laptop, and say you're living in one of those lovely areas where you have to dial the area code to call the Chinese restaurant across the street, then after Step 3, click the Area Code Rules button. A special dialog box appears where you can tell Windows when and how to dial area codes for where you live. This setting works whether or not you're on the road.

✔ You use the Dialing Properties dialog box whenever you use Windows to dial the modem. This can be for an Internet connection or a local system.

✔ By telling Windows the area code and location from which you're calling (plus the other information), you save yourself from having to re-input that information each time you visit that location.

✔ Save the Default Location item for wherever your laptop is most of the time.

Chapter 17

The Singing PC

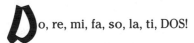o, re, mi, fa, so, la, ti, DOS!

Even though the first IBM PC had a speaker, it could only *BEEP*. Games could play silly songs but nothing symphonic. Fortunately, a few companies began creating *sound cards,* mostly so game players could hear music and antediluvian space grunts. Then, over time, the sound circuitry became part of the motherboard. Throw in a pair of stereo speakers and a subwoofer, and you have the melodic PC of today.

This is your PC sound chapter. Face it, sound is *fun!* Of course, you can tut-tut yourself and claim that you use sound for *business presentations* and *educational uses,* but what you really want to hear is the *THWOK!* as the club makes perfect contact with the ball in the famous Microsoft Golf game.

Sound in Your PC

Nearly every PC today has built-in sound circuitry. And it's good stuff, much better than the state-of-the-art computer sound cards of ten years ago. And although older models may have their sound abilities included on an expansion card, newer PCs have the sound built right into the motherboard.

"How can I tell if my PC has sound?"

Too many people write me questions about whether or not their computer can bleep and squawk with a sound card. How can you tell if your sound card is installed? Easy: Look 'round back.

Your PC should have sound connectors on its rump if it has a sound card installed. You should be able to find three tiny jacks — called mini-din; they accept tiny ⅛-inch audio plugs. The jacks will be labeled Mic, Line In, Line Out, or Speakers.

If your PC has the jacks, then it can produce sound. Whether the sound is working at that point is a software problem. (You should check with your computer dealer if you still can't hear the sound.)

The sound card

When your PC has a sound card, either an expansion card or circuitry on the motherboard, it's capable of doing more than beeping through the speaker.

The first thing the sound card does is to play *wave sounds,* which are the recorded sounds you hear when you turn on the computer or run a program. These are also the sounds you hear when you play a computer game: a ding-dong for a correct answer, the sound of your opponent going "ouch," or the sound of spent 9mm shells hitting a concrete floor. They're all wave sounds.

The second thing most sound cards can do is play music. Included with the basic audio circuitry is a complete musical synthesizer. You can use this synthesizer to play MIDI files, which produce near-realistic music over the PC's speakers.

Finally, sound cards amplify and play music from your computer's CD-ROM drive.

✔ With a microphone and the proper software, you can also use the PC's sound card to record your own voice. See the section, "Recording your voice," later in this chapter.

✔ The sound card and CD-ROM were once packaged together as a PC's *multimedia upgrade.* This is why you need a sound card to hear music from the CD (or you can just plug headphones into the CD's headphone jack).

✔ Today, nearly all sound cards are Sound Blaster-compatible, whether or not they share the Sound Blaster brand name. Some high-end sound cards may not be compatible, but they're used mostly with custom sound engineering software.

✔ MP3 is a special wave file format that plays high-quality music on your PC's speakers. See Chapter 28 for more information on MP3 files.

✔ Digital sound takes up huge amounts of room on a disk. That's why most digitized sounds are limited to short bursts like golf swings and grunts.

Speakers

Your computer needs speakers so that you can hear the sounds the sound card makes. Most PCs now come with speakers or offer them as options. If not, buying a set of speakers with a subwoofer costs $80 or more at your local computer store.

✔ The quality of the speakers really isn't important. Unless you're a die-hard audiophile, I see no point in spending too much money on PC speakers. However, I do recommend external speakers over the built-into-the-monitor type. The quality is better.

✔ It's best to run your speakers electrically instead of through batteries. If your speakers didn't come with an AC power adapter, you can usually buy one at any computer store.

✔ Subwoofers? These boxes sit on the floor beneath your PC and amplify sounds at the low-end of the spectrum. They really give oomph to the base in music, and the thud of your enemy dropping in a game has all the more impact. I recommend them!

✔ If you put speakers on your desk, remember that they contain magnets. If any stray floppy disks come too close, they may lose their data.

Having Fun with Sound in Windows

If you have time to waste, you can turn your smart business computer into a goofy business computer by adding sounds to Windows. I'm not going into any detail here, because this is an area wide open for play. But I will show you the playground:

1. Open the Control Panel.

From the Start menu, choose Settings⇨Control Panel.

Sounds

2. Open the Sounds icon.

Double-click the Sounds icon to open it. The Sounds Properties dialog box is revealed, as shown in Figure 17-1.

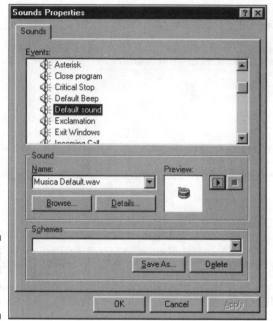

Figure 17-1:
The Sounds
Properties
dialog box.

3. Mess around.

In the Events list are various things that Windows and some of your applications do. You can apply a specific sound to each of these things. So, for example, when Windows opens a window, you can have the sound of something unzipping (or a balloon popping or a rubber band snapping) play on your PC's speaker.

Ah, yes. Fun.

You select sounds by using the Sound area in the dialog box. This area is rich for fiddling.

You can pluck out a sound scheme in the Schemes area. Schemes are collections of sounds that came with Windows or the Plus! package. I enjoy the Robotz Sound Scheme, but I mix in a little Musica and Utopia for my own pleasure.

4. Click OK to get back to work.

You can create your own sounds using a microphone and your sound card. If you want to record stuff from a sound effects CD or your stereo, use the sound card's Line In jack, not the Microphone jack.

Oh, there's tons of sound software to mess with. It would take another book to cover it all. *PC Sound For Dummies?* Maybe.

How do I rid myself of sounds?

Q: I am having trouble getting rid of my PC sound scheme. I had the Space theme but changed it to something else. Yet I still have the sound of the Space theme. How do I get it out?

A: In the Sounds Properties dialog box, select No Sounds from the Schemes drop-down list (near the bottom). Then you can re-add the sounds you like using the list at the top of the dialog box.

✔ Don't be embarrassed when you call tech support for some reason, and each time that they tell you to open this or that window, Mary Poppins says, "Spit-spot?"

✔ Never, under any circumstances, play the Microsoft Sound sound. It will make you gag.

Playing a wave file

BAMBOOM

Wave files are earmarked by specific icons in Windows, shown in the margin. To play these files, open 'em up! Double-click the Wave icon, and Windows plays the sound for you. Nifty.

Playing MIDI music

take five

You play MIDI music by opening those icons, shown in the margin. This action may run the Windows Media Player program, shown in Figure 17-2, or it may run other MIDI-playing software, depending on your PC's sound card.

Figure 17-2:
Windows
Media
Player plays
a MIDI file.

Why are MP3 files so big?

Q: There is something that I don't understand. Why are MIDI files smaller than MP3 files, even though the MIDI files are about as long as the MP3 files? Isn't MP3 newer and more compressed? So why is it so big? A three-minute MP3 file is about 3MB, but a similar MIDI file is only 30KB. I am very confused.

A: A MIDI file merely contains instructions to play the PC's internal synthesizer. You know:

"Play D# for .125 seconds," which is only about four bytes of code. The MP3 files, however, are compressed audio recordings that play back through the speakers. Typically MP3 files are 1MB for each minute of sound — which is actually fairly good when compared with other sound file formats.

- ✔ MIDI stands for Musical Instrument Digital Interface. It's the standard for recording electronic music.

- ✔ MIDI files don't contain recorded music. Instead the files contain notes plus information about the instruments that play those notes. In a way, the MIDI file "plays" the synthesizer on your PC's sound card.

- ✔ Using the proper software, plus maybe some MIDI musical instruments, you can create your own MIDI files.

Recording your voice

If you hook up a microphone to your PC, you can record your voice. Aside from the microphone, you need software. Recording software may have come with your PC or sound card, or you can use a Windows program called Sound Recorder.

Run Sound Recorder from the Start menu by choosing Programs⇨ Accessories⇨Entertainment⇨Sound Recorder. The Sound Recorder's window appears, as shown in Figure 17-3.

Figure 17-3:
The Sound
Recorder.

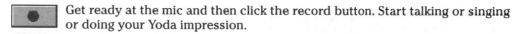 Get ready at the mic and then click the record button. Start talking or singing or doing your Yoda impression.

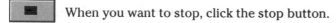 When you want to stop, click the stop button.

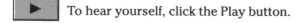 To hear yourself, click the Play button.

You save your work to disk by choosing the File⇨Save As command, just as you would any file in any application.

- ✔ If you can't find Sound Recorder on the Start menu, use the Find command (covered in Chapter 7) to find the file named SNDREC32.EXE.

- ✔ If the Find command can't locate Sound Recorder on your computer, you can add it from the Windows CD. Your favorite book on Windows should have this information in it, or you can visit the following Web page for more information:

  `www.wambooli.com/PCs_for_Dummies/Sounds`

- ✔ Better, more sophisticated sound-recording programs than Sound Recorder often come with your PC's sound card.

- ✔ Sound files are huge! While playing and collecting sounds is fun, be aware that they occupy lots of space.

- ✔ If you have a Zip drive, know that Zip disks make excellent storage for sound files.

- ✔ Sound Recorder can also record sounds from the Line-In jack on your PC. Just click the Record button and start playing the sound.

Can It Talk?

Your PC cannot talk, mainly because Windows doesn't contain any talking software. It may in the future, but because your PC's operating system doesn't talk, you need to find other software to get the thing talking.

- ✔ Many sound cards do come with text-file readers. They allow you to open a text document on disk and then have the computer read aloud the contents of the file. It's amusing . . . for about ten minutes.

- ✔ Sound Blaster used to come with software called *Text-olé*, which could read text files aloud using one of several voices. I'm not aware whether this software is still included with Sound Blaster hardware.

- ✔ Other talking software may be available on the Internet or at your local software store.

Dictating to Your PC

I'll be brief here: There are programs available that let you talk to your PC. You can dictate to the PC, for example, and the program fairly accurately interprets your speech into text right on the screen. It's actually amazing to watch.

For a fast typist such as myself, talking software doesn't really work. I find talking mode and typing mode to be two different things. Also, I change my mind a lot, which means I'm always editing my own text as I write it, something the dictation software is rather poor at.

If you do want to take a turn at dictation software, I recommend Dragon Naturally Speaking. It's inexpensive and comes with a nifty microphone headset. Setting up and configuring the program does take a few hours, but it works rather well at taking proper dictation.

Note that you need at least a 166MHz Pentium PC with 32MB of RAM for software such as Dragon Naturally Speaking to work properly.

Chapter 18

More Stuff for Your PC (Peripherals)

· ·

In This Chapter

▶ What is a peripheral?

▶ Installing new hardware in Windows

▶ All about scanners

▶ All about tape backup units

▶ How, when, and what to upgrade on your PC

· ·

Scientists claim that the universe is expanding, constantly growing outward in all directions. My question: outward into *what?* And what if the universe isn't expanding? What if everything is just getting smaller? Would we notice?

The PC's universe is ever-expanding. You can add dozens of gizmos and gadgets to a PC. These extra parts are called *peripherals,* gizmos you can add to your computer to make it more useful or more fun — and certainly more expensive. This chapter takes a look at some of the more popular peripherals that attach to a PC.

The Wide, Wide World of Peripherals

Peripheral refers to anything outside of the main. For example, the *peripheral nervous system* is made up of all the nerves in your body outside of your brain (which is called the *central nervous system*). *Peripheral vision* includes things you can see without looking directly at them. And *peripheral nervous vision* is what first-time computer buyers get when they enter the store. With a computer, however, a *peripheral* is any accessory or auxiliary equipment you may buy and connect to the computer.

The variety of peripherals you can buy for your computer is endless. Common peripheral items include: scanners, tape drives, CD-Rs, digital cameras, video cameras, and numerous other toys you can connect to the typical PC.

- Anything outside of the console box is considered a peripheral. The mouse, modem, and printer were all once considered peripherals, similar to how a scanner or PC video camera is viewed today.

- Peripherals enable you to expand your computer system without having to buy a totally new computer. You can add these extra hardware devices yourself or have a guru, computer consultant, or some other overpaid individual do it for you.

- All peripherals are hardware.

- Although the word *peripheral* refers to things outside of a computer, you can also add peripherals internally — inside the PC's console. (In a way, peripheral refers to anything beyond what comes standard in the computer.)

Installing a peripheral

The hardware side of adding a peripheral is really cinchy. Most peripherals sit outside the PC. All you need to do to connect them is find the proper hole and plug the thing in.

Well, granted, you need to follow other instructions when adding a peripheral, but plugging the thing into the proper port is most important.

Because peripherals can also live inside the PC, installing one may involve opening the console and plugging in an expansion card. Again, this process isn't that tough, but it's not the sign of a PC wimp if you pay someone else to do it.

- Most peripherals plug into standard connectors on the back of every PC. See Chapter 9 for a review.

- Generally speaking, whenever you install hardware inside of or onto your PC you should first turn off the computer. See Chapter 2 for the official turning-off instructions.

- USB peripherals are the easiest by far to install. You don't even need to turn off your PC; just plug in the USB cable, and you're on your way.

Telling Windows about your new hardware

This computer thing involves two parts: hardware and software. The hardware installation of a peripheral is a snap. Software installation involves telling Windows about the peripheral.

Fortunately, most peripherals are what's known as *Plug and Play.* When you restart your computer after installation, Windows instantly recognizes the new hardware (unless it's a USB peripheral, in which case you don't have to turn the PC off in the first place).

When Windows finds the new hardware, it has to add special software called a *driver* to control the hardware. This software may be included on the Windows CD or may come on a floppy disk or CD with the hardware itself. At some point in the dizzy search for a driver, Windows may ask if you have a disk. If so, insert the disk into the proper slot and follow the directions on the screen to continue.

- ✔ Keep your eye out for Plug-and-Play-happy peripherals. Nearly all new computers are Plug-and-Play friendly, and just about every hardware doohickey you buy is the same way.

- ✔ If your PC sports a USB port, always check for a USB version of whatever peripheral you're buying: speakers, joystick, scanner, whatever. USB hardware is hands-down the best and easiest to install. Period.

- ✔ According to Microsoft, Windows can identify and properly configure 90 percent of the expansion cards and peripherals out there. It can guess at another 9 percent. And only 1 percent leaves it utterly flummoxed.

- ✔ Yes, you'll probably end up being in that 1 percent.

- ✔ A driver is nothing more than a software program that controls a specific piece of hardware. So when someone says, "Windows needs a new driver," he's not insulting you as the computer operator.

- ✔ Plug and Play isn't foolproof. For that reason, many in the industry have dubbed it "plug and pray."

"Windows is stupid and doesn't recognize my new peripheral!"

In some rare cases, Windows may not recognize your new hardware. The problem could be that the hardware isn't Plug-and-Play compatible, or it could be that you're installing something that doesn't grab the computer's attention directly, like a new external modem.

Add New
Hardware

When Windows refuses to recognize the new hardware, you should run the Add New Hardware Wizard. Open the Control Panel and then double-click the Add New Hardware icon to run the wizard.

Follow the steps in the driver. Read the screen. Click the Next button or select options as necessary. In mere moments, your new hardware should be up and running, and everything will be groovy.

✔ The Big Decision point in the Add New Hardware Wizard is whether to let Windows look for the new hardware or select it yourself from a list. Sometimes it's tempting to taunt Windows: "Go ahead! Find that hardware! I dare you to find it! Double-dog dare you!" Other times plucking the device from a list on your own is easier and quicker.

✔ Windows cannot (or refuses to) find tape backup units, especially the internal models. If you've just added one, don't fret if you notice Windows seems mute to its existence. Instead, run the backup software that came with the tape backup unit. It should locate the device, no problem.

✔ You may need to configure SCSI devices using your SCSI card's setup program. Again, this is why SCSI cards are techy and why I don't really recommend them in Chapter 9. Better have a guru do your SCSI peripheral setup.

Some Popular Peripherals

This chapter gets shorter and shorter with each edition of this book. Back in 1992, modems and CD-ROM drives were considered peripherals. Today the list is short — and may grow shorter still.

The most popular PC peripheral today is the scanner, which has dropped drastically in price over the past few years. Also popular is the tape backup unit. Still on the edge of pheripheralism is the video camera or digital camera. Who knows what could be next? These little boxes called computers are amazing things.

Scan this, Mr. Spock!

Scanners are nifty little devices that work like photocopiers. Instead of copying the image, however, the scanner translates it into a graphics image in your computer. From there, you can modify the image, save it to disk, add it to a document, or send it off as an e-mail attachment.

Most scanners sold today are the flatbed, desktop variety. You place an image into the scanner similar to the way you'd put a picture, piece of paper, or open book into a photocopier. Close the lid. Then use your scanning software to grab the image.

The following are some scanner thoughts to amuse you. Chapter 22 in this book goes over the process in more detail, including using graphics software to edit and save the image.

- ✔ Aside from flatbed scanners, handheld scanners and business card scanners are also available. Unless you see a need for those specialized units, I recommend the flatbed models.

- ✔ A *handheld scanner* looks like a miniature vacuum cleaner. You slide the scanner across a picture, and the picture appears on your screen.

- ✔ You can also use a scanner to *read* a document. This process requires optical character recognition (OCR) software. The document is read in OCR mode and then translated into text you can edit in your computer. As usual, this feature sounds a lot better than it really works.

- ✔ Typical scanner price: $150 to close to $1,000. The more you pay, the better the image. High-end scanners are usually for the graphics industry, though.

- ✔ Try to get a single-pass scanner. They're faster than the multiple-pass scanners.

- ✔ Don't bother with a SCSI scanner unless your PC has a SCSI port.

- ✔ If your PC has a USB port, get a USB scanner!

- ✔ Some scanners also plug into the PC's printer port.

- ✔ Don't let anyone fool you into believing adding a scanner can turn your PC into a photocopier. True, you can scan an image and then print that image. But the process takes more time than it would to drive to the copy store and make a few copies. (Well, maybe not that long, but scanning and printing isn't the fastest thing the PC does.)

Tape backups

A tape drive is a device used to create backups, or duplicates, of all the information on your PC's hard drive. Everything. It's an emergency copy. A safety copy. A just-in-case copy.

Alas, most PCs don't come with a tape backup unit. Because they're optional, many people skip using them and then skip backing up. So when disaster strikes, you have no backup copy of everything, and all your work and all your computer stuff is lost. But I need not dwell on that here.

Adding a backup drive to your PC is simple. Some can be added internally, piggy-backing themselves onto your PC's floppy drive (actually taking over the position of drive B). Others can be added externally, often plugging into the printer port or a USB port.

Then, after you install your tape backup drive, use it! Make a backup copy of your work *at least* once a month. I make backup copies of the books I write *daily*. And the backup software automates everything. All I did was tell it what to backup and when. Oh, it's times like this computers really fulfill everything the brochure promised.

- ✔ A tape backup drive costs anywhere from under $100 to over $1,000 for the fancy, super-duper network backup drives.

- ✔ Tape backup drives come with one tape. Buy more. You need about three to rotate your backup copies.

- ✔ The amount of information storable on a backup tape varies. Some tapes store only 500MB, others over 8GB. Buy a tape backup unit that uses tapes equal to or greater than the capacity of all your PC's hard drives.

- ✔ Windows 98 no longer lets you back up to floppy disks! You must have a tape backup (or other backup device) to use the Backup program.

- ✔ You can also back up to CD-R or CD-RW drives, and those drives usually come with software to assist you in backing up.

- ✔ You can also back up to Zip or Jaz drives. Zip drives, however, are very expensive to back up to; most backups require several Zip disks, which is more costly than a dedicated tape backup unit and a stack of tapes.

- ✔ Speaking of Windows and backing up, I recommend using your tape backup's software and not Windows own software for backing up your hard drive. Windows backup software stinks. Your tape backup drive probably comes with something better anyway.

It's live, and it's living on top of your monitor!

An interesting toy to add to your PC is a video camera. These little mechanical eyeballs perch near your PC, usually on top of the monitor. You can use them to record movies or single images, or to send live images over the Internet — it all depends on the software that comes with the camera.

- ✔ My camera appears to be broken. So much for including a live action shot of me writing this book. . . .

✔ If you want one of those cameras that sends pictures to the Web, what you want is a *Webcam*.

✔ Make sure the software you need is included with the camera. For example, videoconferencing is possible only with the proper software. The camera is just a device; you need software to really play with it.

Everyone say, "Megabyte!" *(digital cameras)*

The latest PC craze is the digital camera. Not only have these wonderful toys come down drastically in price, but the quality of the images they take is rivaling traditional cameras.

Digital cameras range in price from just a coupla hundred dollars to several thousand dollars. The average is about $800, which makes them spendy toys. But scanners were $800 each just a few years back, so the prices will probably come down.

The two things to look for in a digital camera are the resolution and number of photographs the camera can store.

Resolution is measured in horizontal by vertical pixels, the more the better (and pricier) the camera. Don't get anything with a resolution less than 1024 x 768 pixels. Average resolution is about 1280 x 1024, and some of the *nice* digital cameras have a resolution of 1600 x 1200 pixels.

The number of images the camera can store varies from a few dozen to close to 200. An interesting thing to note, however, is that you can delete images to make room for more. The camera is like a computer, so if you don't like one shot, you can remove it to make room for another try. (Or if you take that embarrassing picture of your spouse, you can safely delete it later to avoid sleeping on the couch.)

Choosing a peripheral for backing up

Q: If you cannot back up to floppies using Windows 98, then shouldn't the *first* peripheral you buy be a Zip or Jaz drive?

A: Or a tape backup unit. I'd recommend the tape backup unit over the Zip drive, though a Jaz drive makes a good backup unit as well. Zip disks are just too expensive, and you'd need too many of them to do a proper backup.

✔ These cameras use LCD viewfinders, which means you must hold them away from your face to get an image — like those camcorders that have LCD viewfinders. Same thing.

✔ Beware of digital cameras with too many confusing and poorly labeled dials and buttons. These are the high-end models, suited for professionals.

✔ With some cameras, the resolution depends on how many images the camera can store; the higher the resolution, the fewer the images.

✔ The best cameras have removable storage *flash cards.* Buy more, and the camera can store more images by changing the cards.

✔ You may also need to buy a flash card adapter for your PC, to allow you to easily retrieve the images into your computer.

✔ Some cameras store the images on standard floppy disks. No need to buy an adapter then.

"I Have Some Money, and I Want to Upgrade My Hardware"

Most people don't trade in their cars each year. TVs, VCRs, blenders, and clock radios usually stay put until they break, and then you buy a new one. It's the Bic lighter theory: Why repair something that's cheap, when you can just buy a new one? The same thing applies to most pets. For example, why incur a $35 vet bill on a $1.59 mouse? Toss it out and buy the kid a new one! But I digress. . . .

The computer world, being bizarre and different as we know it, offers updates and upgrades on a monthly basis, if not weekly. It's technology! There's something new and better! And you still have a $1,500 credit on your VISA!

What to buy first

Instead of buying a new computer, upgrading the old one may be cheaper. Or, rather, have somebody else upgrade your old computer for you. But where do you spend your money first? Too many enticing things can get in the way of a sane decision. Let me help.

Memory: Your first upgrading priority should be memory. It's not that expensive, and installation isn't a major headache. Just about all your software will enjoy having more memory available.

✔ Increased memory can make these programs work faster and handle larger chunks of information. It also lets the computer handle more graphics and sound.

✔ More memory is the best thing you can buy for your PC.

✔ For more information about memory stuff, read Chapter 11.

Hard drive: Buy a second hard drive. Make it a big one. Most PCs can handle two hard drives. And by the time you need another one, you'll know exactly how many more megabytes of storage you need.

✔ If you don't have room in your PC for a hard drive, you can always buy an external hard drive or replace one of your current drives. This is a complex process, because you must copy all the files off the old hard drive and onto the new one.

✔ If you have a SCSI hard drive system, you can have up to six hard drives total in a PC (up to two inside and four outside the box).

✔ By the way, larger hard drives don't take up any extra room in the computer's case, so don't worry about needing a bigger case.

Monitor: Buy a big monitor, like a 21-inch jobbie. These things are *great*. You can really see a lot of windows on the screen at once without feeling crowded. Oftentimes, just replacing the old monitor is easy. In fact, you can do the whole operation yourself but have someone with an expendable back hoist the thing up for you.

✔ For more information on monitors, see Chapter 12.

Microprocessor: Upgrading the microprocessor is something I don't recommend. Generally speaking, it's just better to buy a whole new computer. That way you get *all* new components at a cost cheaper than buying a new PC one bit at a time.

I stand corrected!

Q: I just read your book *PCs for Dummies* and enjoyed it for its straightforward information. I have one suggestion for the next edition. In your chapter on peripherals, you referred to *peripheralitis* as a condition in which a computer owner can't buy enough peripherals. I am a veterinary medical student and suggest you use the term peripheralphobia for fear of peripherals and peripheralphilia for love of peripherals. The suffix *itis* means inflammation of.

A: I have removed the "Peripheralitis" sidebar from this edition but thought this letter amusing enough to include it.

My opinion is that you're better off adding more memory to your system or installing a bigger hard drive. These two upgrades give you instant results, whereas a faster microprocessor may or may not be noticeable right away. Of course, this is my opinion, and if you're dead-set on doing an upgrade, go for it.

When to buy a new computer

Plan on this: Every four or five years, replace your PC. By then, the cost of a new system will be cheaper than any upgrading you do.

Your PC is essentially out of date the moment you purchase it. Somewhere right now in Silicon Valley, they're devising new microprocessors and better motherboards that will cost less money. Maybe not the *minute* you purchased your PC, but sooner or later your leading-edge technology will be yesterday's kitty box.

But do you really need to buy a new computer? Maybe not. Look at the reasons you bought it in the first place. Can the computer still handle those needs? If yes, you're doing fine. Upgrade only when you desperately need to. No sense in spending more money on the monster.

- ✔ Computer technology grows faster than fly specks on a clean windshield. But, unless your computing needs have changed drastically, your computer can still handle the tasks you bought it for.

- ✔ Most people buy newer computers for the increase in speed. Yet speed doesn't always mean increased productivity. For instance, most word processing time is spent pondering the right choice of words. A faster computer can't help there. Faster computers do help those applications that need the extra horsepower: graphics, animation, desktop publishing, and programs of that ilk.

- ✔ Compare the price of a new computer with the amount of time you'll save at a faster processing speed. If you spend a lot of time waiting for your computer to catch up with you, an upgrade may be in order.

- ✔ Avoid the lure and seduction of those techy computer magazines that urge you to Buy! Buy! Buy! the latest PC. Remember who most of their advertisers are.

Part IV

The Non-Nerds
Computer Guide
to Software

"SOFTWARE SUPPORT SAYS WHATEVER WE DO, DON'T ANYONE START TO RUN."

In this part . . .

Computer software makes the computer hardware go. It's the real brains of the operation, even though it comes later in this book than computer hardware. Why? Because you must have one before you can use the other. Software needs hardware like a symphony needs an orchestra. After all, what's the point of a bassoon without music to play? And isn't the word *bassoon* fun to say?

Bassoon.

I would love to go on and on about the bassoon and how I believe it was inspired by an attempt at amateur indoor plumbing in the seventeenth century, but this part of the book is about PC software and not musical instruments. So enjoy your PC software and learn to play the bassoon if you have the time.

Chapter 19

Using Software

. . . .

In This Chapter

▶ How to buy software

▶ Stuff in the software box

▶ Installing software

▶ Uninstalling software

▶ Updating software

▶ Whether or not to upgrade Windows

▶ Learning software tips

. . . .

*U*sing software means using your computer. You may punch the Enter key on the keyboard, but it's some piece of software that gives that action significance — running a word processor, launching an intercontinental ballistic missile, or erasing every last file on your hard drive. Yeah, verily, software hath the power.

Tons of tomes have been written on how to make software work for you. To document all of that here would be silly. Instead, this chapter focuses on the getting-started aspect of software: how to buy it, set it up, get used to it, and uninstall it if you hate it.

A journey of ten thousand steps would be shorter if father would only use the map.
                                                                                            —Lao Tsu

A Few Words on Buying Software

Buying software is part of the computer buying process. You pick out your software *first* and then the hardware to match. But with so many software packages available, you can easily feel like you're making a dopey decision.

To prevent that foreboding and dread, you can always comparison shop for software. Better still, I recommend seeing what other people are using. What do they use at the office? What do your computer-literate friends enjoy using or recommend? Make sure that you get what's right for you, not just what's cheap and popular.

- ✔ Try before you buy software.
- ✔ Have someone at the store demonstrate the software for you.
- ✔ Always check out a store's return policy on software.
- ✔ Check the software's requirements. They should match your computer's hardware inventory.
- ✔ Check out *Buying a Computer For Dummies* (IDG Books Worldwide, Inc.) for more information on buying software.

What's This Stuff in the Box?

Surprisingly, many large software boxes contain air or cardboard padding to make the boxes look bigger and more impressive in the store. I suppose the idea is to push the competition off the shelf. Or it could be to justify paying $279 for what ends up being a CD and a pamphlet.

The most vital things inside the software box are the discs. Nearly all software comes on one (or more — many more!) CDs. Some stuff still does come on floppy disks, however.

After the disks comes the manual, plus some other goodies. Here's the rundown:

Disks: Never toss out the CD-ROM or floppy disks! I always keep them in the box they came in, especially after installation, which makes finding the disks easy should I ever need them again in the future.

The Hideous Manual: Most programs toss in a printed manual, typically the size of a political pamphlet and about as interesting. More than one manual may be included. Look for the "Getting Started," "Installation," or "Setup" section of the manual first.

Registration card: Resembling a postcard, though it could be larger, this is what identifies you as a user of the product to the manufacturer. Fill in the blanks on the card and then mail it back to the company. The company then (supposedly) notifies you of any defects, including nonfunctional commands or air-bag problems. Some companies require you to fill out the registration card before they'll offer technical support over the phone.

Quick reference card: The manual works fine for explaining everything in great detail, but you'll find yourself continually repeating some commands. A quick reference card contains those useful commands; you can prop it up next to the keyboard for quick sideways glances. Not all software comes with these cards, however.

Quick installation card: Computer users thrive on instant gratification: Push a button and watch your work be performed instantly. Nobody wants to bother with slow, thick manuals, especially when installing the software. A quick installation card contains an abbreviated version of the manual's installation instructions. By typing in the commands on the card, you can install the software without cracking open the manual. Victory!

License agreement: This extensive batch of fine print takes an average of 3,346 words of legalese to say four things: 1) Don't give away any copies of this program to friends — make them buy their own programs. 2) If you accidentally lose any data, it's not our fault. 3) If this software doesn't work, that's not our fault, either. 4) In fact, you don't even own this software. You merely own a license to use the software. We own the software. We are evil. We will one day own the world. Ha-ha!

Read me first: When the company finds a mistake in its newly printed manual, it doesn't fix it and print out a new manual. It prints the corrections on a piece of paper and slaps the headline "Read Me First!" across the top. Staple that piece of paper to the inside cover of your manual for safekeeping.

Unsolicited junk: Finally, some software comes with company catalogs and *free* offers from related companies for their stuff. You can toss all this stuff out if you like.

Some additional, meandering thoughts:

✔ Sometimes a manual isn't included. You may find an installation card or pamphlet. The manual is *on the disk.* Egads!

✔ If your software comes on a CD but your PC lacks a CD-ROM drive, then you can order the floppy disk version of the product. Stand back! The program can be anywhere from 2 to 36,000 floppy disks.

✔ Sometimes the licensing agreement is printed on a little sticker on an envelope; you have to tear apart the agreement before you can get to the disks inside. Whether or not this means you accept the agreement is up to a battalion of attorneys to discover.

✔ In addition to the registration card, many products let you register online using your modem. Or you can print out a list of information to fax to the company, if you prefer not to modem anything.

✔ Thank goodness software boxes aren't junky like those magazine publisher sweepstakes things. You can never find the things you need to fill in, stickers to place over the TV set or on Ed's head, or options to clip. What nonsense! Software boxes are much neater by comparison.

Software Installation Chores

The first step in installing software is simple:

1. **Get someone else to do it for you.**

   Enough said.

   Or:

1. **Read the *Read Me* blurb.**

   When you first open the box, scrounge around for a piece of paper that says "Read Me First!" and follow the first instruction: Read it. Or at least try to make some sense of it.

   Sometimes the Read Me First sheet contains a sentence or two left out of the manual's third paragraph on page 127, "Dwobbling your shordlock by three frips." If you don't understand the sheet, don't throw it away. It may come in handy after you've started using the program.

2. **Set the manual(s) aside.**

   Say, "There," when you do this.

3. **Put the Installation disk into your disk drive.**

   Find the disk marked with the words *Installation* or *Setup* or *Disk One,* (or the only disk if there is just one) and place that disk in the disk drive where it fits.

   Hopefully it will be a CD. If not, it will be a 3½-inch disk. Like cockroaches, it's the first of many.

   If you're installing from floppy disks, put them in a neat stack, in order, first disk on top. That way you can easily feed them, one after the other, into the disk drive without having to rummage for the next disk later.

4. **Start the Installation program.**

   If you're lucky, the installation program runs automatically when you insert the CD into the CD-ROM drive.

   Add/Remove
   Programs

   If the installation program doesn't start automatically, you need to run it yourself. You can do this by opening the Add/Remove Programs icon in the Control Panel. Click the Install button to direct Windows to hunt down and run the installation program.

5. **Read the screen carefully; click the Next button as necessary.**

   Watch the instructions carefully; sometimes they slip something important in there. My friend Jerry (his real name) just kept clicking the Next button instead of reading the screen. He missed an important notice that said an older version of the program would be erased. Uh-oh! Poor Jerry never got his old program back.

6. **Choose various options.**

The software asks for your name and company name, and maybe for a serial number. Type all that stuff in.

Don't freak if the program already knows who you are. Windows is kinda clairvoyant in that respect.

When asked to make a decision, the option already selected (called the *default*) is typically the best option. Only if you know what's going on and *truly care* about it should you change anything.

You can find the serial number inside the manual, on the CD-ROM case, on the first disk in the stack of 3½-inch disks, or on a separate card you probably threw away even though I told you to keep everything in the original box.

7. **Files are copied.**

Eventually, the installation program copies the files from the CD-ROM drive onto your hard drive for full-time residence.

If you're unlucky enough to be installing from floppy disks, keep feeding them, one after the other, into the floppy drive. Make sure that you get them in the proper order (they're numbered). Make sure that you remove one disk and replace it with the next disk.

8. **It's done.**

The installation program ends. The computer may reset at this point. That's required sometimes when installing special programs that Windows needs to know about. (Windows is pretty dumb after it starts.)

Start using the program!

✔ These steps are vague and general. Hopefully your new software comes with more specific instructions.

✔ You can get software from the World Wide Web on the Internet. This process is known as *downloading,* and Chapter 28 covers it.

✔ Keep the quick reference card next to your computer immediately after installing the program; it's more helpful than the manual.

✔ If the software has a serial number, keep it! Write it down in the manual. Don't lose it! With some software, such as Adobe PageMaker, you cannot order the upgrade unless you have a proper serial number.

Why are computer manuals so horrid?

Computer manuals have a bad rap. Things are better today than they were years ago. Back then, everyone was a nerd. Most manuals just began, "Flip these switches to enter base hexadecimal address pairs for IPL." And *that* was considered user-friendly.

Why are the manuals so bad? Many reasons. Primarily the manual is written as an afterthought. The software developer spends more time and attention on building the product. The manual is given to someone reluctant to create it, often the product manager or programmer. They're far too familiar with the product to compose a useful manual, and they don't care about getting it done properly.

Manuals must also be completed well before the product is done. Printing 10,000 manuals takes more time than copying off 10,000 disks. Therefore, the manual is often inaccurate or vague.

Size is an issue. Most manuals are slim because their weight adds to the product's shipping cost. Some places don't even bother with a manual, instead putting everything on disk in *read me* or *help* files. (Obviously the developer's intention isn't to ensure that you enjoy and use the product to its full abilities.)

People who write computer manuals are often technical writers paid by the hour. They don't have a vested interest in their work. This is why books on the subject are far better than manuals; the author is trying to make money by writing a successful book.

Uninstalling Software

To remove any newly installed program, you use an uninstall program. This program is not a feature of Windows. Each software program must come with its own uninstall feature. Otherwise removing unwanted software is dern tough (see the sidebar, "Out software, out!").

You uninstall software by running the uninstall program. Typically you can find that program on the Start menu right by the icon where you start the program. Figure 19-1 shows such an arrangement; the Norton AntiVirus software is shown in a submenu on the Start menu. Right there, you see the Uninstall Norton AntiVirus option, which removes the software.

If your software lacks an obvious uninstall program, you can attempt to use Windows to rid yourself of it. You can open the Control Panel's Add/Remove Programs icon to try to uninstall software. Opening the Add/Remove Programs icon displays the Add/Remove Programs Properties dialog box, as shown in Figure 19-2.

Figure 19-1:
The Norton
AntiVirus
submenu on
the Start
menu.

Figure 19-2:
The
Add/Remove
Programs
Properties
dialog box.

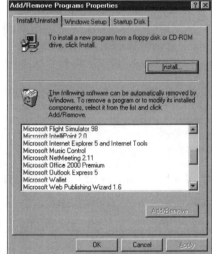

The list of programs Windows knows about and can uninstall is listed at the bottom of the dialog box (refer to Figure 19-2). Click one of those programs, the one you want to uninstall. This selects the program for action. Then click the Add/Remove button.

A warning dialog box appears before Windows yanks the cord on your program. Click Yes to zap it to Kingdom Come.

✔ Do not attempt to uninstall *any* software by deleting it from your hard drive. You should never delete any file you did not create yourself. (You can, however, delete any shortcuts you create.)

✔ The Norton AntiVirus is a third-party program the author paid for and installed on his own computer. It does not come with every Windows computer, so you may not have such a menu on your PC.

✔ You can also use the Add/Remove button to add individual components to your programs. For example, you can click Microsoft Office to add a new component or piece of that software, something you didn't choose to install way back when.

✔ For adding components missing from Windows, click the Windows Setup tab in the Add/Remove Programs Properties dialog box.

Updating Your Software

After a novel's written, it's finished. Subsequent reprints correct a few misspellings, but that's about it. But software's never finished. It's too easy to change. Most software packages are updated about once every year or two.

The reason software is updated used to be to fix problems or to introduce new features. But, honestly, most of the reason new versions of programs appear today is to make more money for the software developer. Upgrading means that everyone who owns the software might buy a new version and generate revenue for the company. Yup, it's greed.

My advice: Order the update only if it has features or makes modifications you desperately need. Otherwise, if the current version is doing the job, don't bother.

Out software, out!

The best way to remove unwanted programs — especially those without uninstall programs — is to get a third-party disk-cleaning program. I recommend CleanSweep, currently available from Peter Norton/Symantec.

CleanSweep goes out to disk and tries to find every possible component installed with a program. It gives you a list so you can check and uncheck which components you really want

deleted. Further, it creates a backup copy of the uninstalled program so you can *undo* what CleanSweep does.

CleanSweep and other third-party uninstall programs work best when they monitor a program's installation. This way they know exactly what to remove and what to reset to bring your PC back to the shape it was in before you installed your software.

- ✔ "Software never gets obsolete." —Bill Gates

- ✔ Consider each upgrade offer on its individual merits: Will you ever use the new features? Do you need a word processor that can print upside-down headlines and bar charts that show your word count? Can you really get any mileage out of the *intranet version* when you're a sole user sitting at home?

- ✔ Something else to keep in mind: If you're still using DoodleWriter 4.2 and everybody else is using DoodleWriter 6.1, you'll have difficulty exchanging documents. After a while, newer versions of programs become incompatible with the older models. If so, you need to upgrade.

- ✔ In an office setting, everybody should be using the same software version. (Everybody doesn't have to be using the *latest* version, just the *same* version.)

Some Tips for Learning a Program

Using software involves learning its quirks. That takes time. So my first suggestion for learning any new software is to give yourself plenty of time. Sadly, in today's rush-rush way of doing everything, time isn't that easy to come by. It's a big pain when the boss sends you down to the software store expecting you to come back and create something wonderful before the end of the day. In the real world, that's just not possible (not even if you're an expert).

What about upgrading Windows?

Upgrading Windows is a *big deal.* Why? Because everything else in your computer relies on Windows. Therefore it's a major change, something to think long and deep about.

Often the newer version of Windows has many more features than the older version. Do you need those features? If not, don't bother with the update.

One problem you may have if you decide to upgrade is that your software may not work properly. None of my Adobe applications worked with Windows 95 when it first came out. I had to wait months and pay lots of money for upgrades before things got back to normal.

When Windows 98 came out, I opted not to upgrade so I wouldn't have to go through the same hassle and expense.

After a time, you may notice newer software packages coming to roost on the newest version of Windows. The new stuff will be better than your current stuff, meaning you'll need to upgrade if you want to take advantage of it.

So where does this leave you? *Don't bother updating Windows!* Just wait until you buy a new computer, and that PC will have the newest version of Windows, all preinstalled and set up nicely.

Most software comes with a workbook or a tutorial for you to follow, which is a series of self-guided lessons on how to use the product. It also tells you about the program's basic features and how they work. I highly recommend going through the tutorials. Follow the directions on the screen. If you notice anything interesting, write it down in the tutorial booklet and flag that page.

Some tutorials are really dumb, granted. Don't hesitate to bail out of one if you're bored or confused. You can also take classes on using software, though they may bore you as well. Most people do, however, understand the program much better after the tutorial.

After doing the tutorial, play with the software. Make something. Try saving something to disk. Try printing. Then quit. Those are the basic few steps you should take when using any software program. Get to know it and then expand your knowledge from there as required.

- ✔ Some businesses may have their own training classes that show you the basics of using the in-house software. Take copious notes. Keep a little book for yourself with instructions for how to do what.

- ✔ Take notes whenever someone shows you something. Don't try to learn anything; just note what's done so you won't have to make a call should the situation arise again.

- ✔ Never toss out your manual. In fact, I recommend going back and trying to read the manual again several weeks after you start to learn a program. You may actually understand things. (Consider that the fellow who wrote the manual knew the product about as well when he first sat down to write about it.)

- ✔ Computer books are also a good source to learn about programs. They come in two types: references and tutorials. The tutorial is great for learning; references are best when you know what you want to do but aren't sure how.

- ✔ This book is a reference. All ...*For Dummies* books are references.

Chapter 20

Software Tips for the Home

● ●

In This Chapter

▶ Financial software

▶ Using Quicken to write checks

▶ Playing games

▶ Working with old DOS games

▶ Educational and training software

● ●

*W*ho would have thought that a computer would once be part of a home's furnishings? When you speak of furniture in the home, you typically use words like ottoman, chinoiserie, or credenza. But a computer desk? And just what is a credenza anyway? It's fun to say. Not as fun as *bassoon,* but close.

Home users have different interests than business users, which is why I've written this whole chapter about things most people use PCs for in the home. This list includes: education, entertainment, and personal finance software. People also do work at home, but I cover that in Chapter 21. And most popular of all is using the Internet at home, which I cover in Part V.

Personal Finance

The old reasons for getting a computer were quaint and impractical: You could balance your checkbook, keep track of your recipes, and create a Christmas mailing list. Sheesh. They should have said: You can meet the mate of your dreams, dial up the Pentagon and launch a weapon, or kill a million space gremlins without getting blood on your tunic.

Even so, one of the most popular software packages of all time is called Quicken. It's essentially a home (and business) accounting package that makes keeping track of your money easy and fun — yes, fun, in that most people actually sit down and balance their checkbooks because it's so dern easy.

✔ Quicken can also do finances for a small or home business. For larger businesses, other financial software is available.

✔ Beyond Quicken is the Microsoft alternative, Microsoft Money. But even Microsoft conceded that Money isn't as nice as Quicken; when Microsoft had the chance to buy Intuit (Quicken's developer), it dropped Money like it was made of plutonium. Therefore, the following sections discuss Quicken only.

Writing checks in Quicken

You can start using Quicken at any time; you don't need to open a new bank account or change anything. Just fill in some information from your last bank statement, and you're ready to roll.

Quicken's first function is to be your electronic checkbook. Creating a check on the screen works just like it does on paper (see Figure 20-1). Writing checks on the computer has some advantages, of course: Quicken remembers previous checks you've written, so if you start typing in **Pho**, Quicken automatically suggests *Phone Company* for you.

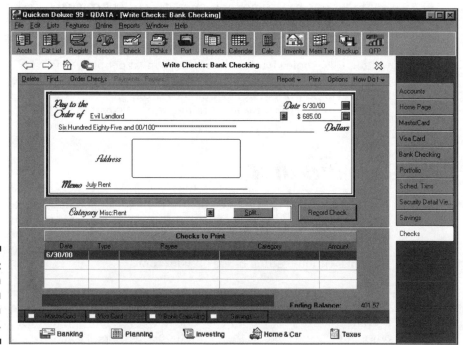

Figure 20-1:
Quicken helps you write a check.

Quicken also lets you categorize checks. In Figure 20-1, the check is filed under Rent. These categories allow you to review your expenses, and they also link into various end-of-the-year tax preparation software.

- When you're done writing checks, you can print them out. Stuff the computer checks into your printer and print away.

- Don't forget to sign your checks! This is a common Quicken boo-boo. Just because the computer filled out the check doesn't mean you're done with it.

- With the checks in the computer, reconciling your account is — dare I say it — fun!

- As long as you put checks into the proper categories, you can get a grip on your spending.

- Quicken even has a home banking feature that pays regular checks for you automatically. It also contains an electronic check-printing feature where the checks are printed and mailed for you. This information is hidden amongst the flurry of papers that accompanies the software in the box.

Oh, and by the way, we also sell checks!

Quicken is an amazing program. Most of the time it comes free when you buy a home PC. And I remember it once selling for $19.99 or being available as a freebie on a TV offer.

The reason Quicken was free — or cheap when compared with other financial software — is that the money to be made is not in selling the software but in selling the *supplies* you need to run Quicken. Chiefly, you need computer-ready checks to print.

You can run Quicken using your checkbook if you like. Just write out the checks later by hand. But if you have *computer checks,* you can write and print checks right from Quicken. And isn't that what a computer is for, making life easy?

I'm not out to dish Quicken for selling checks. The truth is that the program isn't really complete unless you're printing checks. The cost of the checks does, however, come as a surprise to many folks.

- Computer checks don't come cheap. Expect to pay about $100 for a batch of them.

- You can also order computer checks from other companies, including your bank. Deluxe makes nice preprinted checks.

✔ Different types of checks are available for different printers. Don't get the fanfold checks unless you have an impact printer.

✔ I like using the one-check-per-sheet type of computer checks. Other checks come three to a sheet, in which case you're wasting two checks if you need to print only one.

✔ I recommend getting the computer checks *without* preprinted lines on them. The lines are fine when you're writing a check by hand, but they're distracting when the computer prints out a check.

Managing your portfolio

If you dabble in the stock market, you can use Quicken to keep track of your stocks. This feature isn't the easiest thing to set up, but once you do, Quicken keeps a historical record of your stock's performance. It can even remind you of when to sell or buy.

✔ Quicken's portfolio feature has an Internet access function that lets you check stock quotes online.

✔ You cannot (at present) use Quicken to buy or sell stocks. You need an account with a broker to do that.

Other stuff Quicken does

One of my favorite Quicken features is the planner. You can schedule out a loan, figure out how much refinancing your home would save you, or calculate how much a month you need to put away so your 6-month-old can attend Harvard. Fun toys!

Quicken also keeps track of your credit card expenses (see Figure 20-2), which I always find a challenge because I don't always have all my credit receipts.

Then you have the budgeting functions, which I've yet to figure out. I suppose if I were serious about keeping a budget it would help. . . .

Games and Entertainment

Financial software comes first. Serious stuff should take priority for the home because the PC is a big investment. Games? They're second. You just can't justify a PC purchase based on your need to destroy some creature that seriously desires to suck the brains from your head.

The ugly truth is, playing computer games is what PCs are really all about! The PC is a great game machine! Even I play games! Gadzooks!

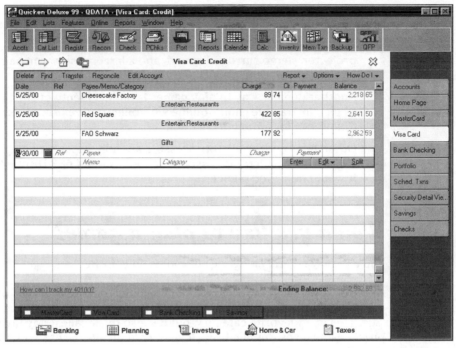

Figure 20-2:
Quicken also allows you to track your credit accounts.

To play a game on your PC in the best possible way, your computer should be equipped with the following:

- ✔ At least a Pentium. A Pentium II with MMX (or a Pentium III) is better!

- ✔ A large hard drive.

- ✔ A CD-ROM drive. Nearly every game comes on a CD.

- ✔ A powerful graphics card. 3-D graphics is better. More memory on the graphics card (upwards of 8MB) is even better.

- ✔ A sound card. Gotta hear the crunch of your enemy's skull under the tank treads.

Optionally you might also need a joystick, though you can play many games using some combination of the mouse and the keyboard. If you do get a joystick, ensure that it's fully compatible with the game. Many of the flight-simulator games are geared to work best with a specific brand of joystick. If you know that before you buy, you'll get the best possible configuration.

- ✔ Games are disk-hogs. Read the box before you buy to see how much disk space they need. Even if you have a 2GB hard drive, expect your extra storage to dwindle fast after you install two or three games.

✔ I recommend using drive D for games, if your PC has a drive D. Most people don't use drive D, which makes all its storage space up for grabs.

✔ The game lord's dream: a high-octane PC connected to a wall-sized video projector, stereo surround sound, and a large, cushy armchair to sink into. Disconnect the phone. See you in a week.

✔ Another popular way to play games is online. Plenty of sites allow you to play interactive games online with one or more other folks. See Chapter 26 for more information.

✔ Other, non-Pentium microprocessors are fully capable of playing games. As long as the microprocessor is flagged as MMX or 3-D-something, then it would be a good choice.

Would you like to play a game?

You can play several categories of games on your PC:

Arcade: These are the classic games, the shoot-'em-ups, puzzles, or maze games similar to the ones you used to drop quarters into back in the early '80s. This is my favorite category, but it's also the smallest. My favorite puzzle game: Lode Runner. I also love the old *arcade packs* that let me relive my wild, quarter-spending youth.

Simulation: The most popular type of game in this category is the flight simulator. Just like flying a big jet (flying in Figure 20-3), you take off, climb to cruising altitude, navigate, see the sights, and then plow into a shopping mall as you attempt to land. Other popular simulators involve golf (do 18 holes on your butt!), war and battle simulations, sporting games (which used to be in the arcade category), and the ever-popular SimCity-like simulations where you create and manage an artificial world, watching it grow.

Virtual reality: Once these were the *little man* games. You know: You'd navigate a little man across the screen, traversing various obstacles, picking things up, and, eventually, reaching some goal. With today's powerful PCs, now *you* are the little man. You see what he sees, you walk through his world, and you suffer from his enemies and graphically see them destroyed. Games like Doom, Duke Nukem, Descent, Quake, Half-Life (shown in Figure 20-4), Myst, and a host of Star Wars games are popular in this area. But be warned: These games can get violent!

Figure 20-3:
Microsoft
Flight
Simulator is
about to
take off into
the Hancock
building.

Figure 20-4:
A large
beast
attempts to
bake you in
Valve's
Half-Life.

Rating the games

Nothing can be as disappointing as buying what you think is a nice, engaging
computer game for your 9-year-old, only to find him frothing at the mouth as
he controls a character on the screen who's ripping the spine from its electronic opponent. To prevent such shock (to the parent, not to the electronic
opponent, who really doesn't feel a thing), two rating systems have evolved
to allow parents or any PC game buyer to know what to expect before buying
anything.

The Entertainment Software Review Board (ESRB) uses a five-level scale similar to movie ratings for its games (I'd show you the graphics here, but they're trademarked, and I'm too lazy to get permission):

- **EC:** Early Childhood means the game is designed for young children and would probably bore a teenager to tears.

- **K–A:** A G-rated game for kids to adult.

- **T:** A teen game, with some violence and language, but nothing too offensive.

- **M:** Mature audiences only, preferably 17 years old or older. This is the type of game the teenager actually *wants*.

- **AO:** Adults only, with strong sexual content or gross violence.

Competing with the ESRB is the Recreational Software Advisory Council (RSAC). Unlike ESRB, which reviews software submitted to it, the RSAC is a voluntary rating decided by the software developer. It has three categories: Violence, Nudity/Sex, and Language. For each category, a tiny thermometer rates the content at four levels, with level 4 being the most offensive. (I'm personally striving for a level 5 in any category.)

As an example, a game I purchased recently has an RSAC Advisory label proclaiming that the game has a Violence rating of 3 and a Language rating of 2. The explanations given on the software box are, for Violence, "Blood and gore" and for Language, "Profanity." (Now please don't draw any conclusions about what type of game I like to play based on my "research." Ahem.)

You can get more information from the following Web sites:

- **ESRB:** www.esrb.org/
- **RSAC:** www.rsac.org/

Getting that old DOS CD to boot

DOS was the game champion, and quite a few games still require DOS. When you attempt to run these games in Windows, you may get a message claiming that the game works best in MS-DOS-only mode. The PC attempts to restart itself and play the game. If it works, great! If it doesn't, you need to try something else.

The best way to run some very stubborn games is to boot the computer into DOS and ignore Windows altogether. To do this, you need an emergency boot disk. Refer to Chapter 30 for information on creating this disk.

Stick the emergency boot disk into drive A and then restart the PC. See Chapter 2 for restarting instructions, but keep the boot disk in drive A! You want to start the computer from that disk.

Two paragraphs about Direct-X

DOS was the game champion of all time. Most of the classic PC games were written for DOS, mostly because DOS was so feeble that the game's software could just push it out of the way and grab control over the entire PC for full-on game-playing power. Youza!

Windows is trying to one-up DOS by coming up with various standards to make game playing more Windows-friendly. One such trick you may read about is Direct-X. It's basically a way programmers can achieve DOS-like access to the computer without shoving Windows aside, which makes the game fit in line better with other software.

When the computer starts, you see a special text menu on the screen. Select the option that reads, "Start computer with CD-ROM support." Press the Enter key.

Don't be alarmed by any of the startup messages; it's an *emergency* boot disk you're using. Normally you would use this disk if something disastrous happened to your PC. Instead, you're being sneaky and using the disk to start in DOS mode with CD-ROM support.

After the hoopla stops, you see the DOS A-prompt:

```
A:\>
```

At this point, you can insert the DOS CD into your PC's CD-ROM drive and proceed to play the game. All your hard drives are there, as are all your files, but note that your CD-ROM drive may not have the same drive letter as it does when you're using Windows.

When you're done with the DOS game, quit. Then restart the PC by pressing its reset button or use the Ctrl+Alt+Delete key combination (which is okay in DOS).

✔ If you need further help, I can only implore you to pick up a copy of *DOS For Dummies,* the book that started it all, from IDG Books Worldwide, Inc.

✔ Keep in mind that you may not be able to play some old DOS games on a Pentium-class PC. One of my old favorites won't run because it was geared to run on a 4.77MHz IBM PC only. That may happen to you, too. Just toss up your arms and say, "Oh, well!"

Teach Me Something New Today

Computers have always had educational software. It may not have been as flashy or as animated and noisy as it is today, but it's a grand old tradition. And don't just think identifying shapes or learning ABCs is all that educational software can do; it can teach you anything from typing to reading music to connecting a 24,000-volt transformer to your cell phone.

Like games, educational software comes in different types. Mavis Beacon (oh, Mavis!) teaches typing through a series of drills cleverly disguised as games. Dr. Seuss's ABCs is a read-along computer book that educates as it entertains. My least favorite type, however, is the book-on-the-screen software. No one wants to sit there and read text on the computer screen. It's just not fun.

✔ The best way to find good educational software is to ask around. Discover what others are using. Ask what the schools and preschools recommend. Family magazines, both computer and noncomputer, offer reviews and recommendations as well.

✔ Try to avoid game software that masks as educational. A hefty chunk of software designed for young children is really silly games, puzzles, and painting software with some educational bits tossed in as an afterthought. Your kids may have fun, but they won't be learning as well as they would otherwise.

✔ If you ever find yourself justifying a computer game with the catchphrase *hand-eye coordination,* then be aware that something better is probably available. In fact, the best way for your kids to develop hand-eye coordination is to play catch or hit a ball with a bat.

✔ Another type of software in the educational category is reference software. The best example I can think of is Microsoft's Encarta encyclopedia. It's like a regular encyclopedia, but with animated references, sounds, and links to related topics. A great way to waste time and learn something all at the same time.

Chapter 21

Software Tips for the Office

● ●

In This Chapter

▶ Working with words

▶ Using a text editor

▶ Knowing your word processing

▶ Understanding desktop publishing

▶ Using your PC as a calculator

▶ Working a spreadsheet

▶ Organizing stuff in a database

▶ Getting a mailing list

▶ Doing everything at once with office software

● ●

Computers need software like the Frankenstein monster needs an electrical storm. It gives the big, hulking beast of a computer life! *Life!* And without it, the computer would just be a collection of, er, *parts*.

This chapter describes the variety and flavors of business software available. Well, it's not really *business* software as much as it's productivity software, the workhorse stuff for the PC. You can use these applications in the home or at the office, or when you take work home.

↙ Home versions of business software don't really exist. They tried to market such products years ago, but home users showed they want the powerful stuff just as much as the business people do.

↙ Mary Shelley wrote *Frankenstein* when she was 19 years old. It was her first book.

The Wordy Stuff

Just about everybody wants to use the computer to write something. Whether it's a thank-you note to Aunt Sally, a letter to the wacko liberal editor of your local paper, or a 500,000-word sweeping romance novel about two entomologists in Bolivia, computers make the writing process much easier.

- ✔ Word processing is writing.
- ✔ Three types of word processing software are available: text editors, word processors, and desktop publishing software.
- ✔ If this book were *USA Today,* a little box nearby would say that 70 percent of all computers are used for word processing.
- ✔ The best part about writing on a computer is that you can change what you've written without messing up the printed page. Editing *on the screen* means that each printed page will be perfect. Or as near perfect as you and the computer can make it.

Text editors

A text editor is a bare-bones word processor. It probably won't let you set the margins, and forget about formatting the text or using different fonts. So why bother with a text editor?

Text editors are so simple that they're fast and easy to use. Instead of writing a gargantuan novel on the history of the agrarian society in Europe, you would use a text editor to create or edit a plain text (or ASCII) file on disk. Sound dumb? Well, it turns out *lots* of plain text files are on the hard drive, quite a few of which you'll end up editing from time to time.

Figure 21-1 shows Windows text editor, Notepad, in action. In it appears a tiny list of things you may not put in a blender.

Figure 21-1:
Notepad is
Windows
cutesy li'l
text editor.

- ✔ A text editor is basically a no-frills word processor.
- ✔ Text editors save their documents as plain text or ASCII files. No fancy-schmancy stuff.

- ✔ Actually, any word processor can be a text editor. The secret is to save the file as a *plain text* or *text only* type of file. Refer to Chapter 6 for more information on saving files of a certain type.
- ✔ Why should Freon cost anything?

Word processors

The word processor is the natural evolution of the typewriter. No longer are words written directly on paper. Instead, they're *words electric,* which you can toss around and fiddle with on the screen to your heart's content. Editing, fixing stuff up, spell checking, formatting — computers were made for this stuff. It's no wonder IBM sold off its typewriter division.

- Word processors work with text just like text editors, but they add formatting, styles, proofing, and a whole grab bag full of features that no one ever takes the time to learn.

- The files that word processors save are commonly called *documents.*

- In the early part of this century, Vladimir Nabokov wrote by hand while standing up. In the latter part of this century, he probably would have used a word processor — but standing up anyway.

- Windows has a word processor called WordPad. It's like an early version of Microsoft Word. In fact, WordPad has features that people would have drooled over ten years ago. Today, it's considered ho-hum. (But it's free with Windows, and besides, people don't drool as much as they used to.)

Desktop publishing packages

Desktop publishing, or DTP if you're in a hurry, was once a type of application that mixed text and graphics to create documents. Today's word processors, like Microsoft Word or WordPerfect, can also do that. In fact, the everyday run-of-the-mill word processor today is far more powerful than the first desktop publishing programs were. So what's the deal?

The deal is that desktop publishing programs work with text and graphics far better than a mortal word processor. Although the word processor does allow you to paste in graphics or double-up text into columns, desktop publishing programs just do it *better.*

The word processor is for composing text. The graphics program is for creating graphics. The best way to merge the two is in a desktop publishing program.

- Desktop publishing software is expensive. Cheaper, *home* versions are available. But the stuff the pros use is some of the spendiest software in the biz.

- This book was created using PC software. The original text was composed in Microsoft Word. Graphics were captured from the screen by a program called HiJaak 95. Adobe Illustrator was used to create some of the graphics. Finally, everything was put together in a desktop publishing program called Quark XPress.

The Numbery Stuff

I hated computers in college and never took a computer course, which was sad because I have a natural understanding of the beasts. Still, I was afraid that computers were all about math, and I wasn't any good at math. So why bother?

Today you know that computers do more than numbers. They also work words, graphics, sounds, videos, and communications. Still, at the core of the PC is a great calculator. If you want to work some numbers, the computer is more than capable. Even more so, because contrary to my college-age fears, the *computer* does the math, not the operator.

It's a calculator!

If your computer is merely a large calculator, why do you have a calculator by your computer desk? Don't give me that "I don't know what you mean?" look. There! Right there is a calculator. It could be something you paid money for or something free with your title company's name on it. Whatever. *What is it doing there?*

Your computer is its own calculator. For small operations, you can use a program called Calculator that comes with Windows.

Start Calculator by choosing Programs⇨Accessories⇨Calculator from the Start menu. The Calculator window appears, as shown in Figure 21-2. Work it just like that freebie calculator: Click buttons to get a result. Duh. There it is!

Figure 21-2:
The
Calculator.

> ✔ The Calculator uses the standard computer characters for addition (+), subtraction (-), multiplication (*), and division (/).
>
> ✔ The result from the Calculator's window can be copied and pasted into any other Windows program. Choose Edit⇨Copy to copy the result.

✔ Choosing View➪Scientific from the menu displays the calculator's advanced techy mode, with more buttons to scare typical college freshmen.

✔ Quicken has calculators all over the place. Just about any time you enter a value in Quicken, you can use one of the calculator keys around the keypad (* / + -) to figure out some result. See Chapter 20 for more information on Quicken.

✔ You can purchase more technical calculator software if you really want to go all-out nerd on this.

Numbers from A1 to infinity (spreadsheets)

Calculators are fine for quick and dirty calculations, things your grandparents could have done in their heads but now scoff at you for having to use electronics. For larger operations, you need a real number-crunching tool. You need a *spreadsheet*.

A spreadsheet uses a large grid of box-like *cells* on the screen (see Figure 21-3). Into those cells, you can put text, numbers, or formulas.

The formula part is what makes the spreadsheet so powerful: You can add various cells, compare values, and perform any number of odd or quirky mathematical operations or *functions*. The whole spreadsheet is instantly updated, too; change one value and see how it affects everything else. Millions of dollars have been embezzled this way.

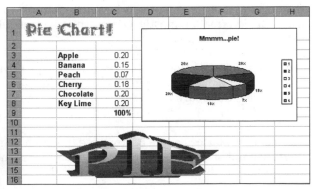

Figure 21-3:
A typical
spreadsheet.

✔ More than numbers, spreadsheets can really handle any information that fits into a grid. For example, when doing my vacation schedule, I often use a spreadsheet because its grid is easier to work with than the tabs in Microsoft Word.

✔ Spreadsheets are also quite adept at doing graphics. The pie chart in Figure 21-3 took maybe 20 seconds to create, after answering some simple yes-or-no questions. Amazing stuff. Good pie, too.

✔ Don't be shy about using color in a spreadsheet — especially if you have a color printer!

✔ The files saved by spreadsheets are called *worksheets*. A worksheet is created by a spreadsheet. Even so, many people refer to worksheets as spreadsheets. Ain't no crime in that.

✔ Most spreadsheets can convert the numbers into graphs and charts, making it easier to visualize how much money the CEO is *really* making.

✔ All worksheets you create are blank, ready for you to fill them in. Some worksheets are not blank. They're called *templates* and have been pre-designed and customized to do specific tasks.

✔ Number crunching = using a computer to work mathematical problems.

The Databasey Stuff

Because the word and number processing chores are snapped up by word processors and spreadsheets, database programs are required to mangle every other type of data out there.

Two important things about *data* first: It's pronounced *day-tuh*. It's not *dat-uh*. Think *day-tuh*. The second thing is that *data* is just Latin for our word *stuff*. A database contains stuff, information mostly. (Data can also mean information, but I like *stuff* better.)

Databases do two things: sort and report. They handle any type of information, whether it's words, numbers, or little-known bits of trivia (the *Lawrence Welk Show* was originally called the *Dodge Dancing Party,* or the scientific name for a gorilla is *Gorilla, gorilla, gorilla*).

✔ Like spreadsheets, databases can be customized to match specific needs. Rather than toil on your own, you can hire a programmer to create a database perfectly suited to your line of work.

✔ Oh, heck, just put the programmer on the payroll; those guys never finish their work.

✔ Databases and spreadsheets can sometimes replace each other's jobs. If the fields in a database contain mostly numbers, a spreadsheet may work better. If a spreadsheet contains more labels and text, a database may be in order.

✔ Of all the computer software, databases are about the slowest. Especially if you have particularly huge files, fetching information from the database takes a lot of time.

Database programs come in three unimportant types

Just as you can use different programs to write text, you can use different programs to store data. Three different types, in fact:

Free-form database: Perhaps the simplest database, it works best when you're organizing a big file heaped full of random information. When you type the word **eggs**, the database retrieves every paragraph mentioning eggs, whether it's a grocery reminder, a favorite recipe, or the evil Egghead from the old Batman TV series.

Flat-file database: A flat-file database helps retrieve information that's been organized into fields, records, and files. So you can type in a request or query, and the database then retrieves information about people named Thomas who drive Yugos and vote Democratic. It's more powerful than a free-form database, but it requires the information to be relatively organized to begin with.

Relational database: The most powerful database, which I don't know much about, but they tell me it's expensive.

Do you need a database?

No, you don't need a database. You could probably benefit from one, but fewer people use databases than use spreadsheets.

The mailing-list database

One type of database I can suggest to just about everyone is the *mailing-list database,* which is a primitive type of database containing names, addresses, phone numbers, and other information about people. The primary purpose of a mailing list database is to print out a list of people for special occasions.

The mailing-list database software category has no major player. The shelves at the local Software-O-Rama are filled with simple little programs designed to store, sort, and print names on a list.

✔ Managing a small mailing-list database is easier than struggling with the names in your word processor.

✔ You can buy special mailing labels for your printer. Some mailing-list database programs even come with a few sample sheets.

Those Office-Type Programs

To make even more money, the software developers have come up with so-called *office suite* types of programs. These suites are actually several software programs sold as a single unit. You can buy them cheaper that way, plus the software company makes oodles of money selling you upgrades from time to time (more on upgrading in Chapter 19).

Office packages are great when you're starting out. But you might not consider one if you're buying it for just one piece of pie. For example, if you're just buying Microsoft Office to run Excel or Word, consider buying them separately. I see no point in junking up your hard drive with stuff you'll never use.

✔ Most people buy Microsoft Office to run Word. That's it! They pay for the other programs but never use them.

✔ I might also mention that installing programs you don't plan on using is a waste of disk space.

✔ Most office programs allow you to select which of their applications you want to install when you set them up. You always have the option of adding the other applications later, so at first you should just select what you need.

✔ A good office program should offer: a word processor, spreadsheet, database, and graphics or presentation program, plus — and this is the most important — the ability to integrate each of those items. Everything should work together smoothly.

Chapter 22

Playing with Graphics

· ·

In This Chapter

▶ Using various graphics applications

▶ Knowing the difference between paint and draw

▶ Creating photographic and 3-D images

▶ Taking an image from the Web

▶ Scanning photographs and other images

▶ Editing a scanned image

▶ Cropping an image

▶ Using special effects

▶ Saving an image in another file format

▶ Graphics file formats

· ·

*E*ven if you can't draw a stick figure with a crayon, you can use your PC to make beautiful graphics. It's cinchy. The power of the Pentium combined with plentiful graphics software brings out the Picasso in any doodler. And you don't even need to start from scratch: Affordable scanners allow you to *import* images that you can play with to your heart's content. Now everyone can get into the act.

This is the graphics chapter. It's a quick-and-dirty introduction to the method and madness of PC graphics software. Plus, just because almost everyone has a scanner, I also divulge the secrets of scanning. And if you still want to doodle while you talk on the phone, that's possible too.

Graphics Software Overview

The computer is *the* thing for graphics and art. Hundreds of illustrious warriors, in fact, have already swapped their oils and acrylics for computers. Never mind that most of them use the Macintosh. The same software is available for your beloved PC.

Graphics programs come in varying degrees of sophistication, each with a different target audience in mind. There isn't a *best* or *better.* Most graphics professionals use more than one, depending on what type of result they want.

The following sections briefly describe various graphics programs.

Painting programs

Also known as *pixel painters,* painting programs are the electronic equivalent of a box of crayons. You can draw basic shapes, doodle, fill things in, and otherwise splash color on the screen.

Windows comes with a simple pixel painter called Paint (or MS Paint), as shown in Figure 22-1. It contains various simple drawing tools and lets you create anything from basic stick figures to complex color drawings. However, paint is best for the quick and dirty, or for doodling while you're on the phone.

Figure 22-1:
The
Windows
Paint
program.

Advanced painting programs have better features and tools than Paint. You can use them to create stunning pictures and illustrations, even some three-dimensional stuff. The bag of tricks is quite amazing.

- ✔ The Paint program creates and edits bitmapped files. If you ever hear someone say, "That's a bitmap file," then you know it's one that can be created or edited using Paint.

- ✔ Paint can also create and edit JPEG (JPG) files. These files take up less disk space, which make them ideal for the Internet.

- ✔ The wallpaper image you see on the desktop is most likely a bitmap image, one that was created with Paint.

> ✔ The advanced painting programs, such as Fractal Design Painter, offer much better painting tools than Paint, but cost a ton. These programs are best used by professionals.
>
> ✔ You can find more information on graphics file formats in the section "Saving the image in a specific format" at the end of this chapter.

Drawing programs

Drawing programs differ from paint programs in that they create objects. Unlike a painting program that just splashes down pixels, a drawing program creates things that can be moved, resized, or changed after they're created.

Figure 22-2 shows a drawing program that comes with Microsoft Office. It's available in Word, Excel, and other office programs to let you create images in your documents. You can resize or move the drawing program's objects, as well as change the colors and the order they appear on the screen (beneath or on top).

Beyond basic drawing programs come professional illustration programs like Adobe Illustrator and CorelDraw. These programs are primarily used by graphics artists to create illustrations — like the ones you see in *USA Today* or on wine bottles or posters advertising art shows. You know the type.

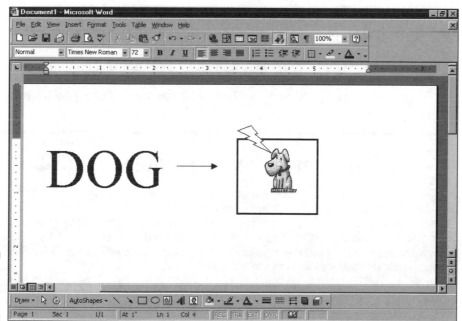

Figure 22-2:
A drawing
program.

- Drawing programs work best for illustrating things. Painting programs work best for pictures and images.

- Drawing programs work with lines. The lines can have different thicknesses or colors or be linked to form geometric shapes.

- Painting and drawing programs can be mixed. You can create an image in a painting program and paste it into a drawing.

Photo-editing programs

Coupled with most scanners is some type of photo-editing software. These programs are essentially painting programs, though they have tools customized to work with photo images. For example, one popular package is a tool that lets you remove red eyes or scratches from scanned photographs.

See the section, "Using Photo-Editing Software on a Scanned Image," later in this chapter, for more information on photo-editing programs.

3-D and animation programs

The latest editions to the PC graphics software roundup are 3-D and animation programs. Sometimes they're the same program, sometimes different programs; sometimes each is an add-on program for the other. However these programs come, they let you design and manipulate images in three dimensions.

3-D programs are actually a special type of drawing program. They let you create lines and shapes in three dimensions, being able to view the artwork from many perspectives. Figure 22-3 was created using such a program.

The best drawing program is a CAD

CAD is an acronym for computer assisted (or aided) drafting. This type of software handles extremely detailed or technical drawings. It lets engineers do such scientific things as design new three-tray microwaveable containers for frozen New Orleans–style chicken and broccoli.

CAD is a unique animal. The software is expensive, though cheap versions exist if you just want to experiment. The granddaddy here is AutoCAD — a monster of a program, but just about anyone who needs CAD software has it.

Figure 22-3:
A 3-D image
whipped out
in no time
using fancy
software.

Animation programs are often coupled with 3-D design programs. Basically you create the 3-D image and then use the program to move the image around. These programs can be used to create computer-animated movies. Some of them even rival the computer animation work done in the 1980s on supercomputers.

Getting the Image

You can get an image into your PC four ways: Scan the image, use a digital camera, create the image on your own, or steal the image from somewhere else.

To create the image on your own, you can use one of the many types of graphics packages available, as described in the previous sections. The following sections cover the other three methods.

Image theft

Stealing *some* images is not really theft. Certain images, such as popular clip art and other images, are considered public domain. You can copy and use the images all you want. Other images may be owned, but the owner lets you use the image as long as you give the owner credit. Of course, all of this is fuzzy; few people I know really ask before they steal an image.

The quickest way to get images is to purchase clip art. You can often find a CD full of thousands of images available for you to use, such as the one shown in Figure 22-4.

Images can also be stolen from the World Wide Web. By right-clicking on an image in Internet Explorer, you get the image's shortcut menu. Choosing the Save Picture As command (see Figure 22-5) brings up a Save As dialog box, from which you can save the image to your hard drive.

Figure 22-4:
The cliché
"monitor
head" clip-
art image.

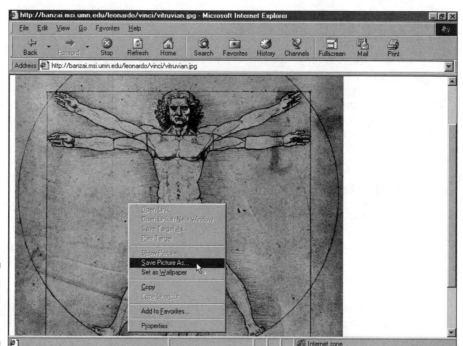

Figure 22-5:
Grabbing an
image from
the Web.

Not every image on the Web is free for the taking. The law on this is called *fair use*. Apparently you're able to take most images and do with them what you will personally, but you're not allowed to repackage or sell the image as your own. Or something along those lines.

Snapping a digital picture

Grabbing an image with a digital camera is yet another way to soak graphics into the PC. You remove the flash card or disk from the camera, chock full of pictures. Then you *read* the images from the card or disk into your PC. Special software should help you here; many cameras come with *gallery* type programs that let you review, print, or otherwise mess with the images.

Try to keep a place on your hard drive for the images you grab from the camera, such as a Photos folder inside the My Documents folder. Further, you may want to create subfolders in the Photos folder for trips, family stuff, and other categories of photos you take. The gallery software that comes with your camera may, in fact, do this automatically for you.

Scanning images

Scanning is fun, albeit time-consuming. Scanning any image on paper, a picture from a magazine or newspaper, a photograph, or even a slide, delivers it right to your computer screen.

To scan an image, you need to run a program in which you can edit the image. You don't just scan an image and then save it to a file. No, no, no, no, no. The image must be scanned and then *appear* in an application. Only then can you save it to a file.

The following steps are loosely based on most common scanning programs, though the software that comes with your scanner may be subtly different:

1. **Activate the scanner.**

   This may be an automatic step. Some scanners pop on when you raise their lids or use the scanning software. Other types must be switched on.

2. **Start your software.**

   Most scanners come with software, such as Adobe PhotoDeluxe or Photoshop or Microsoft Picture It! or PhotoDraw. These image-editing programs include scanning as a way to get the image that you want to edit.

3. **Place your image facedown in the scanner.**

   Most scanners scan from the back to the front, and they'll tell you which corner is the *upper right.* Try to place your image snugly against that corner — though this is not a hard and fast requirement.

   If you're scanning an image from a book or magazine, open it up and lay it on the glass just as you would in a photocopier.

4. **Choose the proper command to get a scanned image.**

   The command may be called Acquire, Place, or Scan. Most likely it sits in the File menu.

   If you choose the Acquire or Place command, you may have to choose an additional command from a submenu, such as Twain or the name of your scanner.

   The PhotoDeluxe software that came with my scanner has you click a Get Photo button and then click a scanner icon to start the scanning program.

   Some programs require you to select a scanner before you can scan. For example, the Imaging program that comes with Windows has a File⇨Select Scanner command that you use to select a scanner. After that, choose the File⇨Scan New command to actually scan the image.

5. **Preview the image.**

   Using the scanning program software, preview the image. In Figure 22-6, my UMAX USB scanner's program has a large Preview button on it. Clicking that button activates the scanner to show me the image I've placed there.

Figure 22-6:
Scanning
software.

In some scanner programs the Preview command may be called Prescan.

You preview the image so that you scan only the information you want. For example, if you're scanning Uncle Richard's boat but don't want Uncle Richard in the picture, you can tell the scanner not to scan him in.

6. Select the part of the image you really want.

In Figure 22-6, I would select only the parts of the photo that I wanted to scan, not the excess to the right, for example.

Use the scanner's selection tool to lasso only that part of the image you want scanned. Drag the lasso over the image, or use the mouse to drag the lasso's edge in or out.

You may need the magnifying glass tool to inspect the image in detail, ensuring that you're getting only what you want to scan.

7. Make adjustments for the type of image.

In Figure 22-6 (the *beginner* mode), four options are available: Color Photo, Printed Matter, Text/Line art, and Web Image. Some scanner programs may list options for scanning in black and white or color. Some may list resolutions. Whatever. Select the options that best describe the image you're scanning.

- You want to tell the scanner which type of image you're scanning so that it shows up properly. One setting isn't good for everything.

- Line art is an illustration, mostly black and white. If the image isn't crystal clear, then select another way to scan.

- Web image options scan color images but do so in a way that makes them look good when posted on the Internet.

- Most scanning software has advanced options that take out the weird patterns that appear when you scan images from a magazine or newspaper. Refer to your scanner documentation for which command that is (it's called *diffuser* in my program).

8. Scan the image.

Click the Scan button to do this.

In Figure 22-6, in the beginner mode, you click the button associated with the type of image you're scanning. For example, to scan the photograph of Jonah, I would click the Color Photo button (the one with the lady and the stupid hat on it).

The scanner may take a few moments to warm up or calibrate itself.

Scan . . . scan . . . scan. . . .

(I apologize for not having an appropriate scanner noise to insert here.)

9. Place the image into your application.

Some scanner programs have an OK button. If so, click it. That action puts the image into the application for editing, saving, or printing.

Your scanner may automatically place the image into the application. If so, you don't have to click anything!

Some scanner programs may stay open after placing the image. If so, close that window or switch to your photo-editing software by clicking its button on the taskbar.

10. **Fuss with the image.**

Now you're ready to edit, print, or save the image.

For more information on editing an image, see the next section.

✔ You may be able to scan several photographs at once: Scan the lot and then use the photo-editing software to crop out and save each individual photograph. This technique takes less time than scanning each image individually.

✔ Refer to Chapter 18 for more information on scanners as hardware.

✔ Special hardware is needed to scan slides. This hardware is either a special slide-scanning device or an attachment to a traditional scanner. You cannot, unfortunately, put your slides of that Bermuda trip into a flatbed scanner and have them appear as anything other than a black rectangle.

✔ TWAIN is an acronym associated with scanning graphics. It stands for Technology Without An Important Name. No, I'm not making that up.

Using Photo-Editing Software on a Scanned Image

Most scanners come with photo-editing software that lets you modify or edit the image you've scanned. Some, such as Adobe PhotoDeluxe, are quite easy to use.

Entire books have been written on photo-editing software, and I encourage you to check them out if it's something you're into. Otherwise, you probably only want to do a handful of things with the image, some of which I cover in the following sections.

Cropping the image

Cropping is the same as trimming — what you would do with a pair of scissors to a photograph. It allows you to clip the image to contain only the part you want.

Often the crop tool, similar to the one shown in the margin, is used to identify this command.

In PhotoDeluxe, the command is called Trim, which is shown in Figure 22-7. To crop the image, select the Trim tool and drag over the part of the image you want to keep. Complete the command by clicking in the image or pressing the Enter key.

Changing the image's dimensions

For some weird reason, scanned images are *huge*. A 4-x-6 photograph I once scanned was larger than my computer's 19-inch monitor. Go figure. (I suppose it has something to do with pixel depth or something scientific.)

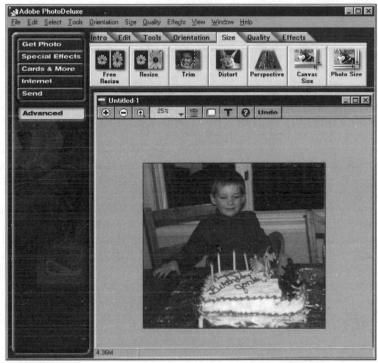

Figure 22-7:
The PhotoDeluxe image-editing program.

You *really* don't want to post an image that humongous to your Web page; loading it would take *hours*. Instead, you can make the image smaller by using various resize commands, such as those shown on the toolbar in Figure 22-7.

In PhotoDeluxe, the command to change an image's size is Photo Size (it's a button on the toolbar). In other programs, it may be called Image Size or just

Resize, or it may be a menu command. Whatever, you want to make sure you're changing the size of the entire image, not just part of it.

After clicking the Photo Size button on PhotoDeluxe's toolbar, a special dialog box appears, as shown in Figure 22-8. Note that the image is scanned at 4-x-3-something inches — but that's a whopping amount of pixels — 3.96MB according to the figure.

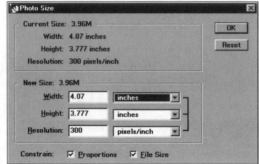

Figure 22-8:
The resizing
dialog box in
PhotoDeluxe.

To change the image size, enter a new value in the dialog box. The value can be in inches, centimeters, or pixels. I recommend selecting pixels, especially when saving the image for a Web page.

A good pixel size for an image is 300 pixels wide. If you enter that value, you may notice that the program automatically adjusts the height to a value that keeps the image in proportion. Click OK, and the image is resized.

If you're saving the image to be used as your Windows desktop wallpaper, make it the same size as the desktop: Right-click on the desktop and choose Properties from the shortcut menu. In the Settings tab of the Display Properties dialog box, note the size of the Screen area. Resize your image to those exact dimensions.

Special effects

Programs like PhotoDeluxe are loaded with special effects you can apply to your image. I won't go through the whole list here, but Figure 22-9 shows how one such effect works. What you see is the Find Edges tool in action. Other commands do other, amazing things. It's a great toy! Just don't forget the Undo button. . . .

Figure 22-9:
An interesting variation that took only one click to create.

Saving the image in a specific format

The final chore for your scanned image, edited or not, is to save it to disk.

If you choose just to use the Save command — watch out! Most photo-editing programs use their own formats for the images. For example, if you save an image in PhotoDeluxe format, not only will it be very large on the hard drive, but only people who have PhotoDeluxe will be able to view the image. No, it's best to select a file format best suited to what you're doing with the image.

✔ If you're going to be sending the image to a friend on the Internet via e-mail, or posting it to a Web page, it's best to save in the JPEG or GIF format.

✔ If you're going to place the image into another program, such as a desktop publishing program, word processor, or other application, save the file as a TIFF.

✔ If you're going to use the image as Windows wallpaper, save the image as a bitmap file, BMP.

To save in these formats, use the Save As or Export command.

If you use the Save As command, select the proper file type from the Type drop-down list.

The Export command, called *Send To* in PhotoDeluxe, usually displays a submenu full of file formats. Select the proper one from the list.

If you quit after exporting, the program may warn you that the image is not saved. That's okay! The program means the image is not saved in its own format. You're not required to do that if the image was saved in another format (and I wish the program would wake up and realize that, but I'm only a small voice in the wilderness).

Chapter 23

Even More Software!

· ·

In This Chapter

▶ Programming software

▶ Using utility programs

▶ Understanding shareware and freeware

· ·

*I*t used to be that you could have just one computer, and on that computer, you could have a sample of every type of software on the market. Not any more. Programs have grown so complex and occupy so much disk space — not to mention they get downright grumpy with each other from time to time — that having them all just isn't possible. You can try but probably won't succeed.

This last chapter in the software part of the book wraps up the discussion with the loose ends of software, which all happen to be programs that computer nerds really enjoy! Maybe you will, too, should you have the time or desire.

Software for Geeks

Of course, I use the term *geeks* fondly. And so do they, when you get to know them. There is a certain delight in being enamored with a computer. Those who love their PCs call themselves nerds or geeks. They're terms of pride.

One day, you may become a computer nerd. Maybe not. If you do, you may end up programming the computer. Or you may just enjoy ogling over utility software, which I also cover in the sections that follow.

✔ Remember, computer geeks *create* the hardware and software you use. You can be quick to blame them when things are hard to understand, but be just as quick to thank them when you find something easy or enjoyable.

✔ Just because software is branded for one type of person doesn't mean you shouldn't try it. For example, graphics software can be fun and the results amazing, even if you don't wear a beret.

Tell the stupid thing what to do with itself (programming)

Computers are excellent at obeying dimwitted instructions. Just ask any programmer! You can program a computer to sit and do nothing, and it will do so to the point you have to reset to regain control. It's not being stubborn; the computer is just obeying a programmer's instructions.

Anyone can do computer programming. I have 9-year-olds who read my *C For Dummies* books and send me the programs they've written. They aren't experts at math; they just know what they want the computer to do and use a programming language to carry it out.

Varying degrees of programming languages are available, from the easy to learn to the utterly baffling.

The simplest programming language to learn is BASIC. Microsoft distributes a product called Visual Basic that makes building programs as easy as cut and paste. The BASIC language is easy to learn as well; most of the words are English, so the instructions read like commands you'd give a dog, for example:

```
PRINT "I am stupid"
```

And the computer diligently displays I am stupid on the screen. (It doesn't send the text it to the printer, which would make sense. Work with me here.)

Digital peerage

When it comes to terms describing computer users, a certain pecking order exists. Here's a small sampling:

User. Someone who uses a computer.

Nerd. Someone who uses a computer and loves it.

Geek. A nerd who also programs or builds hardware.

Wizard. A geek other geeks refer to when they need help.

Guru. The person a wizard refers to for help.

Lord. A person who disseminates information used by Gurus. Lords are not spoken to directly, but merely consulted like the oracles of ancient Greece.

God. The person who thought of the concept originally, whom the Lords write about and the Geeks, Wizards, and Gurus praise.

Note that there is no such thing as a *computer genius.* Too many people are quick to label others computer geniuses simply because they know a trick or two. That's ridiculous. Most 4-year-olds would be computer geniuses if that were true.

The C and C++ languages are more difficult to learn, but more programmers use them. Figure 23-1 shows a screen shot of Borland C++ with some windows floating about full of sample C code.

C is a good place to start, and from there, it will be easier to learn C++, the programming language in which nearly all the Windows programs are written. The product to get here is Borland's Builder, which I feel is a better product than Microsoft Visual Studio (or whatever they're calling it nowadays).

- ✔ Before you set out to program, understanding what a variable is and how it's used helps. For that, a wee bit of algebra is good.

- ✔ When you program, the computer does the math. You merely tell it the problem, and the computer solves it.

- ✔ BASIC is an acronym for Beginner's All-Purpose Symbolic Instruction Code.

- ✔ Microsoft started its software existence selling a version of BASIC. For years, GW BASIC was available free with DOS. Many early PC users actually wrote their own programs. Weird, huh?

- ✔ You can use many languages to program your PC. The list is huge, but beyond BASIC and C are Pascal, Assembler, Java, Perl, Prolog, COBOL, and a host of others.

- ✔ Java and Perl are used primarily for Internet-based applications.

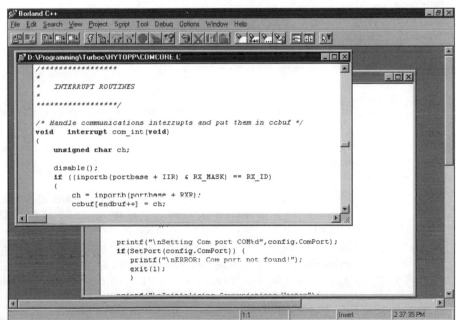

Figure 23-1:
The Borland C++ programming environment.

The utility stuff

Most software is designed to help you get to work. Utility programs help your *computer* get to work. Basically, a utility helps a computer accomplish a chore, whether it's organizing the hard drive or figuring out why it's not working right. In fact, most utilities are disk utilities.

Windows comes with many of the utilities you'll need. To see its portfolio of disk utilities, right-click on a disk drive in the My Computer window and choose Properties from the pop-up menu. Click the Tools tab, and you see three disk utilities you can (and should) run from time to time. Figure 23-2 shows the Tools tab in the disk drive Properties menu.

Figure 23-2:
Windows
disk utilities.

- ✔ On the Start menu, you can find Windows utilities in the Programs⇨ Accessories⇨System Tools submenu.

- ✔ Windows comes with a few handy utilities, but that doesn't mean you shouldn't buy any more. A lot of the third-party utilities are tons better than the stuff Windows has.

- ✔ One utility that Windows doesn't come with is a virus checker. These utilities scan your hard drive for any evil programs and wipe them out before the viruses try some nasty trick. Virus checkers are mondo important if you download lots of files from the Internet. See Chapter 24.

- ✔ Although Windows comes with a backup program (for making safety copies of the files on your hard drive), it's kind of lame. I recommend buying a separate backup program. If you buy a tape drive for your PC, then backup software comes with it. Good stuff.

✔ Even though Windows can, supposedly, uninstall software, you may consider buying an uninstall program. These programs do a much better job than Windows by itself, often saving you lots of disk space in the process. I recommend CleanSweep from Norton/Symantec as an excellent uninstall program.

Software for (Almost) Free

Frustrated by the system, some programmers give away their programs for free. Seriously! But there's a catch: They ask you to send them money on the honor system if you like their program. Because they're bypassing the traditional, expensive way to sell software, they don't ask for much; most charge from $5 to $45 for their software. When you mail in the check, the programmer mails back a code to *unlock* the program, plus maybe the latest version of the software and a manual.

Actually several types of this freebie software are available, each of which has its own cutsie acronym:

Public domain software. This is absolutely free stuff, written for the good of the people. No charge is ever made for the software, and you're free to do whatever you like with it.

Freeware. This software is also free for the taking, but the author retains ownership. You cannot modify the software or repackage it without permission.

Shareware. This is software you can try free. The software may have a special startup screen begging for money, or some feature may be disabled. After you pay for the software, you get the full program.

You can find most free or near-free software on the Internet, which I cover in Chapter 24. You may also be able to find the software at a computer store or swap meet or at a user's group.

✔ Always get your software from a reputable source. Avoid programs sent to you at random and given by "friends." These programs often contain viruses. See Chapter 30 for more information on viruses.

✔ If you use shareware, pay for it. I do.

✔ Software will state that it's public domain or freeware. If it doesn't say so, it ain't free.

Part V

The Non-Nerd's Guide to the Internet

The 5th Wave   By Rich Tennant

"QUICK KIDS! YOUR MOTHER'S FLAMING SOMEONE ON THE INTERNET!"

In this part . . .

The Internet has become such a big thing that its growth threatens to comsume us. Eventually phone wires will encircle the globe to a degree that vacationing space aliens will go out of their way to see the giant ball of cable in the galaxy. Maybe it won't be that bad, but when you sit in a movie theater and everyone there gets a joke about something-dot-com, you know the Internet is a big deal, and its jokes are more effective than all those "hard drive" puns I made in the '80s.

This part of the book covers the Internet. It's the Web! It's e-mail! It's pictures of your dog sent to everyone you know! Well, that and a whole lot more. These chapters give you the whirlwind tour. Ladies, please remove your hats.

Chapter 24

Doing the Internet Thing

● ●

● ●

*Y*our telephone, TV, and computer collide at a certain point in space and time. That point has been given the name *Internet*.

The Internet has grown from a way for computer scientists and researchers to share information to a way for you to interact with the world using your PC. Taking things one step at a time, this chapter tells you how to *get on* the Internet. Nothing can happen until you make that initial connection, which as you may suspect, just isn't as easy as picking up a phone and punching in a number or working a TV's remote control.

The 23¢ Description of the Internet

It's easy to describe the Internet by what it's not:

The Internet is not a piece of software.

The Internet is not a single computer.

No one person owns the Internet, though Bill Gates is trying as hard as he can.

The Internet is really thousands and thousands of computers all over the world. The computers send information. They receive information. And, most importantly, they store information. That's the Internet.

✔ The idea behind using the Internet is to get at that information.

✔ The best way to get at the information stored on the Internet is by using a piece of software called a Web browser. I cover browsers in Chapter 25.

✔ Information is also exchanged via e-mail, which is used by more people than the Web. (Believe it or not, e-mail is number one, and using the Web is a distant second.)

✔ Chapter 27 covers e-mail. Actually Chapter 28 does as well. E-mail is a big topic.

The Five Things You Need to Get on the Internet

To access the Internet from your very own computer, you need five things. Chances are that you already have four of the five.

You need a computer. Any computer will do. Because the Internet comes through your PC's modem, it doesn't matter how fast your PC is.

You need a modem. Speed counts here. Get the fastest modem you can afford. (See Chapter 16 for more modem mayhem.)

You need Internet software. Windows comes with nearly all the software you need.

You need money. Access to the Internet costs you, just like cable TV. Expect to pay anywhere from $5 to over $100 a month to get on the Internet, depending on which type of service you get. The average cost is about $20 a month.

You need an Internet service provider (ISP). This is the only item you probably don't have. The next section covers obtaining an ISP.

As an alternative to an ISP, you can use a national online service, such as America Online (AOL). These services have some advantages and disadvantages, which I rant about in the sidebar, "AOL pro and con."

✔ Though I hate using acronyms, ISP for Internet service provider is becoming popular enough that I feel I must. Not only is it easier to type, but many people today use ISP and don't even know that it stands for Internet service provider.

✔ Though the Internet isn't a program, you need special software to access the Internet and to send or retrieve information.

✔ Though Windows comes with nearly all the Internet software you need, alternatives are available. These alternatives are covered in the appropriate chapters that follow.

✔ For this book, I stick with the software that comes with Windows.

✔ If you work for a large company, it may already give you Internet access through the network at your office. Ditto for universities and some government installations.

The Internet service provider (ISP)

The best way to get on the Internet is through an ISP. ISPs give you a direct connection to the Internet, plus they may offer 24-hour help or classes to get you started.

The ISP should provide you with the following:

✔ A *getting started* booklet, class, software, or other information to ease you onto the Information Superhighway.

✔ A local phone number to dial.

✔ An e-mail account. Some ISPs offer more accounts in family or office plans. Everyone needs an e-mail account. Get the login names and passwords, too, if they're not provided in the booklet.

✔ Service (the *S* in ISP). The ISP should provide a number to call or classes, or have some form of *human* help available. This is key, especially for beginners.

I rave about ISPs that offer those getting started pamphlets. The pamphlet should contain everything you need to know about connecting to the Internet, all the secret numbers you need, plus the phone number and your passwords and other information. This is a must.

Beyond the basics, try to find an ISP that offers most of the following:

✔ **Unlimited access time.** Some ISPs charge by the hour. Avoid them. If they charge by the block of time, get a plan where you can have 100 or more hours a month. Only the very sturdy can be on the Internet for more than 100 hours in a month.

✔ **Access to newsgroups.** The more the merrier. Currently tens of thousands of newsgroups are available, about a third of which are in English. Avoid an ISP that censors newsgroups; you are your own best censor.

✔ *Web space* **or disk storage space.** This is a small amount of the provider's disk storage you can use for whatever. If the provider offers it, you can use the space to create your own Web page at some point in the future.

✔ Bonus goodies: These apply only if you're creating your own Web page: FTP access, Real Audio/Video abilities, CGI programming, Web page statistics, and a whole grab bag of other goodies that are way too complex to get into now but not bad things to find out about when you're starting.

✔ Don't get a shell account unless you enjoy using UNIX.

If your area has more than one ISP, shop around. Find the one that gives you the best deal. Oftentimes, the cheapest ISP lacks a lot of features that other ISPs offer (but it won't tell you that unless you know what you're missing). Also, paying quarterly or annually (if you can afford it) is cheaper. These places can wheel and deal with you — providing that you know a bit about what you want.

Don't be afraid to change ISPs if yours doesn't work out. I did this. My first ISP was snoozing and never told me about any of its new features. Heck, it didn't even offer newsgroups. Changing to a new ISP was no problem.

✔ Most communities have several ISPs offering access to the Internet. You can find them in the yellow pages under *Internet*. Some of them even advertise on TV, usually late at night along with the 1-900 psychic babe hotlines.

✔ Your Internet login ID and password will be different from the user ID and password you use to get into Windows. You need a different ID and password for each system you access.

✔ Your ISP may give you two IDs and passwords: One may be required when you first connect to the service, another for when you access your e-mail. Write them both down. (Put the paper away in a safe place.)

✔ I might add that ISPs with 24-hour service rank high on my list. If your e-mail dies at 11:00 p.m. and you need to get online, it's nice to have someone there who can help you.

✔ If the ISP does give you a disk, make sure that it's for your version of Windows. The older Windows 3.1 Internet stuff should not be used on newer Windows 95 and Windows 98 PCs.

Configuring Windows for the Internet

Setting up your PC to do the Internet is not all that hard, provided you have the following three things:

✔ A silver bowl

✔ A ceremonial knife, preferably bejeweled

✔ An unblemished goat

No. Wait. You needed those things in the *old days*, back before Windows came with an Internet Connection Wizard. Now all you need is some information from your Internet service provider:

- ✔ The phone number to call.

- ✔ Your ISP's domain name — the `blorf.com` or `yaddi.org` thing.

- ✔ Your Internet login ID and password.

- ✔ The number for your provider's DNS (Domain Name Server). This is a four-part number separated by periods, like this: `123.456.789.0`.

- ✔ The name of your ISP's e-mail server, which involves the acronyms POP3 or SMTP.

- ✔ Your Internet e-mail name, address, and password.

- ✔ The name of your ISP's news (NNTP) server.

Fortunately, your ISP should have provided you with *all* of this information when you signed up. It should be handy on a sheet of paper for you or located inside a booklet. All you need to do is tell the Internet Connection Wizard about the numbers. It does the rest.

To start the Internet Connection Wizard from the Start menu, choose Programs➪Internet Explorer➪Connection Wizard.

AOL pro and con

I'm not a big AOL fan. Believe me, I've tried. I used it back in the '80s on my Macintosh when it was called AppleLink. And I've had several accounts since then. For me, in the world of high-speed ISPs, AOL seems like a throwback. But how can 20 million users be wrong?

Pro. AOL is great if you're just starting out. The software is free, and it's easy to set up. Access is available all over, which means you can get your mail and go online when you travel. And AOL is widely supported by many companies, news organizations, and online retailers.

Con. Using AOL is slower than directly connecting to the Internet through an ISP. You're limited by the AOL software, through which Web pages are funneled, as opposed to viewing them directly with a true Web browser. Though AOL's phone lines may not be as busy as in days past, AOL is still subject to outages. And AOL's help system is impersonal.

I favor a local ISP because you often get hometown service and the fastest Internet access possible. All of your Internet software works, and you're not restricted to certain places or prevented access because the system is busy.

My advice. If you use AOL chiefly for e-mail, great! But if you use AOL for Internet access, consider moving to an ISP in the future. The price may be cheaper, and you may end up with better access to the Internet.

Or you can find the wizard here: Programs⇨Accessories⇨Internet Tools⇨ Connection Wizard.

Or in Windows 95, it could be here: Programs⇨Internet⇨Get on the Internet.

Or you may just want to run the disk provided by your ISP, which connects you automatically.

For AOL, just install the AOL software from the CD. You're done.

Run the Wizard and answer the questions using the information provided to you by your ISP. Start by selecting the option that tells Windows you already have an Internet account (the middle option, as shown in Figure 24-1). This option tells the Wizard you've already found your ISP and have all the information you need to set up an account.

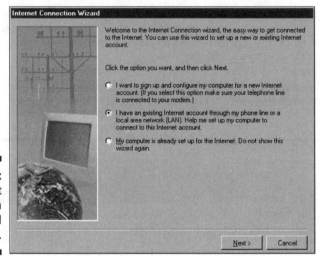

Figure 24-1:
The Internet
Connection
Wizard
window.

Keep working through the dialog box, filling in information until you finally click the Finish button.

Dial-Up
Networking

After everything is done, you have a new folder in the My Computer window: Dial-Up Networking. This folder contains the icon you can use to connect to the Internet. However, if you're running Windows 98 and using Microsoft's Internet Explorer, the connection is automatic.

  ✔ Read the screens! Never just click the Next button and assume everything is okay.

  ✔ Connecting to the Internet is covered in the next section.

✔ You need to run this wizard only once. Well, if you change ISPs, you need to do it again. And if you switch over to Netscape, you need to do it again.

✔ Don't toss out the booklet or sheet of information your ISP gave you! You may need those numbers later.

✔ 111,111,111 x 111,111,111 = 12,345,678,987,654,321.

Connecting to the Internet

To connect to the Internet, you do two things. First, you direct your PC to dial up the Internet service provider (ISP). When you connect with the ISP's computer, you computer is actually *on* the Internet. Then (second), you use Internet software on your computer, which enables you to access information on the Internet.

In Windows, you can combine both steps. By running any Internet software, Windows automatically dials up your ISP and makes the connection. Follow thcsc stcps:

1. **Start your Web browser.**

In Windows, the browser is Internet Explorer. Double-click the Internet Explorer icon on the desktop, or choose <u>P</u>rograms⇨Internet Explorer⇨ Internet Explorer from the Start menu.

The Web browser (Internet Explorer) is merely one Internet program. In Windows, you can run any Internet program to connect: Outlook Express, Telnet, an FTP program, a Web page editor, or anything that accesses the Internet (which is just about everything today).

2. **Fill in the connection dialog box (if it appears).**

After the Internet software starts (the Web browser in this case), you may see the Connect To dialog box, as shown in Figures 24-2 and 24-3.

Figure 24-2:
The older
Connect To
dialog box.

Figure 24-3:
The newer
Dial-up
Connection
dialog box.

Which dialog box appears depends on which version of Windows you have installed. Whatever type of dialog box it is, fill in the boxes as necessary: Enter your Internet username and password.

- Click in the Save Password box if you don't want to be troubled to type in the password each time you log on. However, for laptops and in open office environments, I recommend deselecting that item.

- Windows 98 lets you connect automatically without seeing a dialog box first. To select that option, click in the Connect Automatically box.

3. Click the Connect button to direct your modem to dial.

Again, this step may be optional; if you've configured Windows to connect automatically, you don't need to click anything. The modem just dials by itself:

Boop-beep-doop-dap-dee-dee-dee.

4. Wait while the modem connects.

A dialog box appears, as shown in Figure 24-4, monitoring your progress as you connect to the Internet.

Hopefully you're connected and logged into your ISP, ready to do the Internet. If not, Windows gives you four more tries to make the connection (refer to Figure 24-4). After that, you have to start over. (Refer to Chapter 16 if you're having trouble dialing.)

5. Work the Connection Established dialog box (if it appears).

After you're connected, you may see the Connection Established dialog box, shown in Figure 24-5. You're there! Welcome to the Internet. Read the dialog box. Click in the Do Not Show This Dialog Box in the Future check box if you want. Then click Close.

Figure 24-4:
The Dialing
Progress
dialog box.

 After closing the Connection Established dialog box — or even if it doesn't appear — you should notice a new teensy icon in the system tray (on the right end of the taskbar), looking like the graphic in the margin. That's your Connected To Whatever teensy icon indicator, telling you that you're online with the Internet and ready to run your Internet software.

Figure 24-5:
The
Connected
To
Whatever
dialog box.

Continue reading in the next section.

- To connect to AOL, start the AOL software. Choose your screen name and type in your password in the Welcome dialog box. Click the Sign On button to connect. See? Simple.

- Remember to turn on your external modem (if you have one) before you dial.

- Windows 95 and Windows 98 each handle connecting to the Internet differently. Also Internet Explorer Versions 4 and 5 are a bit different on Windows 98. Because of these variations, the connection dialog box may be different from what's shown in this book. Even so, the preceding steps will work to get you on the Internet.

- Use the Work Offline button to tell Windows *not* to connect to the Internet. That way you can use your Web browser to view documents on your computer or read your e-mail without connecting to the Net.

- ✔ If it bugs you later that Windows connects automatically to the Internet, you can always turn off that option. When the Dialing Progress dialog box appears (automatically), as shown in Figure 24-4, click the Cancel button. That action redisplays the connection dialog box, where you can deselect the Connect Automatically check box by clicking in it.

- ✔ Keep an eye out for the Connected To Whatever teensy icon indicator on the taskbar! It's your reminder that your PC is talking with the Internet.

- ✔ Internet connections are *stored* in the Dial-Up Networking folder, which you can find in the My Computer window. You can open the connection from that window to access the Internet, but starting some Internet program is easier than going through those extra steps.

Doing Something on the Internet (Using Internet Software)

After you've made the connection to your ISP, you're ready to run any or all of your Internet software. Fire up your Web browser, e-mail package, news-group reader, or any of a number of applications designed for fun and folly on the Internet.

- ✔ Internet programs are just like any other programs on your PC; the only difference is that you must be connected to the Internet before you can run them.

- ✔ As long as you have the Internet connection, you can run any program that accesses information on the Internet.

- ✔ Yes, you can run more than one Internet program at a time. I typically have three or four of them going at once. (Because the Internet is slow, I can read one window while waiting for something to appear in another window.)

- ✔ You can also stay on the Internet while using an application program like Word or Excel. Just don't forget you're online.

- ✔ Close your Internet programs when you're done with them.

Adios, Internet!

To wave bye-bye to the Internet, follow these steps:

1. **Quit all of your Internet programs.**

   This step isn't a must, but it's a starting point. If you want to keep your programs open (say, to read a long Web page), that's okay too; just don't close that window, and move on to the next step.

2. **Tell Windows to hang up the phone**.

Chances are Windows will want to hang up automatically when you quit your Internet programs. A dialog box appears, such as the one shown in Figure 24-6. Click the disconnect button, Disconnect Now (or it may be labeled only Disconnect). You're disconnected.

Figure 24-6:
A
disconnect
dialog box.

If a disconnect dialog box doesn't appear, such as when you want to keep a window or two open, then you must *manually* disconnect. To do this, double-click the Connected To Whatever teensy icon indicator in the system tray. A window appears, looking like Figure 24-7. Click the Disconnect button. You're done.

Figure 24-7:
Click the
Disconnect
button to bid
farewell to
the Internet.

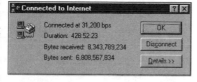

✔ For older versions of Windows, summon the Connected To Whatever dialog box. The window may be minimized, so click its button on the taskbar to bring it up and center. Click the Disconnect button. You're done.

✔ On AOL, you can choose Sign Off⇨Sign Off from the menu to disconnect but continue using the AOL program. Choosing File⇨Exit disconnects as well as quits the AOL program.

✔ Never forget to disconnect from the Internet.

✔ Do not disconnect by turning off the modem. In some rare cases, the ISP's computer may think you're still online and charge you for connect time. Only by properly disconnecting are you certain to avoid that fate.

✔ Big hint that you're no longer connected to the Internet: The little Connected To Whatever teensy icon indicator disappears from the system tray on the taskbar.

✔ You can keep track of how much time you've spent online by viewing the Connected To Whatever dialog box. This information is important when you eventually grow to spend several more hours on the Internet than you originally intended. Just double-click the Connected To Whatever teensy icon indicator in the system tray. View the time. Exclaim, "My goodness, that's a long time!" and then click the OK button.

The perils and praise of Auto Disconnect

Windows has a built-in feature to automatically disconnect you from the Internet should you tarry too long.

This feature is nice, for example, if you get up to go eat or play ball in the yard and forget to hang up; the computer hangs up automatically for you. It's not nice if you're online and suddenly see the *Hey! Are You There?* dialog box that threatens to knock you offline if you don't do something.

If you don't like the dialog box, click in the Don't Use Auto Disconnect check box. Click Stay Connected and never be bothered by it again.

To set the timeout limit, open the Control Panel's Internet or Internet Options icon. (The difference is whether or not you have Internet Explorer 4 or 5.)

Click the Connection (or Connections) tab in the Internet Properties dialog box. Click the Settings button. This action displays the Dial-Up Settings dialog box. (If not, click the Advanced button.)

The dialog box should contain a Disconnect if Idle For check box and time area. Select that check box if you want Windows to automatically hang up the modem for you. Optionally, set the time to something you think would be long enough. (I set mine for 35 minutes, which seems to be okay for me.)

If you do not select the Disconnect if Idle For option, then the computer stays online all the time. (You can still manually hang up, of course.) Click OK to close the various dialog boxes and, eventually, close the Control Panel's window.

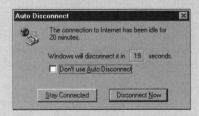

Chapter 25

Browsing the Web

● ●

In This Chapter

▶ Introducing your Web browser

▶ Going somewhere on the Web

▶ Typing in a Web page address

▶ Clicking a hyperlink

▶ Using the navigation buttons

▶ Refreshing reasons to refresh

▶ Visiting your home page

▶ Quitting the Web browser

● ●

*T*he Internet never really caught on until the World Wide Web was introduced in the early 1990s. Even then, the Internet was brimming with information, but the problem was accessing all that stuff. Most of the software used to access the Internet was based on UNIX, which can be an ugly and intimidating operating system. Then along came the World Wide Web (WWW) or *Web* for short.

Using special *browser* software, accessing information on the Internet through the Web became as easy as reading a magazine. The older, crazier ways of getting information from the Internet began to fade away, letting the Web dominate just about everything. Today, with its friendly text, graphics, and connections, the Web is quickly becoming *the* thing to do on a computer. It's like Internet software with nice hair.

Say Hello to Your Web Browser

Prepare to dip yourself into the cool waters of the Internet. . . .

The chief piece of software used to access information on the Internet is a Web browser, or *browser* for short. Fortunately for all of mankind, Microsoft has deemed that Windows is, in fact, a Web browser. That means you don't

The story of Netscape Navigator

Once upon a time, you could choose from several different browsers to surf the net. The most popular one was known as Netscape (the software was officially called *Netscape Navigator* or *Netscape Communicator*). Netscape was beloved of everyone and popular with all the creatures of the forest.

Then came the sound of angry unhappiness in the kingdom of Microsoft. King Bill was throwing a terrible tantrum! "What is this thing called the Web?" he cried out. "Why does Netscape have an 80-percent market share?!" The king was very sore, and there was much frowning and rocking back and forth.

So all the king's horses and all the king's men toiled and churned. Eventually they came out with an inferior product called Internet Explorer.

The friends of Netscape laughed at Explorer. It was weak and feeble. But soon came several new versions. And soon King Bill gave it away free. And soon after that, Explorer suddenly became the left hemisphere of Windows' brain. And there was fear of Explorer in the kingdom.

The people had to decide: Which was best?

Netscape was best, of course! But Windows 98 was a sneaky thing. And with Internet Explorer well hidden in that leafy tree, people soon came to realize that it was a Microsoft world. And, lo, Netscape lost her beauty. And her friends. And she was sold to AOL for a given amount of stock.

King Bill was pleased. Netscape *could* run on Windows 98, but not very well. Not as well as Explorer. And the king rejoiced. And as long as the surfers could surf, they were content.

---

really need to buy any more software to access information on the Internet. Aren't we all lucky?

- ✔ This chapter (and the next) assumes Internet Explorer (IE) is the Web browser of choice.

- ✔ You can also browse the Web in AOL, and I present information on that subject where appropriate.

- ✔ Windows either comes with a Web browser or *is* a Web browser. It's up to lawyers to decide whether Internet Explorer is a separate program or really the core of Windows.

- ✔ Lawyers are good at deciding things like what is a Web browser versus what is an operating system. In the early part of the 20th century, lawyers convinced the United States Supreme Court that the tomato is a legally a vegetable. (Scientifically it's a fruit.)

Starting Internet Explorer

Open the Internet Explorer icon on the desktop to start your Web browser. If you're not already connected to the Internet, you will be (refer to Chapter 24). And soon, Internet Explorer's main window fills with a *page* of information from the World Wide Web (see Figure 25-1).

The first page you see is called the *home page*. It's merely the first page you see when you start your Web browser. (It's not your own personal page on the Web, but you can change it to that page if you like; see the section "Take me home!" later in this chapter.)

Unless you've already messed with the Web, the home page you probably see is Microsoft's home page.

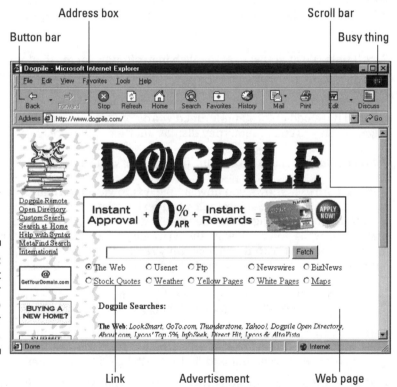

Figure 25-1: The Internet Explorer Web browser program.

You should notice a few things in the Web browser window:

Button bar. Below the menu bar, you find a series of buttons. You use these buttons to visit various places on the Web and do basic things with your Web browser.

Busy thing. The far right of the button bar has what I call the *busy thing.* The busy thing becomes animated when the Web browser is doing something, which usually means that it's waiting for information to be sent from the far parts of the Internet. That's your signal to sit, wait, and be patient; the Web is busy.

Address box. As in the days of DOS, you can type in various commands to make the browser visit certain places on the Web. These commands are officially known as *URLs,* though I call them Web page addresses. Either way, what you type is cryptic, but you can get used to it.

Web page. The contents of the Web browser (what it displays) is a page of information on the Web. In Figure 25-1, you see the home page for *Dogpile,* a place to find things on the Web. Arf.

Scroll bars. What you see on the Web may often be larger than your browser's window. So you don't miss out, scroll bars allow you to move the Web page's contents hither and thither.

Links. Those odd-colored underlined words or icons or graphics on the Web page. When you click them, they display another Web page.

Advertisements. Can't avoid 'em. They're everywhere.

The Web browser shows you how simple it is to view information on the Internet. What you see are graphics and text — almost like a magazine. In addition, some Web pages may have animation on them. Many Web pages also play music while you're viewing them (which can be annoying). Also, you do most of your input with the mouse. Only rarely do you have to type anything. I suppose that's why it's called *browsing* and not *hunting and pecking.*

✔ The busy thing will be busy a lot. It's often said that the World Wide Web should be WWWW, the fourth W being Wait.

✔ You pronounce only the letters in URL: *You Are El.* It's an acronym for Uniform Resource Locator. Essentially it's a command that you give the Web browser to go out and find something on the Internet.

✔ Most URLs you type start with `http://`. That cryptic doodad is actually an Internet command. The text that follows `http://` is the address of that information — its location on some computer somewhere in the world. Think of it as the *location* of a file on the Internet, much like the location of a file on your hard drive.

✔ Only rarely will you type in a Web page address. Normally, you can do most of your navigation on the Web by clicking various *links* located on a Web page or by choosing a Web page from your list of bookmarks or favorites. More on that in a sec.

✔ In AOL, type a Web page address into the navigation bar just below the row of buttons just below the menu bar. Click the Go button to open the Web page.

 ✔ Web pages can be wider and very often longer than what you see displayed in your browser's window. Don't forget to use the scroll bars! Better still, maximize the browser window to get the full-screen effect.

Visiting Somewhere Webbish

An estimated 100,000,000 pages of information are on the World Wide Web. Why not visit them all?

To visit a Web page, you have two choices. First, you can manually type in the address of some page somewhere on the planet — you know, all those `http://www-slash-dot-com-dot-slash-dash` things you see all over the place. Second, and more easily, you can click a link, which is a piece of text or graphic on one Web page that takes you to another Web page.

Manually typing in an address (the painful part)

To visit any Web page in the known universe, you can type in its address. Often this is necessary when visiting a new place. Bear with me, and follow these steps:

1. **Click the mouse in the address part of the Web browser window.**

   This action should select whatever text is already there. If not, select the text manually by dragging over it with the mouse.

   If you don't see the address part of the Web browser window, choose <u>V</u>iew⇨<u>T</u>oolbar⇨Address Bar from the menu. (For Netscape, choose <u>O</u>ptions⇨Show <u>L</u>ocation.)

2. **Press the Backspace or Delete key to erase whatever text is already there.**

   Thwoop!

3. **Type in a new address.**

How do I delete those pesky adult sites?

Q: Uh, I recently visited one of those adult sites and would like to remove it from the Web browser's history list. Any help?

A: Choose Tools⇨Internet Options in Internet Explorer 5. (In older versions of IE, the command is View⇨Internet Options.) In the General panel of the Internet Options dialog box, click the button that reads Clear History.

If the offending address still shows up, you need to find someone who knows the Windows Registry or can use the REGEDIT program. Have that person find the entry HKEY_USERS\Default\Software\Microsoft\Internet Explorer\TypedURLs. Once there, he or she can remove the offending address.

As an example, type in the following:

```
http://www.cnn.com
```

Type **http**, a colon, two forward slashes, **www**, a period, **cnn**, another period, **com**. You don't need to type a final period at the end of that address. Just type it in like it looks, weird stuff and all.

4. **Press Enter.**

   Immediately, the Web browser searches out CNN's Web page on the Internet.

The Web page loads, displaying text, graphics, and the latest news from around the world.

If the Web page doesn't load, you may see some type of error message. First thing you should do is try again! The Web can be busy, and oftentimes when it is, you get an error message.

If you get a *404* error, then you probably didn't type in the Web page address properly. Try again!

> ✔ The keyboard shortcut for getting to the address box is Ctrl+L. When you press that key combination, a dialog box appears into which you can type a Web page address.

> ✔ In the Now He Tells Us Dept.: The http:// part of a Web page address is optional. The browser automatically assumes you mean to type in http:// even when you forget. The www part is required on most Web sites. In fact, you should always type in the full Web page address as listed.

> ✔ On the other hand, if a Web page address starts with ftp:// or gopher://, then you're required to type in those commands.

Clicking a link (the simple part)

It's called a *Web* because nearly every page has a link to other pages. For example, a Web page about the end of the world may have links to Web pages about Nostradamus or that guy who walks around with a sandwich board that says, "Doom is near." Click the link to see more information.

Most links on Web pages are text. The text appears underlined and usually in a different color from other text on the screen.

 Links can also be graphical; some pictures are links. The only way to know for certain is to hover the mouse pointer over a link. If the pointer changes to a pointing hand, then you know that it's a link you can click to see something else.

> ✔ Links are designed to display related information.
>
> ✔ Quite a few Web pages are simply collections of links.
>
> ✔ Clicking a link takes you to another Web page, just like typing in a new address but without typing in a new address.
>
> ✔ Any good, informative Web page will have links relating to other topics. You find most links at the bottom of the Web page, though some Web pages have the links laced throughout the text.
>
> ✔ Link is short for *hyperlink* — yet another bit of trivia to occupy a few dozen neurons.

Going back, way back, forward, and stop

Following links can be fun. That's the way most people waste time on the Web. For example, I found a Web page recently that explained all the lyrics to Don McLean's *American Pie*. I don't know how I got there; I just ended up there after clicking a few dozen links. Unlike Hansel and Gretel, I neglected to leave bread crumbs along the Information Superhighway. Fortunately, the Web browser does that for you.

 To return to the Web page you were just ogling, use your Web browser's Back button. You can continue clicking the Back button to revisit each Web page you've gawked at, all the way back to the first page you saw 18 hours ago.

If you really need to dig deep, click the down arrow by the Back button. A list of the last several Web pages you've visited appears. (In Netscape, you can also use the Go menu to see the past few pages.)

 And if you need to return from going back, you use the Forward button. Back. Forward. It's like learning to drive, but no hills.

Finally, if you accidentally click a link and change your mind, click the Stop button. The Internet then stops sending you information. (You may need to click the Back button to return back to where you were.)

 ✔ These buttons are also found on AOL's navigation bar.

 ✔ The American Pie link:

```
http://urbanlegends.com/songs/american_pie_
              interpretations.html
```

Ah! How refreshing

Your browser's Refresh button serves a useful purpose in the world of ever-changing information. Refresh merely tells the Internet to resend you the information on a Web page. That's it!

The reasons for clicking the Refresh button:

Changing information. Many Web pages have updating information on them. Clicking the Refresh button always gets you the latest version of the Web page.

Missing pictures. Occasionally a graphic image may not appear. In that case, a *blank* icon shows up, telling you the image is missing. Oftentimes, clicking the Refresh button works some magic that causes the image to reappear.

Accidental click of the Stop button. Oops! Click Refresh to unstop and reload the Web page.

Take me home!

To visit your home page, click the Home button. This action takes you back to the first page you saw when you connected with the Internet.

The beauty of the home page is that you can change it. For example, I use Yahoo! as my home page. (Yahoo is a portal site, described in Chapter 26.) Here's how you, too, could Yahoo!:

1. **Choose the Internet Options command from the menu.**

   For Internet Explorer 5.0, the command is Tools⇨Internet Options. For earlier versions, it's View⇨Internet Options. (Really early versions used View⇨Options.)

2. **Click the General tab in the Internet Options dialog box.**

The General tab is the first tab, so it should appear first, as shown in Figure 25-2. The top area of the dialog box is where you set Internet Explorer's home page.

3. **Type the new home page into the Address box.**

For example, type **http://www.yahoo.com,** or whatever home page you like.

If you have a personal page on the Internet, you can make that your home page if you like.

4. **Click OK.**

The new home page is now set. And you can change it again at any time. After all, it's *your* home page!

Figure 25-2:
The Internet Options dialog box.

We All Have Our Favorites

Often you'll find some Web place you love and want to visit again. If so, drop a *bookmark* on that page. That way you can visit it any time by selecting the bookmark from a list.

To drop a bookmark, use the Ctrl+D command. D for drop.

This command places the bookmark on the Favorites menu. (You can also find a copy of this menu off the Start button's menu — for some strange reason.)

To revisit that Web page, merely pluck it from the Favorites menu. Cinchy.

> ✔ You can do a lot of organizing and such in the Favorites menu. The Favorites⇨Organize Favorites command does this. (Due to space limitations, I cannot explain fully how it works here.)
>
> ✔ If you have the time, organize your bookmarks into their own proper submenus.
>
> ✔ Feel free to delete any favorites that Microsoft pre-installed on the Favorites menu. Those bookmarks are from companies that paid money to have their products advertised there. Feel free to look them over. Feel freer to delete them.
>
> ✔ I really wish Microsoft would call *favorites* by their proper name: bookmarks. Every other Web browser uses bookmarks instead. That name is just so much more descriptive than *favorites*.
>
> ✔ To add a Web page (or any place in AOL) to your AOL favorites list, click the *heart* button located in the window's upper-right corner. In the dialog box, select the Add It to My Favorite Places item.

Quitting Your Web Browser

After you're done browsing the World Wide Web — meaning that it's 4:00 a.m. and you need to get up in 90 minutes to get ready for work — you should quit Internet Explorer. This is easy: Choose File⇨Close from the menu.

A dialog box may appear, asking if you want to close the connection (meaning *hang up*), as shown in Figure 25-3. Yes, disconnect. Go to bed. Get some sleep.

Figure 25-3:
The Auto
Disconnect
dialog box.

Chapter 26

It's a World Wide Web We Weave

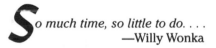*o much time, so little to do. . . .*
—Willy Wonka

The Web is crawling with information. That would be wonderful by itself, but the fact that you can find information in a matter of moments is really something. One minute you're just a regular potato head on the Internet, the next minute you're a well-informed potato head on the Internet.

Still, the Web is more than just raw information. It's also a place where you can shop, invest, buy airline tickets, play games, and enjoy a host of other activities, all of which I cover in this chapter.

Finding Stuff

The Web is like a library without a librarian. And it doesn't have a card catalog, either. And forget about finding something on the shelves: Web pages aren't organized in any fashion, nor is the information in them guaranteed to be complete or accurate. Because anyone can put anything up on the Web, well, anyone does.

You find something on the Web by using a _search engine._ That's a Web page that contains a huge catalog of other Web pages. You can search through the catalog for whatever you want. Results are displayed, and you can click those _links_ to eventually get to the Web page you want. It's all very nifty.

Using Yahoo! to find something

Whenever I search for stuff on the Internet, I start at Yahoo!. It's perhaps the oldest and most traditional of all the search engines (see Figure 26-1).

Visit Yahoo! at `http://www.yahoo.com`.

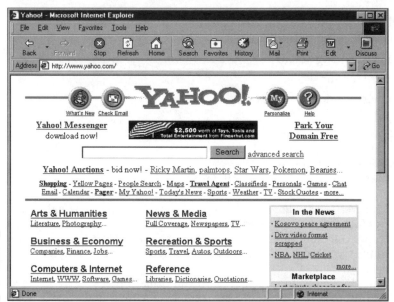

Figure 26-1:
Yahoo! I
found it.

With Yahoo! you have two choices: Type in something to search for in the Search text box or browse the categories by clicking those links with your mouse.

For example, to find all things Gilbert & Sullivan, type **Gilbert & Sullivan** into the Search box. Click the Search button.

In mere moments, Yahoo! displays a list of found items for you. The list may include Category Matches (which are like finding what you find in a library's card catalog) or individual Web pages. These results are all displayed on the next screen you see.

✔ Many other search engines use Yahoo!'s card-catalog approach to searching for information.

✔ If the search engine finds more than one page of information, you see a <u>Next 20 Matches</u> link (or something similar) at the bottom of the page. Click that link to see the next list of Web pages found.

✔ The more information you give in the Search text box, the more accurate the Web page results.

Finding lots of information

When you want to find nuts, Yahoo! works great. But if you want to find that one last cashew in the mixed-nuts tin, you might try another type of search engine.

The entire list of search engines is endless. Beyond Yahoo! are search engines that evaluate a Web page's contents and then show the results of a search based on those contents. I don't have space to list them all, but I can give you a hint of the more popular ones.

For example, the popular GoTo search engine, shown in Figure 26-2, is powerful, yet simple in its design. You can type in a phrase or question, and GoTo runs out to the Web and fetches the answer. For example, "How tall is the Empire State Building?" or "Which is the tallest building in New York City?" The search engine will display a list of Web pages containing information relative to those questions.

Visit GoTo at `http://www.goto.com`.

Here are some other search engines that provide alternative forms of information based on a Web page's content. This is by no means the complete list:

Jeeves, at `http://ask.com`, offers services similar to GoTo, in that you can ask it a question, and it goes out to fetch the answer. For example, "Where can I order that awful album William Shatner recorded in the '60s?"

WebCrawler, at `http://www.webcrawler.com`, is one of the early *search by content* search engines. It's usually my second choice when I want to find something that Yahoo! can't cough up.

Excite, at `http://www.excite.com`, has a special feature that lets you refine your search. As it finds matching Web pages, you can click the <u>More Like This</u> link to display similar Web pages.

HotBot, at `http://www.hotbot.com`, is a Web robot that actually scans individual Web pages for the information you need.

Mr. Tambourinemaaaaaaaaaaaaaan!!!!!

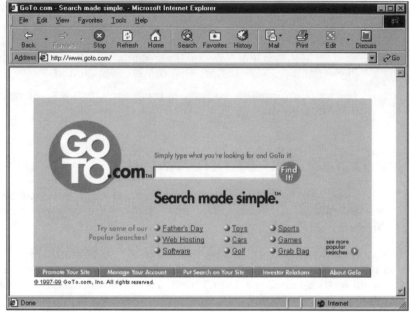

Figure 26-2:
GoTo is
simple yet
powerful.

All-in-one search engines

There are search engines, and then there are search engines for the search engines. No need explaining this further; if you need to find *anything* on the Internet, try these two places:

CNET's Search.com (which I pronounce *search-dot-com*), at `http://search.com`, is a catalog of Web catalogs. At this site, you can find any and every way to search the Web.

Finally, the ultimate search engine is Dogpile, at `http://www.dogpile.com`. It searches *everywhere* for *anything*.

Finding people or businesses

Locating people who use the Internet isn't as simple as finding, say, information on Shakespeare (who doesn't use the Internet). On the Internet, you can still try yellow and white pages for finding people or businesses. Table 26-1 lists a batch of them.

Table 26-1	Web Pages for Finding People or Businesses
Site	*Address*
411 Locate	www.411locate.com
Hoover's Online	www.hoovers.com
Northern Light Search	www.northernlight.com
Switchboard	www.switchboard.com
WhoWhere?	www.whowhere.lycos.com
Yahoo!'s People Search	people.yahoo.com
Yellowpages.com	www.yellowpages.com

✔ Of all the searches on the Internet, finding people is perhaps the least successful. You'll find that most people-searching Web pages require a TON of information about the person you're trying to find. Even then, they don't always find that person.

✔ Don't freak out when you find yourself (and your address and your phone number) listed. Most people-searching places let you unlist yourself quite easily.

Ports of Call (Portal Sites)

The Web is like a huge ice cream sundae. It's so vast. You find fudge dripping here. A cherry there. Whipped cream delicately clinging to the sweet icy mountain. Ahhh. . . . Where do I start?

The best place to start on the Web is a portal site. That's a Web page designed (and begging) to be your center of activity on the Internet, your *home plate,* so to speak.

Portal sites, such as Yahoo! (refer to Figure 26-1), contain lots of links, a search engine, news, online games, personal Web pages and e-mail, shopping, auctions, guides, files, and just about everything anyone would need on the Internet.

Table 26-2 lists some popular portal sites.

Table 26-2	Popular Portal Sites, But Not All of Them
Site	**Address**
AOL	www.aol.com
CNET	www.cnet.com
CNN	www.cnn.com
Excite	www.excite.com
Infoseek	infoseek.go.com
Lycos	www.lycos.com
Microsoft	www.msn.com
Netscape	www.netscenter.com
Yahoo!	www.yahoo.com
ZDNet	www.zdnet.com

This is by no means a complete list. You can find other portal sites for specific interests, hobbies, political convictions, types of people, and parasites.

- ✔ Yes, most portals are also search engines.

- ✔ A portal is a great thing to have as a home page.

- ✔ I recommend checking out a portal for anyone new to the Internet. It's a great place to get oriented.

- ✔ Portal sites don't have to be your home page. But consider this: With a portal site as your home page, you can always quickly return there by clicking the Home button.

- ✔ AOL has a Web page that anyone on the Internet can access, www.aol.com. If you're an AOL user, then AOL itself is your portal or your home page. Ain't no way to change that!

- ✔ Being popular is a tremendous value for a portal site. The more often people visit the portal, the more it can charge advertisers.

- ✔ Though the marketing and Wall Street types like to believe portals hold a key to the Internet's future, studies show that the typical Internet user doesn't put much value in one portal site over another. (I do, but apparently the Mass Herd of Users is more fickle than I am.)

How to Spend Even More Money Online

Shopping on the Web is currently *the thing* to do with a computer. You can buy computers, books, clothes, knickknacks, even real estate from the comfort of your orthopedically designed computer chair. All it takes is a few clicks of the mouse and a credit card number.

Online shopping Q&A

Belay your fears: Shopping online is fast, easy, and "safe." You're just a few clicks away from maxing out your Visa card. . . .

Q: What can I buy online?

A: Anything and everything: groceries, prescription drugs, books, computers, toys, stereo equipment — you name it. (I've yet to see new cars sold online.)

Q: Isn't it a little weird that they sell computers online?

A: Not really. When radio first became popular the commercials all advertised new radios.

Q: How do I shop?

A: You find a Web page that sells something. The most famous is Amazon.com (see Figure 26-3), which started as an online bookstore but now sells other goodies.

- ✔ Amazon.com's address is `http://www.amazon.com`.

- ✔ You can browse various categories in an online store just as you would in a real store.

- ✔ You can also use a search button just as you would in a Web page search engine. For example, to find a set of night-vision goggles, type **night vision goggles** into the Search box and see what comes up.

- ✔ After you find what you want, review the information (similar to what's shown in Figure 26-3). Check the price. Check the discount (if available). Confirm shipping arrangements.

- ✔ Many online retailers have lists of best-selling products. Check them out! Also refer to comments from other users on the products sold, if available. Don't forget the specials! I buy *Web-only* specials all the time. Save money!

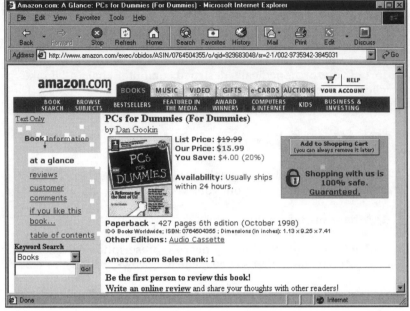

Figure 26-3:
Buying a
good
book at
Amazon.
com.

Q: How do I pick out something?

A: You pick out a product by adding it to your *virtual shopping cart.* You click a button, which places the item into a *bin* that you can check out later.

Q: How do I pay for it?

A: Just as you pay for items at a store, you open your shopping basket window (usually by clicking a shopping basket link) and review the items listed there. Follow the instructions on the screen for checking out, which usually involve filling in personal and shipping information, as well as a credit card number.

Q: Is my credit card information safe?

A: Very safe. Most shopping sites and Web browsers use special encryption technology to ensure no one snags your credit card on the way to the store. (This process is much safer than, for example, handing your credit card to a waiter in a restaurant.)

Always pay by credit card. That way if you don't get what you want, or get nothing, then you can easily cancel the debt. A credit card is a good form of protection in case the online retailer turns out to be a phony.

Q: What about *cookies?*

A: I don't know if you can buy them online or not.

Q: No, I mean the cookies that some Web pages create on my PC?

A: *Cookies* are files that a Web page saves on your computer. They're safe. They contain information that can be read only by that same Web page. Oftentimes when you go online shopping, the cookies keep information about you: your shoe size, your shipping address, and other information. That just makes it easier to return to that Web page and do more shopping later.

Q: How can I find online stores?

A: Use any search engine. Look for online retailers.

Q: Do you buy stuff online?

A: Absolutely. Lots of stuff. Books and computers, mostly. I once bought a new PC entirely by using the Internet. When I had a problem with the monitor, I e-mailed the company my complaint, and it e-mailed me back a return notice. I got a new monitor and now use the new computer and have never spoken with a human from the company.

Q: What about returning things?

A: This is very important: Check the store's return policy. Some places are very good and quick to accept returns. If possible, try to find a place that has a no-questions-asked return policy. But watch out! Some places are cryptic and hide return information. Always check!

Some other advice tidbits I could not fit into the Q&A format:

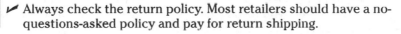

- ✔ Check for a real phone number or an address for the online retailers you work with. No major online scams of note have occurred, and most companies online are legitimate. Those that aren't probably won't have a phone number or address listed.

- ✔ Some online retailers offer payment alternatives if you fear paying online. You may be able to phone-in an order or direct the company to phone you for confirmation. Some places may let you print out and fax an order.

- ✔ Always check the return policy. Most retailers should have a no-questions-asked policy and pay for return shipping.

✔ Beware of buying some types of computer hardware online. Occasionally, the original manufacturer rather than the online retailer provides service for some hardware. If the hardware breaks, you may have to run around a bit before you can find someone to help you.

Auctions without the auctioneer

Two types of auctioneers exist. First there's the rapid-fire auctioneer who spews out numbers like a machine gun, *budda-budda-budda-budda*. Then there's the Sotheby's or Christy's type of auctioneer, very polite: "I'm bidding $35-point-2 million for the Van Gogh. Do I hear 35-point-3? Mr. Gates?"

Online auctions don't have auctioneers, per se. In most cases, the auctioneer is the Web page itself. It works like a combination search engine and online retailer.

The search engine lets you look up whatever trifle you're trying to buy, say that 1977 vintage Darth Vader still in the box. The seller offers a price and you bid on it, sending off how much you want to pay to the Web page. Hundreds of people bid on it every hour, so the price goes up and up. Eventually you get your trifle, and the seller gets money.

One of the most popular online auction sites is eBay. It lets you buy or sell just about anything (see Figure 26-4). After registering, you can enter the fray, searching for some tchotchke you want to buy or posting information about one you want to sell.

You can visit eBay at `http://www.ebay.com`.

In addition to eBay, Amazon.com and Yahoo! also offer online auctions. Visit `http://auctions.yahoo.com` or `http://auctions.amazon.com`.

✔ The online auction site makes its money off commissions collected from the seller.

✔ After a given time, if you hold the winning bid, you and the seller decide on payment and shipping terms (or they may be dictated in advance).

✔ To avoid being ripped off, many of the better online auction sites offer information about the seller, including comments from other buyers.

✔ You can also use an online escrow service if you want to hold your payment until you receive the merchandise. One such service is I-Escrow at `http://www.iescrow.com`.

Figure 26-4:
eBay is the
world's most
popular
online
auction.

Saving and Investing

Not everything you do online involves spending money. One of the early dreams of the PC (and an argument to buy a modem before the Internet) was that you could do all your banking from the convenience of your home. Many banks have online services or started them up in anticipation of the flood.

The problem? Online banking was expensive. Extra charges were involved, and getting connected was a hassle. For example, my bank charged $25 for the online banking services, and then if you wanted to do anything other than check your balance, you had to phone into the bank for verbal confirmation. That didn't seem very online to me.

Today's online banking is easier, thanks to the Web. Inquire with your bank or financial institution about online banking. Find out what's involved and what the fees are. Also find out if the bank can work with financial software such as Quicken or Microsoft Money. If you can pay your bills by having Quicken phone-in the list of checks to print, then it really makes it all worthwhile.

Checking Those Stocks

In addition to online banking, you can also wheel and deal with the stock market online. Basically you find an online trading service (or maybe your current broker offers a service) and sign up. Then you buy and sell stocks until you're broke! Or until you retire to that island you bought in the Caribbean.

If you're not into wheeling and dealing, you can still use the Web to check your stock prices. Yahoo! and many other portal sites offer methods for checking stock quotes throughout the day. Figure 26-5 shows Yahoo! Finance (`http://finance.yahoo.com`), where you can check the market, read financial news, or look up stock quotes.

By the way, I do not own any stock in Yahoo!, even though I tend to recommend it a lot. (Just being fair.)

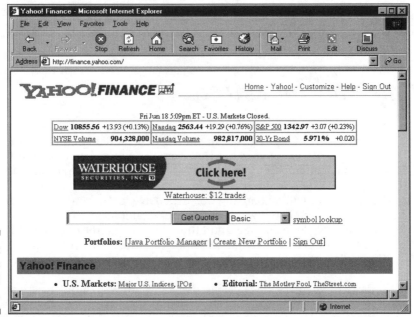

Figure 26-5: Yahoo!'s financial page.

Planning a Trip?

You can go online to buy a notebook computer. You can make a million dollars trading stocks. Why not use that money to go on a vacation? Sure, from the same chair you shopped and played the market in, you can also plan a vacation. The Web makes an excellent travel agent.

Working an online travel agent is just like shopping: Find out where you want to go and then browse the details.

Some online travel agents, like Yahoo! Travel (http://travel.yahoo.com), let you set up everything. You can plan a trip or buy a package tour. Fill in a form and check out flight availability and rates.

Another good site to try is Microsoft's Expedia (http://www.expedia.com), shown in Figure 26-6.

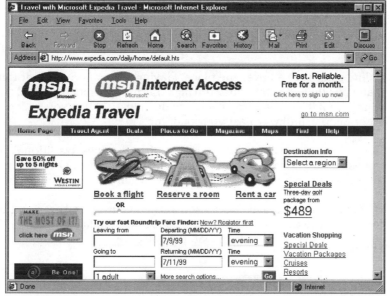

Figure 26-6:
Start your vacation at Expedia.com.

> ✔ After setting up, organizing, and paying for your trip, your tickets are mailed to you.
>
> ✔ You may also be issued an *e-ticket,* which is a method of travel where you don't have any tickets but are issued a boarding pass at the gate.

Playing a Game Online

Online games are of two types. First is the game that actually runs on a Web page. You sign up, you're given a little man or dealt a hand of gin, then you play with other people all over the world.

The second type of game is software on your PC that uses the Internet to connect with other people playing. Games such as Doom and Quake have these online death matches, where they basically use the Internet to connect, but use software on their own machines to play.

The following sections detail these two types of online games.

Online games to play

Playing games online is nothing new. I knew a guy who signed up for CompuServe back in the early 1980s. He spent hundreds of dollars a month playing some type of space war game with other people online. Amazing. And addicting!

Online games are all over the place. Playing them often costs nothing more than your time. You find one. You sign up. You download special software to your PC. (If it asks, you say it's *OK* to download.) Then you play games with other people until way past your bedtime.

Yahoo! has a game area that offers lots of card games, traditional board games, fantasy games, or games of chance (visit `http://games.yahoo.com`). After signing up, you click a link to select a game.

Yahoo! has to download special software to your PC so that you can play the game. You'll see a Security Warning dialog box, similar to the one shown in Figure 26-7. Click Yes to download the software.

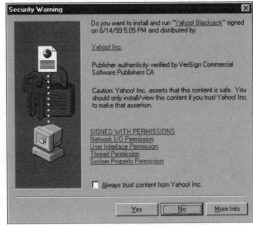

Figure 26-7:
You must have this program to play blackjack on Yahoo!.

After the software is installed, you join a table and play away. In Figure 26-8, the author is playing blackjack (21) with several other people who are online (and I don't know who they really are, but they seem to be losing quite a bit, don't they?).

- ✔ Games can be addictive.

- ✔ When you play a gambling game (poker, blackjack) on Yahoo!, you play with what I call *Yahoo! dollars*. You start out with $1,000 and then gamble that away quickly. Yahoo! keeps track of how much money you have. Seeing how far in the hole some people get is amusing!

- ✔ Yahoo! dollars aren't worth anything! You cannot redeem them for prizes, and Yahoo! won't break your kneecaps when you cross the $100,000 barrier. (The most in debt I've ever seen anyone online is $150,000; the most Yahoo! dollars I've seen someone have is $56,000.)

- ✔ Yahoo! also lets you chat with other players (refer to the bottom of the screen in Figure 26-8). Chatting can be almost as fun as playing the games! See Chapter 29 for more information on chatting online.

- ✔ Other Web sites besides Yahoo! offer online games. Use a search engine to find them all!

- ✔ Try `http://www.won.net`, the World Opponent Network, for some fun online games.

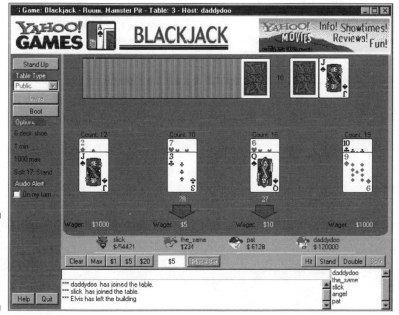

Figure 26-8:
Hit me!
(Playing
online
blackjack.)

Taking your PC's game online

You can duke it out with the computer, or you can take your game online and play others via the Internet. Most popular games (Quake, Duke Nukem) let you do this. In fact, some people only play the games online and rarely work the mazes or shoot the bad guys in single-player mode.

Each game accesses the Internet differently. Basically, you find a game server (a specific place on the Internet) to log into. Then you run the game software, and the server connects you with other players elsewhere on the Internet.

You can also play the game over a local area network (LAN), which means that you can use the office network after hours to play with your coworkers. Or you can play during office hours, if you dare to risk it.

After making the connection, game play proceeds in several modes. Team play is a mode where you pair up with others to battle computer or human enemies. Another mode is the popular death match mode where it's a free-for-all and the last person standing wins.

✔ Alas, I can't get any more specific here, because each game plays differently.

✔ Start playing online by connecting to the Internet *first*. Then run your game and select whichever option hunts down a game server.

✔ You may want to turn off the Auto Disconnect feature (see Chapter 25), just in case the computer is dumb and logs you off in the middle of a game.

Chapter 27

Mail Call!

· ·

In This Chapter

▶ Starting Outlook Express

▶ Sending e-mail

▶ Understanding Cc and Bcc

▶ Reading e-mail

▶ Replying to a message

▶ Forwarding e-mail

▶ Managing your e-mail folders

▶ Using the Address Book

· ·

*N*othing perks up your Internet day like getting fresh e-mail. If you have AOL, then you get the mellifluous, "You've got mail!" greeting you at the start of a productive day. *Ahhhh, people care enough about me to write! I'm loved!*

This chapter is about e-mail. I secretly believe, though I have no data to back this up, that more people use the Internet for e-mail than for surfing the Web. And if they're not sending messages, then they're waiting despondently for new mail to arrive. It can be an obsession.

- ✔ This chapter centers around using Outlook Express (Version 5), the Windows e-mail package.

- ✔ Outlook Express is *not* the same program as Outlook, which is another e-mail program made by Microsoft and distributed with Microsoft Office.

- ✔ Also see Chapter 28, which covers e-mail file attachments. Chapter 29 covers setting up Web e-mail accounts.

- ✔ Oh, and this chapter mentions AOL, though the subject here is really Outlook Express.

Starting Your E-Mail Program

Outlook Express

Start Outlook Express by opening the Outlook Express icon on the desktop (shown in the margin). You may also find the icon on the Quick Launch bar.

If you aren't already connected to the Internet, starting Outlook Express connects you. If not, refer back to Chapter 24 for information on connecting to the Internet.

You cannot send or recieve e-mail unless you're connected to the Internet.

The first thing Outlook does is check for new mail. Refer to the section "Reading Your E-Mail," later in this chapter, if you *really* can't wait to get started. Outlook also sends any mail you have waiting.

Figure 27-1 details the Outlook Express screen. It consists of three parts:

Folders list. On the upper left of the window is the list of folders where sent, received, trashed, and filed mail goes.

Contact list. On the bottom left is a list of *contacts,* people with whom you may normally communicate. Refer to "The Valued Address Book," later in this chapter, for more information.

Message summary. On the right is a "home page" of sorts for messages, newsgroups, and stuff. You may or may not see this screen. Instead, you may configure Outlook to display your Inbox whenever you switch it on.

Click in the When Outlook Express Starts, Go Directly to My Inbox check box. Doing so selects the option and changes the display to show your Inbox, shown in Figure 27-2.

The right side of the screen displays the Inbox. The top part shows the queue of e-mail. Bold text indicates unread mail; normal lines indicate read mail (and the open/closed envelope icon confirms this information).

The bottom-right part of the window shows a preview of the message's contents, such as the advertisement in Figure 27-2.

Between the left and right side of the window is a separator bar. You can drag that bar with the mouse, making either side larger. My advice is to drag the separator bar to the left, making the Inbox and preview windows larger.

That's it for your introduction! If you have mail waiting, jump forward to the section "Reading Your E-Mail." Otherwise, continue with the next section on composing a new message.

Folders list   Unread messages

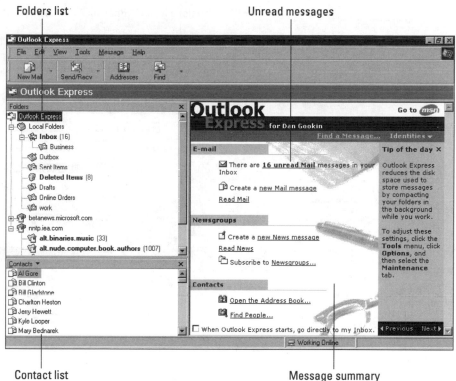

Figure 27-1:
Outlook
Express in
action.

Contact list   Message summary

To quit Outlook Express when you're done, close the program's window. Or choose File➪Exit from the menu.

- ✔ Most e-mail programs look similar to Outlook Express. Often an Inbox displays pending messages in bold type and read messages in normal type. A list of folders is off to the side.

- ✔ AOL has its own e-mail program, and it checks for new mail whenever it starts.

- ✔ You probably won't have any mail waiting for you right away. Oh, you may have a welcome message from Microsoft. Like it cares. . . .

- ✔ Outlook Express is actually a program file named MSIMN on your computer. If you cannot locate the Outlook Express icon, use the Find command (Chapter 7) to locate the file named MSIMN.EXE. If the file isn't there, then you have to use some other e-mail program.

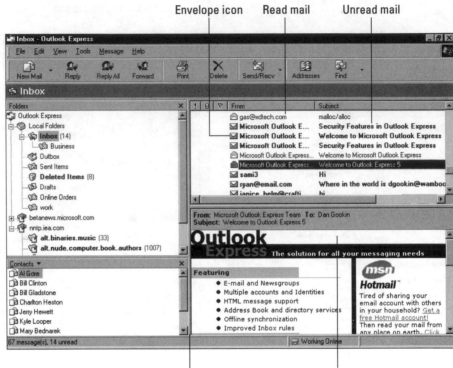

Figure 27-2:
The Outlook
Express
Inbox view.

Sending E-Mail

In order to get e-mail, you must first send it.

Naturally you're popular. People love you. And you give out your e-mail address to everyone you've ever met. Even so, to get a lot of e-mail you have to send a lot of e-mail. Occasionally some people will send you spontaneous stuff, but keep in mind that communication is a two-way street.

✔ To compose an e-mail epistle, you need to know the e-mail address of some other person on the Internet. Your friends and coworkers can give you this information, and it's extremely trendy to put your e-mail address on your business card and resume.

✔ Refer to the section "The Valued Address Book," later in this chapter, for information on keeping e-mail addresses in a special place.

Creating a new e-mail message

To create a new message in Outlook Express, click the New Mail button. The New Message window appears, as shown in Figure 27-3. Your job is to fill in the blanks.

To. Who are you sending the message to? Type the person's e-mail address into the To field.

- E-mail addresses do not contain spaces!
- You must enter the full e-mail address: blah@wambooli.com. Note the single exception: If you have e-mail nicknames set up, you can type the nickname into the To field instead of the full e-mail address.

Type subject here

Type e-mail address here

Send button

Click this to check your spelling

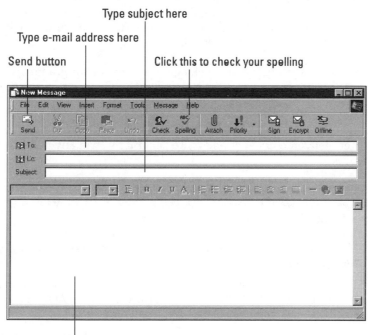

Figure 27-3:
The New Message window.

Message contents go here

- You can type in more than one address in the To field. If so, separate each with a semicolon, as in:

  president@whitehouse.gov;first.lady@whitehouse.gov

- You can also use the Address Book for sending e-mail. See the section "The Valued Address Book," later in this chapter.

✔ If you type in the wrong e-mail address, the message *bounces* back to you. This is not a bad thing; just try again with the proper address.

Cc. The carbon copy field. This field contains e-mail addresses of people you want to carbon copy the message to. See the section "All about Cc and Bcc," later in this chapter.

Subject. Type in the message's subject. What is the message about? It helps if the subject is somehow related to the message (because the recipients see the subject in their Inboxes, just like you do).

The message itself. The last thing to fill in is the contents.

```
No, I don't think the Dutch suspect a thing. . . .
```

When you're done, check your spelling by clicking the Spelling button. Your message is scanned, and potential misspelled words are flagged. Select the properly spelled word from the dialog box — the same drill you go through with your word processor's spell check.

Review your message! Spell checking doesn't check for grammatical errors or potentially offensive outrageous statements. Remember, you can't recall e-mail after it's sent!

Finally, you send the message. Click the Send button, and it's off on the Internet, delivered cheaper and more accurately than any post office on earth.

If you don't want to send the message, close the New Message window. You'll be asked if you want to save the message. Click Yes to save it in the Drafts folder. If you click No, the message is destroyed.

✔ You can start a new message by pressing Ctrl+N or choosing File⇨New⇨ Mail Message from the menu.

✔ In AOL, create a new message by clicking the Write button on the toolbar, or press Ctrl+M. Click the Send Now button in AOL to send your message, well, *right now!*

✔ An e-mail message is sent instantly. I sent a message to a reader in Australia one evening and got a reply back from him in less than 10 minutes.

✔ Please don't type in ALL CAPS. To most people, all caps reads LIKE YOU'RE SHOUTING AT THEM!

✔ Don't write letters begging for people to send you e-mail.

✔ Be careful what you write. E-mail messages are often casually written, and they can easily be misinterpreted. Remember to keep them light.

✔ Ignore people who write you nasty messages. It's hard, but you can do it.

> ✔ Alas, you can't always expect a quick reply from e-mail, especially from folks in the computer industry (which is ironic).
>
> ✔ To send a message you've shoved off to the Drafts folder, open the Drafts folder (double-click it to open it). Then double-click the message to open it. The original New Message window is then redisplayed. From there, you can edit the message and click the Send button to finally send it off.

All about Cc and Bcc

All e-mail must be sent to someone. Normally it's just one person, but if you want to send the message to more than one person, you have several options.

The To field. You can type as many addresses as will fit in the To field. The e-mail message is sent to all those people.

The Cc field. The Cc field is used to carbon copy a message. That's when you want to clue someone into what's going on but not write to that person directly. For example, you send an e-mail to the customer service department and put the company's president on the Cc field. Everyone still gets the same message, but the recipient on the Cc field knows the message was not directly intended for them.

The Bcc field. The sneaky Bcc field is used to blind carbon copy a message. To access this field, choose View➪All Headers from the menu. The people in the Bcc field receive a copy of the e-mail message just like everyone else; however, the people in the To or Cc fields do not see the Bcc field names listed.

As an example of using the Bcc field, consider you're replying to a nasty letter written by a relative dishing your spouse. You can reply and put your spouse's e-mail address in the Bcc field so she knows what's going on, but your relative doesn't know she's snooping in on the conversation.

Composing messages in style

Outlook has the ability to let you compose prettymail. I call it prettymail because the mail looks better than plain-old boring text.

To make prettymail, you can start a new message by clicking the down arrow by the New Mail button. A list of stationery appears, as shown in Figure 27-4. Select a type from the list, and Outlook creates a new message with a special background pattern, picture, or design.

Figure 27-4:
Selecting
stationery
for a new
message.

In the New Message window, you can then use special text formatting tools to add life and color to your message. Figure 27-5 shows such a message composed with lots of obnoxious formatting.

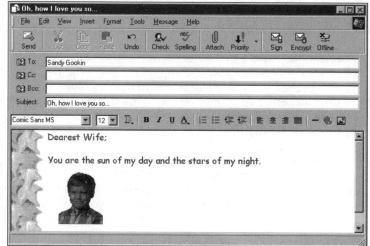

Figure 27-5:
An over-
formatted
message.

To achieve the formatting, use the formatting toolbar. The buttons are similar to buttons you find in your word processor, and they have the same effect on your text.

- Click the Send button to send your heavily formatted e-mail epistle.

- You can find other formatting commands in the Format menu.

- To create your own stationery, choose the Select Stationery command from the New Mail drop-down menu (refer to Figure 27-4). In the Select Stationery dialog box, click the Create New button to run the Stationery Setup Wizard.

✔ Note that not every e-mail program will receive the message formatted the way you see it. If you get a reply claiming that the message looked like jumbled text, then consider composing messages *without* the fancy formatting and stationery.

Reading Your E-Mail

Whenever you start Outlook Express, it lets you know whether you have new mail. Usually a tone plays: *ding-dong*. Then you scurry to your Inbox to see what joyous mail awaits you.

Waiting for mail is never a problem in AOL because you see (and hear) the You Have Mail icon right away. Click it to open up your mailbox and start reading.

Reading a message

To read a message, select it from the list in the Inbox. The message text appears in the bottom of the window, as shown earlier in Figure 27-2.

To read another message, select it from the list. (You don't have to read the messages in order.) Selecting a new message displays its contents in the bottom part of the window.

Excess reading on the columns in the message window

The message window contains several columns that detail information about the message you're reading:

Priority. The exclamation point column tells you a message's priority. For example, an exclamation point there tells you to *read me first*.

Attachment. A small paper clip icon appears next to messages that have file attachments. See Chapter 28 for more information.

Flag. Click this column to put a flag by a message you mean to respond to somehow later.

From. The sender's address.

Subject. The message subject.

Received. The date and time your computer received the message.

Click a heading to sort the messages in the Inbox by that column. Click again to sort in reverse order. (You can also use the View⇨ Sort By submenu to sort your Inbox.)

You control which headings are visible by choosing View⇨Columns. Select the column headings you want to see. Or, for example, you can deselect a column, such as the Flag column, if you don't use it.

After reading a message, you can print, reply, forward, delete, or stow the message. I cover each of these actions in the various sections that follow.

- ✔ Actually, you don't have to do anything with a message after reading it; you can just keep it in your Inbox. There's no penalty for that.
- ✔ New e-mail messages appear in your Inbox in bold text.
- ✔ You can read the messages in any order. In fact, most people scan the list of messages to look for ones they've been waiting for and open them first.
- ✔ Use the scroll bar to scroll through long messages.

Opening a message window

To open a message in its own window, double-click the message in the Inbox. (Any message, read or unread.) A special message-reading window opens, which is similar to the one shown in Figure 27-6.

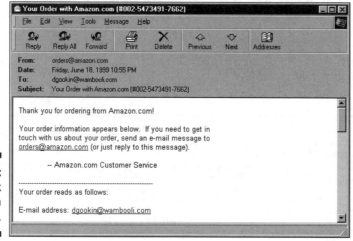

Figure 27-6:
Outlook
Express in
action.

Being its own window, you can resize or drag around the message anywhere on the screen. And you can open more than one message-reading window at a time, which helps if you need to refer to more than one message at a time (those he-said-she-said type of things).

The message-reading window also has two handy buttons: Previous and Next.

Click the Previous button to read the previous message in the Inbox, the one before the current message.

SPAM, SPAM, SPAM, SPAM

Junk e-mail is known as SPAM. It's a reference to an old Monty Python routine, and regardless of protests from the Hormel company (which makes SPAM, the meat product), it's used as a term for widely distributed, unwanted e-mail solicitations.

Don't let SPAM bother you. Everyone gets it. Just delete those messages. Read them if you want but delete them. And *never* reply, even if you're requesting to be removed from the SPAM list; replying to any SPAM signals the sender that you're a *live one,* and your name will be added to the list of suckers. You'll get more SPAM in the future. So don't reply! Ever!

As a tip, you can help squelch SPAM in Outlook Express by choosing Message⇨Block Sender from the menu (when viewing a SPAM message). That way any future messages from the same e-mail address will be immediately deleted before you read them. Pretty nifty, eh?

Click the Next button to read the next message in your Inbox. If you're reading the last message in the Inbox, then clicking the Next button makes an annoying sound.

Close the message window when you're done browsing or reading.

Printing an e-mail message

This one is easy: To print an e-mail message, choose File⇨Print from the menu. The Print dialog box appears; click OK to print.

You can also print a message by clicking the Print button on the toolbar.

Replying to a message

To send an answer or follow-up to an e-mail message, click the Reply button. Or you can use the keyboard shortcut, Ctrl+R. A message-composing window, similar to the New Message window, appears. Figure 27-7 shows a typical reply window.

Note that Outlook Express does several things for you automatically:

- ✔ The sender's name is automatically placed in the To field. Your reply goes back directly to the sender without your having to retype an address.

- ✔ The original subject is referenced (Re) on the Subject line.

✔ Finally, the original message is *quoted* for you. This feature is important because some people receive a lot of e-mail and may not recall the train of the conversation.

Type in your reply.

Click the Send button to send off the reply.

Figure 27-7:
Replying to
a message.

✔ If you like, you can edit the quoted text, splitting it up into relative pieces and replying to each one individually.

✔ You can also edit away the quoted text by deleting it, if you so desire.

Why does my real name appear in my e-mails?

Q: Why is it that when I send e-mail, my real name appears. I got an e-mail today from someone that did not show that person's real name. How do I know who it is REALLY from?

A: Your e-mail program is configured to display your real name on every message you send. You

filled out this information when you set up the program. That name appears in the From line of every message you send.

How do I resend bounced messages?

Q: After typing an inaccurate address on an e-mail letter and having it returned with the message user unknown, can I correct the address and resend the letter?

A: You can forward the returned e-mail to the proper address. The forwarding command is Ctrl+F. Then type in the proper address and maybe an explanation of how you goofed or something. Or you can copy the message and paste it into a New Message window that has the proper e-mail address.

✔ Use the Reply All button when you reply to a message that was carbon-copied to a number of other people. By clicking Reply All, you create a reply that lists *everyone* the original message was sent to so that they can all read the reply.

✔ After replying to a message, the envelope icon in the Inbox changes (shown in the margin). This change is your clue that the message has been replied to.

Forwarding the message to someone else

Forwarding a message is the same as remailing it to someone else. For example, you get the latest list of zingers about how a computer is like a toilet, and you want to send it off to Aunt Ruth. To do that, you forward the message, and she gets a copy.

To forward a message, click the Forward button. Fill in the To field with the address of the person to whom you're forwarding the message. (This part is what makes forwarding different from replying; you must supply a new e-mail address.)

The forwarded message appears *quoted* in the body of the new message. Type in any optional comments. Click the Send button to send it off.

Deleting the message

To delete the message you're reading, click the Delete button. Poof! It's gone.

Well, to be accurate, the message is merely moved into the Deleted Items folder on the left side of the Outlook Express window.

Deleted mail sits in the Deleted Items folder until you clean out that folder. To clean it out, choose Edit⇨Empty Deleted Items Folder from the menu.

Managing Your E-Mail

Vinton Cerf — Father of the Internet and the creator of the @ in all your e-mail messages — said that e-mail can be like barnyard manure; it accumulates if you don't take care of it.

To help you take care of your e-mail, Outlook Express has the Folders window (refer to Figure 27-1). It has five standard folders:

Inbox. This is where all your unread mail messages sit, and also where read mail sits until you delete those messages or move them elsewhere.

Outbox. This folder contains messages waiting to be sent. If you're online, then this folder is empty most of the time.

Sent Items. A copy of all messages and replies you've ever sent is stored here.

Deleted Items. Messages you've deleted are kept here.

Drafts. Any messages you decide not to send are stored here (see "Creating a new e-mail message," earlier in this chapter).

In addition to these folders, you can create your own folders for storing and organizing your messages. The following sections detail the process.

> ✔ Folders with blue numbers in parentheses by them contain unread mail. The number indicates how many messages are unread.

Creating a mail folder

To create your own mail folder, a place for specific types of messages, follow these steps:

1. **Choose File⇨New⇨Folder from the menu.**

   The Create Folder dialog box appears, as shown in Figure 27-8.

2. **Enter a name for the new folder.**

   Type the name into the Folder Name box.

   For example, I have a folder named Online Orders for e-mail receipts sent to me when I order things on the Web. Another good folder to create is a Jokes folder for humorous things people send you.

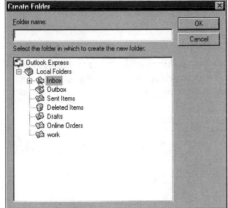

Figure 27-8:
The Create
Folder
dialog box.

3. **Select where you want the folder created.**

   Click the folder in which you want the new folder to be placed. If you select the Local Folders item, Outlook places the folder on the *main level*. Selecting another folder creates a subfolder.

   I keep my folders on the main level, so I select the Local Folders item from the bottom of the Create Folder dialog box.

4. **Click OK.**

   The new folder is created, appearing in the Folder list on the left side of the window.

You manage the folders you create by right-clicking on them. A pop-up menu materializes with commands for renaming or deleting the folders.

To view the contents of a folder, select it from the Folders list. Click once to highlight the folder, and any messages stored there are listed on the left side of the window.

Moving a message to a folder

You can drag messages between folders like you drag icons around in Windows.

From the Inbox, for example, you can drag a message over to the Jokes folder: Click the envelope icon next to the message and drag it to the proper folder on the left side of the window.

Note that you can delete messages by dragging them to the Deleted Items folder.

The Valued Address Book

Whenever you get e-mail from someone new, or when you learn a friend's new online address, you should note it in the Outlook Express Address Book. Not only does the Address Book let you keep the addresses in one spot, but you can easily recall an address for sending mail later.

Adding a name to the Address Book

You can add an e-mail name to the Address Book in one of two ways: manually or automatically.

To manually add a name, choose File⇨New⇨Contact from the menu. Outlook then creates a new Address Book entry (shown in Figure 27-9), which you fill in.

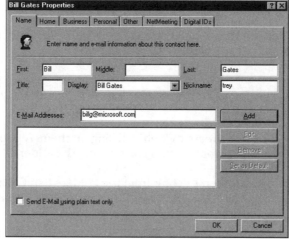

Figure 27-9:
Filling in a new Address Book entry.

The dialog box has many tabs and gizmos for you to work, but you really need to fill in only four items in the Name tab: First, Last, Nickname, and E-Mail Addresses.

The Nickname item is optional, though it can be handy. For example, you can type **goober** into the To field of a new message instead of your brother's full e-mail address. Outlook Express recognizes the shortcut and replaces it with the proper, full e-mail address.

After filling in the four fields (or more, if you're entirely bored), click the Add button and then click OK.

To automatically add a name to the Address book, display an e-mail message from someone whose name you'd like to add. Choose Tools⇨ Add Sender to Address Book from the menu. Outlook instantly adds the name to the Address Book.

Click the Addresses button on the toolbar to display the Address Book window. From there, you can edit or manage the entries in your Address Book.

Using the Address Book when sending a message

The Address Book really comes in handy when you're creating a new message. With the New Message window on the screen (refer to the section "Creating a new e-mail message," earlier in this chapter), click the To field's button, as shown in the margin. A special Address Book window appears, as shown in Figure 27-10.

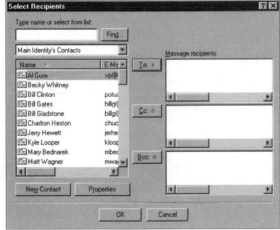

Figure 27-10:
Select
people to
send
e-mail to
from here.

To add someone to the To field, select that person's name and click the To button. Likewise for the Cc or Bcc fields. To select more than one e-mail address at a time, press the Ctrl key and Ctrl+click to select the names.

When you're done, click OK, and the message's To, Cc, and Bcc fields are already filled in for you.

Chapter 28

Files to Here, Files from There!

The Internet was born out of the need to fling files far and wide between the Cro-Magnon computers of the early 1970s. Thank goodness it's much easier to do today. You can send a file to anyone by adding an *attachment* to your e-mail. You can fetch files either through an e-mail message or by grabbing them from a Web page. This chapter tells you all the details.

Grabbing Stuff from the Internet

The Internet is brimming with files and programs that are just waiting for you to grab a copy. Work some magic, and the file is piped into your PC just as if you copied it from a CD-ROM or floppy disk (but not as fast). You can grab files, programs, fonts, graphics, just about anything and everything you want. And it's as cinchy as clicking your mouse.

- Copying a file to your computer is known as *downloading*. When the Internet sends you a file, you *download* it. (Think of the other computer as being on top of a hill; it may not be, but it helps to think of it that way.)

- Sending a file to another computer is known as *uploading*.

- Complaining to your best friend is known as *unloading*.

Saving a Web page to disk

To save an entire Web page to disk, choose File⇨Save As in Internet Explorer. A Save Web Page dialog box appears, similar to the Save As dialog box in any other application. Use the dialog box to save the Web page to disk.

✓ Saving a Web page actually saves what's called an HTML file to disk. That file contains the formatting instructions for the Web page.

✓ You can view the Web page offline using Internet Explorer, or you can edit it using any Web page editor, such as Microsoft Word or FrontPage.

✓ Because HTML is a text-based file format, you can also view the file using a text editor like Notepad. Be aware that Web pages look really ugly this way.

✓ Saving a Web page to disk does not save all the graphics files used on the Web page. You must save those files individually, as described in Chapter 22.

✓ Even though graphics aren't saved with the Web page, Internet Explorer may still display the graphics on-screen. The graphics are saved else-where on disk in IE's *cache.* But don't fret over it: Digging the images out of the cache is a hassle. Grabbing the image from the Web page directly is much easier, as covered in Chapter 22.

Saving part of a Web page to disk

Most Web pages display plain text. You can copy that text and save it to disk just as you'd copy text from one application and paste it into another. Here's how:

1. **Select the text you want to copy.**

   Drag the mouse over the text, which highlights it on the screen. The text is now selected.

2. **Choose Edit⇨Copy.**

   Or you can press the Ctrl+C key combination.

   The text is now copied and ready to be pasted and saved elsewhere.

3. **Start any word processor.**

   You can start Notepad, WordPad, or your word processor, such as Microsoft Word.

4. **Paste the text into your word processor.**

   Choose the Edit⇨Paste command to paste in the text (Ctrl+V is the shortcut key).

5. **Print. Save. Whatever.**

Use the proper menu commands to save or print or edit the text you copied from the Web page.

I've used this technique a number of times, mostly to copy quotes from famous people and paste them into my books. I then attribute the quote to myself and become very famous for it. For example, "All men are created equal." I made that one up.

Searching for programs

The Internet is a vast storehouse for various programs. It contains applications, programming languages, utilities, games, font files, and lots of programs for using the Internet. It's all out there, free for the taking. The problem usually is finding where the programs are kept.

To find programs, you use a file-searching engine similar to a Web page search engine (which I describe in Chapter 26). Several of these engines are available, though the following example uses CNET's Shareware.com.

As an example, suppose you want to find a new Windows card game. Here's how you would search for one:

1. **Visit Shareware.com.**

Type the following address into your Web browser:

```
http://www.shareware.com
```

In a few moments, the Shareware.com Web page appears on your screen. Figure 28-1 shows what it looked like when I wrote this book; it may change looks in the future.

2. **Input the type of program you're searching for.**

Locate the first Search For text box and click the mouse in that box. That's where you type in the name of the kind of program you want — just like you would using any search engine. The more descriptive you are, the better the results, though being vague can help in some circumstances.

For this example, you're trying to find a card game. Type **card game** into the box.

3. **Select your operating system from the drop-down list.**

Choose MS-Windows(all) to search for any Windows programs.

Figure 28-1:
Take a look
at Share-
ware.com.

4. **Click Search.**

   Finding matches may take a few seconds.

   Doh-dee-doh. . . .

   Eventually you see the Search Results page. On it, you find a list of programs you can download along with a brief description. Such as:

   This description tells you that it's a *new* upload (well, it was when the
   screen shot was taken), as well as gives you the file name, type, size, and
   a brief description.

   Pay special attention to the file size. That clues you in to how long it will
   take the Internet to send you the file. With a 28.8K connection, a 500K
   file takes about five minutes to download, more or less. The 4094K
   (4MB!) file shown previously will probably take 25 minutes or more to
   download at 28.8K.

   If more matches are found, you see a link at the bottom of the page titled
   NEXT 25 (or something). Click it to see even more matches.

5. **Select the file you want to download.**

   Click the hyperlink by the file's name. A download page appears, as shown in Figure 28-2.

Figure 28-2:
The down-
load page.

   The download page lists files by their location, both the country and the Internet site where the file is located. A green-square reliability guide tells you which sites are more likely to give you a smooth download.

   If you get an FTP error, or the site is busy, try another site.

6. **Download the file.**

   Select the Save This Program to Disk option in the File Download dialog box. Click OK.

   A Save As dialog box appears, where you tell the Internet where to save the file on your system.

   I recommend creating a Downloads folder in the My Documents folder for saving downloaded files. You can create that folder using the New Folder button in the Save As dialog box. Then use the dialog box's controls to save the file in that folder on disk.

7. **Wait while the file downloads.**

   The File Download dialog box monitors the download process as the file crawls from the Internet into your computer. Depending on the speed of your modem, this process could take days. (Hey! Get that cable modem, already!)

   Don't disconnect from the Internet until the file has been completely sent! If you do disconnect, you won't have the entire file!

   And don't just sit and watch the screen, either. You can visit other Web pages and do other things on the Internet or work in other applications like Word while your computer is receiving the file.

After you successfully download the file, you should run it. Most downloaded files are EXE files, which means they're programs. Running the program usually installs it on your computer. Either that, or it blasts the single file out into many little pieces, one of which is a SETUP program you can run to install. Either way, the program is yours!

- Downloading the file is free. If the file is shareware, however, you're expected to pay for it if you use it.

- Some files you download are called ZIP files. These files are *archives,* or one file that holds several other files as a single, compact unit. After you download a ZIP file, you need to expand or *unzip* it with a ZIP file manager, such as WinZip.

- You can find WinZip at the following Web page:

```
http://www.winzip.com
```

Downloading an MP3 file

In the world of latest things, the Internet is the latest thing. And the latest thing on the Internet is the MP3 file.

MP3, which stands for something, is a file format used to store audio. The quality of the format is such that the music, when played back, sounds nearly perfect. And the file sizes are small, relatively speaking: about 1MB of disk space for every minute of music. That's pretty good; a 5-minute sound on a CD would occupy only 5MB of disk space in MP3 format, as opposed to 100MB or more for other, similar sound files.

To find MP3 music, visit the MP3 Web page:

```
http://www.mp3.com
```

After you find the music you want, click the download link with the mouse. The file is then sent to your computer.

If clicking the download link causes the Windows Media Player to pop up, stop! Close the Media Player, and instead, right-click on the download link. A pop-up menu appears, as shown in Figure 28-3.

Figure 28-3:
Down-
loading an
MP3 file (or
any link).

How do I print an image that's larger than the screen?

Q: I've been trying to print out a copy of the map found on a Web page but haven't had any luck. The map is larger than my screen, and my printer will not print it all. Is it possible for me to print it out even if it takes several sheets?

A: Right-click on the map and save it to disk. Then use a graphics program to print out the

map. Something like Microsoft Picture It! or Imager (which often are included but neglected with Windows) can print out pictures larger than the screen, or they can resize the image to fit on a single sheet of paper.

Choose Save Target As from the menu. Doing so produces a Save As dialog box, which you can use to save the file to a specific spot on disk. (Say! How about an MP3 folder in your Audio folder in your My Documents folder?)

After the file is on disk, you can play it: Double-click its icon to open it and away it goes — provided you have an MP3 player. The latest version of the Windows Media Player will work okay. For other, snazzier players, refer to the same MP3 Web page for some great software to download.

✔ The MP3 Web page (www.mp3.com) is a great resource for all things MP3.

✔ MP3 files are not zipped; you can play them right away after downloading.

✔ You can also download a quality MP3 player right from the MP3 Web page.

Look, Ma! It's an E-Mail Attachment!

E-mail attachments are fun. They're a convenient way to send files back and forth on the Internet. For example, use your vast scanner knowledge to scan in an image of the kids, save it to disk as a JPEG file, and then attach it to an e-mail message to Grandma! Provided Grandma has read this book, she'll be gazing at her beautiful grandkids in mere Internet moments.

✔ Refer to Chapter 27 for more basic information on e-mail.

✔ At some point, you may receive a file your PC cannot digest, a file of an unknown format. If so, and if it's from someone you know, respond to the e-mail and tell the person that you can't open the file and need to have it re-sent in another format.

✔ Beware of attachments from people you don't know! You cannot get a computer virus from regular e-mail, but if someone sends you a program that you run, it could infect your PC. Only accept attachments from people you know. Otherwise, just delete the e-mail message, and you'll be safe.

✔ I do not accept program files or other large attachments over e-mail.

✔ You can send more than one file at a time — just keep attaching files.

✔ Or instead of sending several small files, consider using the WinZip program to archive your files into one handy ZIP file.

✔ Do not send file shortcuts; only send the originals. If you send a shortcut, the people receiving the file won't get the original. Instead they'll get the 296-byte shortcut, which doesn't help.

✔ Try not to move or delete any files you attach to e-mail messages until *after* you send the message. I know this sounds dumb, but too often I'll be waiting for e-mail to send, and (while I'm not busy) I'll start cleaning files. Oops!

✔ This book's word-processor files were written in Idaho, zipped up, and attached to an e-mail message I sent Kyle in Indiana. After editing, Kyle zipped up the files again and e-mailed them back to me for review. Then they were sent back again to Indiana, attached to an e-mail message.

Grabbing an attachment with Outlook Express

The secret of Outlook Express' attachments is the paper clip icon. When you see the paper clip icon next to the message subject, it indicates that the e-mail message has one or more files attached to it.

When you read the message, you'll find a large paper clip button in the upper-right corner of the message's window, as shown in the margin. Click that button to see a list of files attached to the message, as shown here:

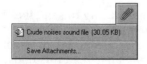

A sound file is attached to the preceding message. Selecting that file from the paper clip button's menu plays the file.

Attached graphics files appear as images below the message body itself. You don't have to do anything; the images just show up. (If not, then the images sent are not JPEG or GIF files.)

All other attached files should probably be saved to disk. To save them, choose the File⇨Save Attachments menu item. A window appears, listing the file(s) attached to the message, as shown in Figure 28-4.

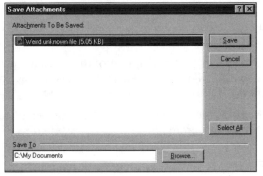

Figure 28-4:
Saving an attachment in Outlook Express.

Note the Save To item at the bottom of the dialog box. Use the Browse button to select another folder; otherwise, the attachment(s) will be saved in whichever folder Outlook Express thinks best (which is a gamble, trust me).

Click the Save button to save the file.

Remember where you saved the file!

With the attachment saved, you can reply to or delete the message as you normally would.

- ✔ I save my attachments in the My Documents folder. After looking at them or examining their contents, I then shuffle them off to the proper folder.

- ✔ Even if Outlook Express displays graphics files right in your message, you may still want to choose File⇨Save Attachments to save them to disk.

Sending an attachment in Outlook Express

You attach a file in Outlook Express by — can you guess? — clicking the big paper clip button in the message composition window. Yup, it's that easy.

Start by creating a new message or replying to a message (refer to Chapter 27 for the details). When you're ready to attach a file, click the paper clip button or choose Insert⇨File Attachment from the menu.

Use the Insert Attachment dialog box to find the file you want to attach. It works exactly like an Open/Browse dialog box. After finding and selecting the file, click the Attach button.

The file you attach appears on a new line in the New Message window, right below the Subject line.

To send the message and the file, click the Send button. And it's off on its way. . . .

- Sending a message with a file attached takes longer than sending a regular, text-only message.

- It's a good idea to ensure that the recipient of the message can read the type of file you're sending. For example, sending a Word file to a WordPerfect user may not meet with the results you want.

- In keeping with my rules mentioned earlier, phone or e-mail someone before you send them a program file so they're certain it's not a random virus being sent.

- Send JPEG or GIF pictures. Any other picture format (see Chapter 22) is usually too large and makes the recipient wait a long time to receive the message.

The World of FTP

The traditional way to send files back and forth on the Internet is something called FTP, which stands for File Transfer Protocol. How the *Protocol* part got worked in there, I'll never know. It should just be FT for File Transfer, which is what the program does. Maybe FT is trademarked, or they didn't want people saying *fort,* or maybe it's a pun on STP. Who knows?

Receiving files with FTP is easy; your Web browser does that, and it operates in a mode you're very familiar with.

Sending files with FTP is tough. I'll save that gristly morsel for the last section of this chapter.

- FTP is File Transfer Protocol. Pronounce it *ef-tee-pee.*

- STP is Scientifically Treated Petroleum. It's the racer's edge.

- Most of the time, you'll use FTP to get files, usually from some vast file archive somewhere on the Internet.

- Sending files to the Internet is kind of rare. It's commonly done when you upload information for a Web page. Also some businesses may have an FTP site where you can upload projects, which is still rare.

Browsing an FTP site

When you point your Web browser to an FTP site, it changes modes and operates more like a disk file tool. The difference is that the files you're look-ing at are on a computer somewhere on the Internet and not on your own PC.

Follow these steps to visit the Simtel FTP site:

1. **Browse to:** `ftp://ftp.simtel.net/`

   Type the preceding command into the Address bar in Internet Explorer. Type **ftp**, colon, two slashes, **ftp**, period, **simtel**, period, **net**, and a slash.

   The `ftp://` command, like `http://`, tells the Web browser to visit a site on the Internet. Instead of a Web page, however, you see an FTP site. In this case, it's the Simtel archive.

   Figure 28-5 shows how Internet Explorer displays the FTP site. Hey! That's just like how Windows Explorer shows folders and files on your disk drive. Amazing.

   If you have an earlier version of Internet Explorer, or you're using another Web browser, you may instead see a list of files. Hello, DOS! Actually, everything works the same, but the display is merely more detailed.

2. **Open the pub folder.**

   Double-click the folder to open it and display its contents.

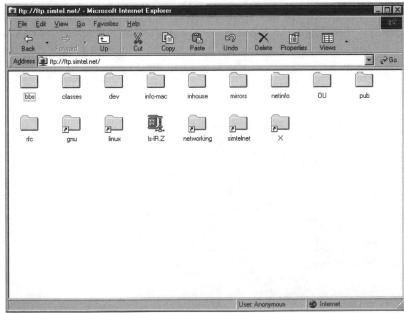

Figure 28-5:
Viewing an
FTP site
with
Internet
Explorer
(Version 5).

3. **Open the simtelnet folder.**

4. **Open the win95 folder.**

   Finally you're at the Windows 95/98 archive on Simtel. What you see in the browser's window is a list of all the folders, each of which contains a certain category of file.

5. **Open the cursors folder.**

   Inside the cursors folder are various cursor files, which you can use to liven up the desktop.

00 index.txt

Most FTP archives contain at least one index file, which describes all the files in the folder. Locate the index file, which on my screen (and in the margin) is called 00_index.txt.

Also notice the other file types. There are mostly ZIP archives, but maybe some EXE, font, or sound files as well.

6. **Open the Index file.**

   Double-click to open and read the information in the Index file.

   Peruse the list and see if you may want to download any of the animated cursor files listed.

   Pay careful attention to the file size! If it's a large file, downloading it takes a while.

   If the index file opens in another window, be sure to close it when you move on to do something else.

7. **Download a file.**

   When you find a file you want to download, open it. (Double-click the file.) The File Download dialog box appears, as shown in Figure 28-6.

   Select the Save This File to Disk option (as shown in Figure 28-6) and click OK. Then use the Save As dialog box to find a spot for the download on disk.

Figure 28-6:
Down-
loading a
file.

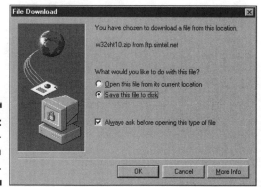

You can continue to peruse the FTP library while the file is downloading, or you can browse the Web, read e-mail — you know the drill. (With Internet Explorer Version 5, use the Back button to return to *Web browsing mode,* or type in a Web page address, or press Alt+Home to get at your home page.)

Numerous FTP archives are on the Web. You can find the Monster FTP Sites List at:

```
http://hoohoo.ncsa.edu/ftp/
```

I'm not making up the *hoohoo* part.

- ✔ Always peruse the Index file in an FTP archive. Note that the Index file may not always be available.

- ✔ As long as you're at Simtel, the compress folder (/pub/simtelnet/win95/compress) contains the latest version of WinZip. Refer to the Index file in that folder for information on other unzipping utilities.

- ✔ Not every FTP site lets you browse around. It has to be an *anonymous FTP site,* which means it lets anyone in for browsing purposes.

A few words on FTP programs

Your Web browser lets you cruise FTP sites and download programs, but it does not allow you to upload programs (send files to an Internet computer). That situation is rare to begin with, as described in this section's introduction. But it is possible, provided you use a special FTP program.

Windows comes with a command line (DOS) FTP program called — believe it or not — FTP. It's an ugly and awkward program based on the original UNIX FTP program. I wouldn't wish it on an enemy.

Beyond Windows lousy FTP program, you can get third-party FTP programs that make sending files back and forth between the Internet and your PC as easy as copying a file to a floppy drive.

One third-party FTP program I use and can recommend is CuteFTP. The shareware program costs only $30, and you can download or purchase it from `http://www.cuteftp.com`. This is the program I use to update my personal and business Web pages.

- ✔ FTP is the way you send a file to an Internet computer.

- ✔ If you have a personal Web page, then the way to get your Web pages *posted* is to send them to your ISP's computer via an FTP program. Chapter 30 discusses the details.

Chapter 29

Other Internetty Things

*Y*ee-ha! Time to round up the rest of the Internet cattle. Entire books are written on the Internet and how to use its programs and access its various secret places. This chapter concludes the Internet part of this book with a summary of several final Internet goodies near and dear to some people, but not required for everyone.

Newsgroups (Usenet)

Newsgroups on the Internet are nothing more than public discussions. In the early days of the Internet, newsgroups existed for various scientists around the globe to discuss things like encryption technology, plasma physics, or where to get good Chinese food in Las Vegas. Today, newsgroups are devoted to any topic or subject, and anyone can read or contribute.

The following sections offer a brief view into the world of Internet newsgroups.

- ✔ Many programs enable you to peruse the newsgroups. This chapter looks at Outlook Express.

- ✔ In AOL, you can get to the newsgroups by typing in the keyword: **NEWSGROUPS**.

- ✔ Usually when people say "Internet News," they mean newsgroups. This is not the same thing as real, this-story-just-in news. To read real news, visit a Web page like cnn.com or wire.ap.org.

- ✔ A newsgroup is similar to a public e-mail system. You can read the messages and contribute (post) messages, if you like.

Browsing newsgroups with Outlook Express

On the Internet, news is provided via a news server. That's a computer or special software that distributes the messages that comprise the various newsgroups.

If your ISP offers a news server, then you probably configured it when you first ran the Internet Connection Wizard. If so, Outlook Express lists the news server in the Folders part of its window.

Figure 29-1 shows two news servers: `betanews.microsoft.com` (a private resource for testing Microsoft stuff) and `nntp.iea.com`, which is my ISP's news server.

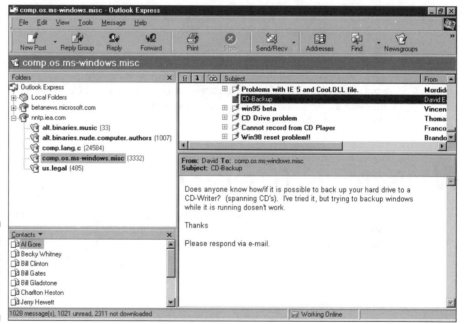

Figure 29-1:
Outlook Express is viewing a newsgroup.

Beneath the news server's name is a list of newsgroups to which I've sub-scribed. This list includes only a handful out of the tens of thousands of newsgroups available.

The right side of Outlook Express lists the messages queued up in the news-group at the top. To view a specific message, click it once, and the contents appear in the bottom part of the window.

Before you can view a newsgroup, however, you first need to subscribe. Click the news server's name in Folders list. A synchronization panel appears on the right side of the window. Click the Newsgroups button. A Newsgroups Subscriptions window opens, from which you can search and select newsgroups to subscribe to.

After you're subscribed to newsgroups, they appear beneath the server's name in the Folders list. Click a newsgroup to list the new messages found there. Then you can browse the messages on the right side of the window just like you read your e-mail.

✔ To post a message to a newsgroup, click the New Post button. The process is similar to creating a new e-mail message, but the post is sent to the newsgroup for *everyone* to read.

✔ To reply and post a message, click the Reply Group button.

✔ You cannot recall a message you've posted.

✔ To reply to the message's author via e-mail, click the Reply button.

✔ You don't have to reply to any e-mail message. You can only read them if you like.

✔ You can forward a newsgroup message via e-mail by using the Forward button.

✔ People who only read newsgroup messages are known as *lurkers*. This is not a negative term.

✔ Posting a newsgroup message almost guarantees that you'll get some SPAM mail. Spammers surf the newsgroups and cull out e-mail addresses for their sucker lists.

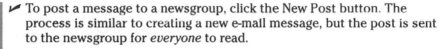

✔ Parents: Be aware that some newsgroups are quite obnoxious. Language can get offensive. Insults are freely hurled. And some newsgroups contain graphic images you probably don't want your children to view.

✔ Yes, you can attach files to a newsgroup message just like you can attach them to an e-mail message. In Outlook Express, you use the big paper clip button to review or download attachments.

✔ Beware of program file attachments! Do not download programs from the newsgroups. Pictures, music, sound files — are all okay. Programs may contain viruses!

✔ News grows. Internet newsgroups sometimes have hundreds of new postings a day. Keeping up is next to impossible (unless you have a cushy job where you can read news all the doo-da-day). On the pleasant side, you don't really have to read everything because the *news* is rather capricious (and experience will prove this to you).

Browsing newsgroups on the Web

If your ISP lacks a news server, then you can use the Web to view newsgroups. Two sites come to mind for this:

```
http://www.deja.com
http://www.remarq.com
```

Each of these Web pages lets you browse newsgroups as you would browse for topics on the Web, or you can search through the newsgroups for specific articles that interest you.

Figure 29-2 shows Deja.com (formerly DejaNews), which you can use to either browse or search for information on a newsgroup.

Figure 29-2:
Browsing
Deja.com
for news-
groups.

Figure 29-3 shows a search result on the hot-button topic of gun control. Clicking the proper links displays messages on the topic.

✔ Most likely, additional resources are available for reading newsgroups on the Web. Use Yahoo! or Ask Jeeves or any of the search engines covered in Chapter 26 to find more of them.

✔ You can also post messages or replies to newsgroups on a Web page just as you can in Outlook Express.

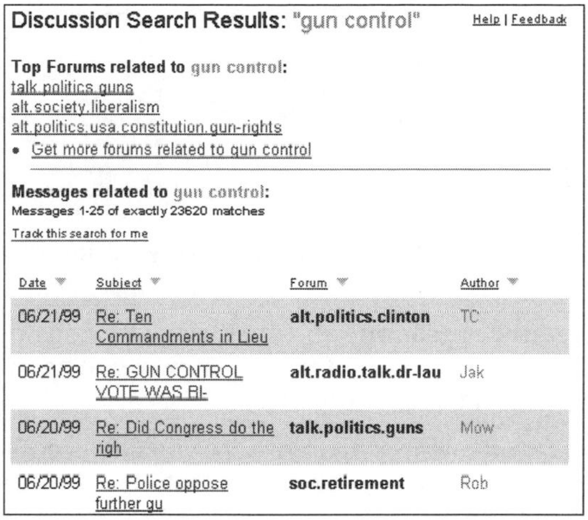

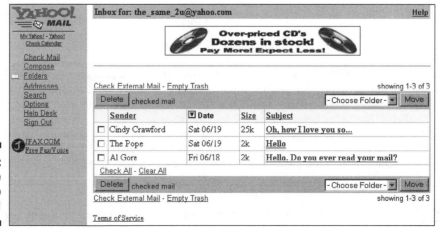

Figure 29-3:
Reading the
news on
Deja.com.

Web E-Mail

Figure 29-4 shows my Yahoo! e-mail account mailbox. After logging in, I can read mail, compose new messages, or do anything I'd do with any other e-mail account.

Unlike a real e-mail account, you browse to a Web page to read your e-mail. You log in. You read the mail. You reply. You can even send and receive file attachments using Web e-mail.

Figure 29-4:
Mail! I've
got Web
mail!

✔ To set up a Web e-mail account, visit any Web page that offers that feature. Here's the short list:

```
http://mail.yahoo.com
http://hotmail.com
http://netaddress.com
http://www.netbox.com
```

Undoubtedly more of these pages exist. Refer to your favorite search engine on the Web for a complete list.

✔ If you and your spouse are sharing an e-mail account, consider getting a Web page e-mail account for each of you. That way you need not be concerned about missing e-mail or snooping.

✔ Web page e-mail is available to you anywhere you can access the Web. It doesn't even need to be your PC; you just log into the Web page e-mail account and read your mail.

✔ My Yahoo! e-mail address is the_same_2u@yahoo.com; however I do not visit that mailbox often enough to make it reliable. Instead, if you want to send me e-mail, use my permanent address: dgookin@wambooli.com. I always answer e-mail there. Promise!

Chit and Chat

One of the more wild aspects of the Internet is the live chat rooms. In these places, you can sit and type back and forth (in real time) with other Internet users.

```
Snooty is here! {[(((((HUGS!!!)))))]}
```

(Pardon me while I grab this air sickness bag.)

Various chat rooms are devoted to certain topics and special events. I've enjoyed debating politics in some chat rooms. Sadly, most chat rooms seem to be dedicated to adult themes or childish tittering, so I generally stay away from them.

Windows 95/98 doesn't come with any specific chat software. Instead, you have to either get (buy or download) chat software from the Internet, or you can use a Web page–based chat system, such as the Chat at Yahoo!.

✔ Chat is also known as IRC, Internet Relay Chat.

✔ If you're a parent, it's probably best to keep your young children out of the Internet chat rooms.

✔ Not all chat rooms are dirty. Quite a few host special events where you can type back and forth with famous people or people who think they're famous.

✔ The following Web page is a great chat resource:

```
http://www.liszt.com/chat/
```

✔ AOL lives for chat rooms. Type the keyword **CHAT**, and you're taken to the People Connection, from whence you can find various chat rooms on certain topics or no topics at all!

✔ A *chat room* is merely a place where a group of people type at each other. When you visit an IRC site, you're shown a list of these rooms along with their topics, and you have the option to join one in progress or sit in an empty room and type to yourself.

✔ Chat rooms quickly make you realize how poorly everyone types and spells.

Making Your Own Web Page

Entire books are dedicated to the subject of creating a Web page, so I'll be brief — and, unfortunately, techy:

You need Web space. Before anything, you need *Web space* to make a Web page. This is disk space on your ISP's server on which you can put your Web page files. Only by transferring your Web page documents to that special Web space can they be accessed by others on the Web.

Typically the Web space is a directory (folder) on your ISP's computer in your own personal directory. The folder is named public_html. Your ISP should set all of this up for you.

Create the Web page. You can use just about *any* program Microsoft makes to build a Web page: Word, Excel, and especially FrontPage, which is the program specifically designed for that task. (It boggles me that you can create a Web page using Excel.)

Whatever you name your Web page is the name that's used on the Internet to visit that page. So if you save the page to disk as Favorites, then Favorites is the place people visit on the Web.

Here is an exception to the Web page name: The main page is always called *index* (specifically, INDEX.HTM or INDEX.HTML).

Uploading the Web page. After creating the Web page, which is simple, you need to send the files to your Web space on the ISP, which isn't simple.

The best (and maybe only) way to send the files is by using an FTP program. I use CuteFTP to send files to my Web page, because CuteFTP works similarly to Windows Explorer. I just drag and drop the files to my Web space. Alas, you'll probably have to use the Windows Ugly FTP Program — if you can stand it. I list abbreviated instructions in the sidebar, "Don't read this FTP information whatever you do!"

View the Web page. Reading the Web page using your Web browser is the final step, the proof that your Web pudding has cooked properly. Most ISP's have your home page address as a tilde, followed by your e-mail or login name. For example:

```
http://www.microsoft.com/~billg
```

Don't read this FTP information whatever you do!

Windows own FTP program is ugly. UGLY! Here are the commands you need to access your ISP and upload a Web page — provided the ISP lets you log on in the first place:

1. **From the Start menu, choose Run.**

2. **Type** FTP **in the box and click OK.**

   A DOS window opens in which FTP runs. The FTP text prompt is ftp>. (Ugly. Ugly. Ugly.)

3. **Type the** open **command, followed by your ISP's domain name.**

   For example, if you were Bill Gates, your domain name would be microsoft.com, which is the last part of your e-mail address. Type it in like this:

   ```
   ftp>open microsoft.com
   ```

   Remember to use your own ISP's domain name, not Microsoft's.

4. **If the open command is successful, you need to type in your login name and password.**

   You're connected to your home directory on the ISP's computer.

If open doesn't work, then check your typing and try again. Also confirm that you're using the proper domain name with your ISP.

5. **Type** cd public_html **at the prompt.**

   This command logs you in to your Web space. FTP should say CWD command successful or something like that, indicating you're ready to upload your Web page files.

6. **Type** put **followed by the full pathname of the file you want to upload.**

   For example, if INDEX.HTML is stored in the c:\My Documents\Web Pages\ folder, you would type:

   ```
   put "c:\my documents\Webpages\
   index.html"
   ```

   That sends that one file to your ISP. For the rest, you're on your own!

7. **To quit FTP, type the** quit **command.**

That isn't a real Web page address, but if it were, you would find Bill G's home page at that address. The file that's displayed is the one named INDEX.HTML and stored in the public_html directory on that computer.

✔ You don't *really* need Web space to post a Web page. Several locations on the Internet, such as GeoCities (`http://www.geocities.com`), let you create your own Web pages.

✔ Refer to Chapter 28 for more information on FTP and CuteFTP.

Other Internet Stuff

Scientists know that atoms work like machines. Unfortunately, the machines are so tiny they can't really see them nor see them at work. So the scientists do what anyone else in that frustrating situation would do: They blow the atoms up and look at the pieces that come out.

As I blow up the Internet in this final section, some random pieces come out. The three worth mentioning are: Gopher, mail lists, and Telnet. The rest have, unfortunately, been blasted into oblivion.

Gopher. Gopher (a variation of *go for*) was the Big Thing before the Web hit in 1993. A Gopher server was an information database you could quickly search, much better than the haphazard way information was stored before then. The Web utterly crushed Gopher, even though you can still browse Gopher sites using the `gopher://` command. A search engine points you to any remaining Gopher sites that haven't been converted to Web pages.

Mail lists. These are popular, shared e-mail accounts that you subscribe to; they're like getting a newsletter. The mail list is sent out to dozens if not hundreds of people. Everyone gets the same message, and your reply to a mail list message is sent to everyone else on the list. Mail lists are designed to serve specific people or interests. I used to belong to one that was subscribed to by computer book authors. You can find other lists at the list of lists, `http://www.liszt.com/`.

Telnet. Windows actually comes with a Telnet program, which is odd given its cryptic nature. Basically Telnet allows you to connect with a UNIX computer on the Internet. Do you know UNIX? If so, then you'll probably use Telnet and won't need me to tell you how it works. If not, that ends the discussion.

Part VI
Something's Wrong!

The 5th Wave   By Rich Tennant

"YEAH, I USED TO WORK ON REFRIGERATORS, WASHING MACHINES, STUFF LIKE THAT—HOW'D YOU GUESS?"

In this part . . .

When we finally invent the perfect, faultless computer, it will be our doom. The PC will turn on us. We will have to serve it. And I don't believe that computers will be as forgiving of us as we are of them!

The biggest problem with computer problems is that people are too quick to blame themselves for their PC's folly. People always assume it's their fault, that they somehow offended the delicate sensibilities of the PC. . . .

Wrong! Computers foul up on the slightest whim. Don't mistake their flakiness for anything you've done. Instead, refer to the chapters in this part for remedies. Make this part of the book your place to turn to when the computer up and dies — or just crosses its eyes and says, "Windows exists, so there are problems."

Chapter 30

Troubleshooting Your PC

●●●

In This Chapter

▶ Checking your system for trouble

▶ Removing dead programs

▶ Resetting to fix things

▶ Using the Safe mode

▶ Checking with the Device Manager

▶ Running a troubleshooter program

▶ Understanding viruses

▶ Creating an emergency boot disk

●●●

*W*hy is it that computers run amok? If cars had the same troubles, no one would drive. Heck, no one would walk, sit, or play anywhere near a road. As humans, we count on things to be reliable and consistent. Life is supposed to be that way. Heaven must be that way. Hell? It's probably floor-to-ceiling computers down there.

For millions of reasons, computers go insane and turn on their owners. (Calling Stephen King! Are you dry on ideas?) I can't list them all here, but I can give you general advice plus a few steps to take for regaining control of the beast.

General, Up-Front, Panicky Advice

When your computer screws up, STOP WORKING ON IT!

  ✔ Any time a program crashes or something doesn't work right, save and shut down. Restart your PC. That generally fixes most problems.

  ✔ Don't be a fool and try to continue to work on the system or even play a game. That's nuts.

> ✔ If you're having disk troubles, try saving your file to disk, but also use the Save As command to save the file to another hard drive, floppy disk, or Zip disk.
>
> ✔ Programs that crash don't go away; their corpses stay in memory. Only by resetting your PC can you get that memory back.

Things to Check

Whenever a computer goes haywire, you should do a few things right away.

Check your hardware

Are all the cables connected? Is the monitor (or printer or modem) plugged in?

Printer cables and monitor cables can wiggle loose. Check them!

Modems must be properly plugged into the wall — which is tough because they all have two phone jacks on the back. Ensure you're using the proper one.

The keyboard and mouse cable can become loose. Check them!

Find out how much control you have

Some programs go gently into the dark night. Others are sucked down into the pit of hell with fingers digging into the linoleum.

When a program dies, you may see an error message, notice that things aren't working properly, or receive no response from the computer. If so, you need to determine how much control you still have over the PC.

Move the mouse around. Does it still work? If so, good. If not, try the keyboard.

What's an illegal procedure?

Q: I have been receiving messages that say that this machine is doing something illegal....

A: *Illegal* is a term widely misused by computer programmers. It means *wrong* or *not permitted* with respect to the way the computer does things. For example, in the filename this:that, the colon is an illegal character. That's just the term they use. Sorry it scared you.

Does the keyboard work? Try popping up the Start menu in Windows: Press Ctrl+Esc to see whether your keyboard is still functioning. (Press the Esc key to make the Start menu go away.)

You may have to wait for Windows to respond; sometimes a misbehaving program tosses a wrench into the gears, which makes the PC slow to respond.

If you have no mouse or keyboard control, your only resort is to reset. Yes, this is the only time you should manually reset the PC. Refer to Chapter 2.

Remove that dead program

Windows has the ability to live with dead programs. Even though the program doesn't respond, you can still use the mouse and keyboard, and you can work in other programs. Still, you should rid yourself of the deadware. Here's how:

1. Press Ctrl+Alt+Delete.

This action brings up the Close Program window (see Figure 30-1).

Figure 30-1:
The Close Program window.

2. Sniff out any recently deceased programs.

You see the words *not responding* in parentheses after the dead program's name in the list. For example:

```
Government (not responding)
```

Click that program's name in the list.

If more than one program is not responding, repeat all of these steps to rid yourself of each of them.

3. **Click the End Task button.**

   The program is killed off.

Be careful not to choose the Shut Down button instead of End Task. Sometimes that makes sense — for example, you want to shut down the AWOL program. But the Shut Down button actually shuts down Windows — and without warning. So don't select it casually!

At this point, the program is gone. It should be removed from the screen, which makes it easier to get at other programs.

Your next step should be to save and shut down other applications you may be running. Then reset your PC.

Resetting to fix strangeness

Resetting is sometimes the best way to cure just about anything weird. If the mouse is missing, reset. If Explorer dies, reset. If a program hangs, reset — even after you get rid of the dead program.

Follow the instructions in Chapter 2 for resetting your PC. Do it. When the computer comes alive again, the problem may be automagically fixed.

- ✔ If you can reset using the Shut Down Windows dialog box (properly), do it. Otherwise, you have to punch the PC's reset button or turn it off and on again (see Chapter 2).

- ✔ Why does resetting work? I have no idea. I think, maybe, the computer just gets tired. It needs to be reset every so often to keep itself awake.

After resetting, check the hard drive

When your computer is up and running after a crash-and-reset, consider running the ScanDisk program. This program checks your hard drives for errors and ensures that the disk system is up to snuff.

To run ScanDisk, just follow these steps:

1. **Start ScanDisk.**

   From the Start menu, choose Programs➪Accessories➪SystemTools➪ScanDisk. ScanDisk's window appears, as shown in Figure 30-2.

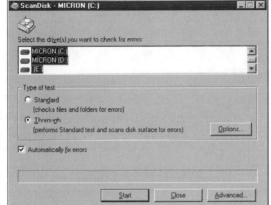

Figure 30-2:
ScanDisk is
used to
check the
hard drives.

2. **Select the hard drives on your computer you want scanned.**

   Selecting all the hard drives in your system — D, E, or F or however many appear in the window in addition to drive C — is a good idea. (You don't need to check the floppy disk or any removable drives.)

3. **Select the Standard option.**

   If you *really* suspect disk trouble, select the Thorough option instead.

4. **Click the Start button.**

   If ScanDisk reports any errors, fix them if they can be fixed; follow the instructions on the screen.

Close the ScanDisk window when you're done.

   ✔ If the choices confuse you when ScanDisk presents an error, just select the highlighted option by pressing the Enter key. (You can avoid this situation by selecting the Automatically Fix Errors option, as shown in Figure 30-2.)

   ✔ ScanDisk is not voodoo. If you have serious disk problems, then it probably won't run at all. In that case, you need to take your PC in for servicing, as covered in Chapter 31.

   ✔ Run ScanDisk every week or so just in case. Windows 98 has a scheduling tool that can run ScanDisk automatically for you. Any good book on Windows will tell you how to do it.

The Perils of Safe Mode

Whenever Windows detects major problems, it starts itself in what's known as Safe mode. Whether or not that implies that normal operation is the *unsafe mode,* I'll leave for the gurus to debate. The point is that Windows has a special mode you can try should you need to wiggle out of a pickle.

Starting safely

Say you screw something up or it screws up by itself. The most common situation I can think of is changing the video display to something you don't want. For example, black-on-black text or maybe text so large that you cannot get to the button to change it back. If so, you need to restart in Safe mode.

Shut down the PC as you normally would. If you cannot access the Start button, press Ctrl+Esc. Then press the U key to access the Shut Down command. The Shut Down Windows dialog box appears.

If you cannot see the Shut Down Windows dialog box, press Alt+R to select the Restart option. Then press the Enter key.

As Windows restarts, press and hold the Ctrl key (on some PCs you need to press the F8 key) to display a special Startup menu:

```
Microsoft Windows 98 Startup menu
=================================

    1. Normal
    2. Logged (\BOOTLOG.TXT)
    3. Safe mode
    4. Step-by-step confirmation
    5. Command prompt only
    6. Safe mode command prompt only

Enter a choice:
```

Search for the Safe mode option (number 3 here). Type that number and press the Enter key.

Safe mode starts, loading only the files necessary to run Windows — it's a no-frills operation. When Windows is finally up, you see it displayed in a low-resolution, low-color mode with the words *Safe mode* displayed on the desktop.

Fix your problem! Safe mode exists to fix problems. Read the dialog box that tells you about Safe mode and how to visit the Control Panel to fix what's bugging you. Generally speaking, all you need to do is undo what it was that you screwed up in the first place.

Starting normally again

If your PC seems to be stuck in *diagnostic* mode, then you may need to manually twist it back into normal mode. Here's how:

1. **Choose the Run command from the Start menu.**

2. **In the Run dialog box, type MSCONFIG and press Enter.**

   This action runs the System Configuration Utility, a handy program to help you troubleshoot startup problems.

3. **Click the General tab and ensure that the Normal Startup item is selected.**

This option ensures that Windows starts normally. (You may notice that the Diagnostic Startup is selected, which is the source of your woes.)

4. **Click OK. Your computer should start normally from here on — unless you have another problem.**

Also note that you can use the System Configuration Utility to remove startup programs that may be causing trouble. My advice is always to use this program under the guidance of a tech-support person or guru; don't mess around there yourself!

When Safe mode starts automatically

If the problem is really bad, Windows may start in Safe mode automatically. Don't let this scare you! Windows has discovered something not quite right in the system and has started in Safe mode to help you fix it.

✔ Safe mode may come up after you install new hardware. That means the software (drivers) required for that hardware is not working properly. Uninstall the software in Safe mode and restart your computer. Contact your dealer to see if new software exists.

✔ Refer to the section "Checking for Device Conflicts" for more information on why Safe mode may have started automatically.

Checking for Device Conflicts

One thing you should check when Windows starts in Safe mode is the Device Manager. It lists all the hardware in your PC and flags any hardware that may be causing trouble.

Viewing the Device Manager

To view the Device Manager, right-click on the My Computer icon on the desktop. Choose Properties from the shortcut menu. In the System Properties dialog box, click the Device Manager tab. What you see may look like Figure 30-3.

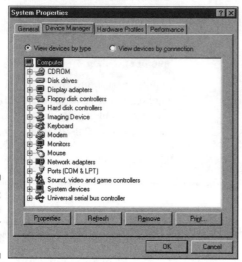

Figure 30-3:
The Device
Manager
window.

If there are any hardware conflicts, they'll be flagged by a tiny exclamation point in a yellow circle:

Standard Floppy Disk Controller

Click a conflicting item to select it and then click the Properties button. In the center of the device's Properties dialog box is an explanation of the problem (in the Device status area).

Sometimes the advice is specific. Sometimes it's just "refer to the device's manual." Sometimes you're asked to run a troubleshooter or conflict manager. Keep reading in the next section.

✔ Close the System Properties dialog box when you're done with it.

✔ Another program to check for system conflicts is the System Information utility: From the Start menu choose Programs➪Accessories➪SystemTools➪ System Information. The Hardware Resources/Conflicts/Sharing page lists any trouble spots the Device Manager may miss.

Running a troubleshooter

Troubleshooters are special Q&A programs included in the Help system for Windows. There is no logical or easy way to start them, other than the following:

1. **Choose Help from the Start menu.**

   The Windows Help thing appears.

2. **Click the Index tab if it's not already up front.**

3. **Type** Trouble **in the text box.**

   The first match, "troubleshooting," appears in the list below.

4. **Double-click the word *troubleshooting*.**

   Another window opens listing Windows various troubleshooters, as shown in Figure 30-4.

Figure 30-4:
Various
trou-
bleshooters.

5. **Scroll through the list to find the troubleshooter that fits your needs.**

   Modem trouble? Scroll down to the Modem troubleshooter. Note that some of the items listed merely point you to *help* in Windows, such as the To Free More Disk Space item.

6. **Select a topic and click the Display button.**

   And you're off!

   Click the various links and put dots in the proper circles to answer questions and work through the troubleshooter.

7. **Don't forget to close the Help and Troubleshooter windows when you're done.**

I've had about 50-50 luck with the Windows troubleshooters. Sometimes they've pointed me right to the problem. Other times, using the troubleshooter was like trying to herd cats.

The it-was-working-yesterday syndrome

I got a flat tire a few months back. Some debris was in the road. I ran over something. I heard the telltale ssp-ssp-ssp as the tire lost air while it was rotating. It was a nice audible clue.

Just like cars, computers should make funny noises before they go south. Computers need thumping thuds or grinding sounds. Or maybe there should be puddles of oil under the mouse. But, no. Computers just stop working. It's maddening.

Sometimes the it-was-working-yesterday syndrome has a cause, only you just forgot it. Ask yourself the following questions:

✔ Did I add any new PC hardware recently?

✔ Did I add any new software?

✔ Have I changed any software?

✔ Have I reset any of the Windows options?

✔ Did I uninstall anything?

Oftentimes you find yourself remembering what happened; that is, "Oh, yeah, I set the printer to print sideways yesterday. No wonder all my correspondence came out looking so funky." Whatever, narrowing down what was changed helps you fix things, or at least leads the tech-support people or your PC guru to the proper cure.

"Does My PC Have a Virus?"

A common question that zips through the mind of a bewildered user facing a silly PC is, "Could this be a virus?" I hate to say it, but yes it could — especially if you can answer *yes* to any of the following:

✔ I downloaded files from a Web page on the Internet, specifically a Web page of a questionable nature.

✔ I ran a program sent to me as an e-mail attachment, something I wasn't expecting or from someone I didn't know or trust.

✔ I ran a program I got from a chat room.

✔ I started a game on my PC from a boot disk in drive A.

✔ I used stolen software my friends and coworkers gave me.

✔ Other people use my PC.

If you answer *yes* to any of these items, you probably have a virus. Those are all nasty habits, and they're just about the only ways that a virus can infect a PC.

Where you cannot get a virus

You cannot get a virus from any of the following sources:

E-mail. Reading plain e-mail does not give your PC a virus. Various scares and scams have surfaced about reading certain messages and getting a virus, but they're all hoaxes. You cannot get a virus from reading your e-mail. Promise! It just won't happen.

A picture file. Picture files cannot infect your PC. JPEGs, GIFs, or even more elaborate graphics file formats cannot infect your PC. Feel free to open these files on the Internet or if they're attached to an e-mail message.

Downloads. Downloading a virus won't infect your computer. The virus must be a program you run. If you download the file and don't run it, then you're safe. (Someone sent me such a virus once. I didn't run the program, so my PC was never infected.)

Retail software. The stuff they sell at the store is not infected.

Known Web FTP sites. Web sites such as Shareware.com or any widely used FTP site will not have infected software on it. And if you doubt that, then download the software and run a virus-checker on it before you run that program. (See the next section.)

Now pay attention: The only way you can get a virus on your PC is to *run* an infected program. That's it! If you don't run the program, you won't get the virus.

Antivirus software

Even if you don't practice any nasty PC program habits, you may sleep better if you get special antivirus software.

Alas, Windows doesn't come with any antivirus software. You need to run down to the Software-o-Rama to buy some or download antivirus software from the Internet.

✔ Antivirus software removes the virus from your PC, as well as assists you in spotting such nasty programs before they invade again.

✔ Antivirus software also tends to slow down your PC. My advice: Run the software first to scan for viruses. Then configure it so that it scans your system only when you start the PC. Then just use the program to scan files you download or get from other people. But try to turn off the options that monitor your PC's activity 24 hours a day.

✔ Believe your antivirus software when it tells you no viruses are in your PC.

✔ On the Web, visit McAfee for a sample antivirus program:

```
http://www.mcafee.com
```

✔ The Windows 98 Plus! package comes with an antivirus program. Unfortunately, I don't cover the Plus! package in this book. Sorry!

✔ No, you can't give your PC a virus by sneezing on the monitor. But you should have a box of Kleenex tissues handy for when that does happen.

Creating an Emergency Boot Disk

The best diagnostic tool you can create for your PC is the emergency boot disk. You may never use this tool. In fact, the only people who might use it are the tech-support people or your PC's guru. (The disk is full of techy programs.) It won't hurt you to create such a disk now:

1. **Open the Control Panel.**

   From the Start menu, choose Settings⇨Control Panel.

2. **Double-click the Add/Remove Programs icon.**

   The Add/Remove Programs Properties dialog box appears.

3. **Click the Startup Disk tab.**

4. **Click the Create Disk button.**

   Follow the directions on the screen.

   Insert a floppy disk into drive A and then click the OK button.

   You may need the original Windows CD for this operation. If so, an annoying dialog box will inform you.

When the program is done creating the disk, remove it from your floppy drive. Label the disk as the PC's emergency boot disk and put it away in a safe place. Pray you never need it.

Chapter 31

When to Scream for Help

· ·

· ·

Should you scream for help? Of course. The decision to scream should never be questioned. I might add, however, that it helps to know who to scream at.

Screaming at a computer doesn't help, even if you scream into the microphone. Computers don't appreciate emotions, and they won't assume, because you're screaming, that you need more help than if you were merely sedated and pressing the F1 key.

No, it helps to have a person to scream at. Further, it helps to scream in a soft speaking voice. Scream calmly. Describe what's going on. And follow the advice in this chapter to help remove the reason for all that screaming in the first place.

Who Is Your PC Guru?

Your personal computer guru is someone — anyone — who loves computers and knows enough about them to offer help when you need it. Your guru is an important person to know and respect. Everyone has one — even the gurus themselves! If you don't have one, you need one.

At work. At the office, the guru is probably the computer manager, but ask around to see whether anyone else can do the job. Quite a few computer zanies may be lurking around the office. If you find one, he or she may be able to offer help and advice more quickly than the computer manager (who goes by a schedule). Especially for help on particular types of software, turn to people who use the programs regularly; they may know tricks they can pass along.

At home. For the home, finding a guru can be more difficult. Usually a neighbor, friend, or relative will know enough about computers to help you install hardware or software, or at least give you advice about some program.

Whatever your situation, identify your guru and keep that person in mind for troubled times or for extracting advice and tips. It's like having a good mechanic handy or knowing a friendly doctor. You may not use your guru all the time, but knowing that he or she is available makes computing easier.

- ✔ Remember that a certain amount of finesse is involved when using your computer guru's talents; a line must be drawn between getting occasional help and taxing your guru's patience.

- ✔ Computer gurus can handle remarkable geekistical operations but only if they know what you're talking about. If you ask them to "check the Kyoowooi for you," they shrug and move off to floss their RS-232 ports. Learn the basics of pronunciation; a *queue* is pronounced *Q,* for example. When in doubt, write it on a card and wave it over your head.

Other Places You Can Look for Help

Computer gurus aren't everywhere. Suppose you live on Pitcairn Island and your PC just came mail order from PCs Limited (along with your absentee ballot for the 1988 presidential elections). Who's going to be your guru? Definitely not the lady who makes festive pot holders out of palm fronds.

When you don't have a real guru handy, look for alternatives. Here's a bunch I can think of right off the top of my head:

- ✔ Some computer stores may offer classes or have coffee groups where you can ask questions. But keep in mind that they're a limited source of information.

- ✔ Local computer clubs dot the nation. Don't be afraid to show up at one and ask a few questions. You may even adopt a guru there or learn about special sessions for beginners. Many computer clubs or special interest groups (SIGs) are designed specifically for questions and answers. Check the local paper or computer flyer at the store.

- ✔ Community colleges offer introductory courses on computers and some software programs. Come armed with your questions.

- ✔ Don't forget the gurus you already paid for: the technical-support people at your computer store or the telephone support you get with every piece of software you buy. Everything comes with support; it's part of the purchase price (or so they claim). Especially for software, call the support department if you're having trouble. (But don't abuse phone support; it's not an excuse for not reading the manual.) Also, watch out for phone support you must pay for, either from the long distance call or on a per-minute charge.

✔ If these traditional avenues fail, consider the unconventional. Search for help on the Internet or access a newsgroup particular to the thing that's bothering you.

Figure Out Whether It's a Hardware or Software Problem

Your guru, or even you, may be able to fix hardware problems: Check the cables, listen for noises, watch for sparks, and so on.

Software problems, on the other hand, can generally be cured by your guru or by a phone call to the developer's technical-support hot line (or wait-on-hold line). But which is which? It's important to know which problem you're experiencing because computer doctors get irked when you hand them a PC with a software problem. Here are the clues:

1. **Does the problem happen consistently, no matter which program you're running?**

   For example, do Word, Excel, and your accounting package all refuse to send stuff to the printer? If so, it's a hardware problem; more specifically the printer is being stupid. Check the power. Check the cables. Check the printer.

2. **Did the problem just crop up?**

   For example, did the Print Preview mode work last week but not today? If so, it could be a hardware problem, it could be a network problem, or it could be a software driver problem — provided that you haven't changed anything on your computer or added any new software since the last time the program worked properly.

3. **Does the problem happen with only one application?**

   For example, does the computer always reset when you try to print using your photo editor? If so, it's a software problem. Call the developer.

Generally speaking, if the problem happens in only one program, it's the software. If it's consistent across all your applications or it happens at random times, it's the hardware.

Calling Tech Support

Tech support can be good or bad — or both! It used to be good and free. There were 800 numbers and lots of eager young people willing to help you to do anything from writing a printer driver to removing the cellophane off the computer box.

Today, tech support is either pay-as-you-go or nonexistent. Before you call tech support, try to find out how much it's going to cost you and how busy the staff usually is. Asking around is the best way to discover this info.

Also, try visiting the company's Web page. Look for support information or a FAQ (Frequently Asked Questions) page. You may find your answer there. I discovered, for example, how best to configure my PC for two monitors by visiting a Web page instead of dialing up the pricey tech support.

If you finally give in and call tech support, you should be armed with the following knowledge:

- ✔ For hardware problems, gather a description of the hardware that's ailing you: how much memory is installed, the microprocessor name and number, the computer type or brand name, and the serial number of the device.

- ✔ For software trouble, they'll want a serial number, version number, and maybe a registration number.

- ✔ Be able to reproduce the problem.

- ✔ Act calm and civil.

- ✔ Be prepared to take advice.

The tech-support person will work you through the problem and provide a solution. Hopefully that will fix the problem.

- ✔ You may want to write down the solution so that you don't have to phone tech support again.

- ✔ Tech support is available for just about every hardware or software product sold. Please don't abuse it! Always try every possible resource (the Web, the manual) before calling up technical support.

- ✔ Never use tech support as a substitute for reading the manual. Too many people did that in the early 1990s, which is probably why all the free tech support disappeared and today you generally have to pay for it.

- ✔ Don't forget your computer dealer! You paid them for service and support. If you're in a bind, the folks there should be who you call first.

Part VII

The Part of Tens

The 5th Wave By Rich Tennant

"OKAY—ANTIDOTE, ANTIDOTE, WHAT WOULD AN ANTIDOTE ICON LOOK LIKE? YOU KNOW, I STILL HAVEN'T GOT THIS DESKTOP THE WAY I WANT IT."

In this part . . .

When caveman Gronk asked caveman Og where his favorite hunting grounds were, Og couldn't decide. So Og began to list where he liked to hunt. To help Og keep track of what he'd already said, he held up his hands. And since his hands had ten fingers, Og felt compelled to rattle off ten places where he liked to hunt. And thus the Part of Tens was born.

To wrap up the discussion of PCs in this book, I've capped this part with various lists. Each list strives to have ten items in it — probably because, like my ancient ancestor Og, I have ten fingers. Where I'm clever, there will be more than ten items. And when I'm stretching it, there will be less. This may or may not be a punishable offense, but at least I'm being honest when I run out of ideas.

Chapter 32

Ten Common Beginner Mistakes

In This Chapter

▶ Not properly quitting Windows

▶ Buying too much software

▶ Buying incompatible hardware

▶ Not buying enough supplies

▶ Not saving your work

▶ Not backing up files

▶ Opening or deleting unknown things

▶ Booting from an alien disk

▶ Replying to SPAM

▶ Opening a program attached to e-mail

Sure, you can make a gazillion mistakes with a computer, whether it's deleting the wrong file or dropping the printer on your foot. But I've narrowed the list down to ten. These are the day-to-day operating mistakes that people tend to repeat until they're told not to.

Not Properly Quitting Windows

When you're done with Windows, shut it down. Choose the Shut Down command from the Start menu, click OK, and wait until the screen says that it's safe to turn off your PC.

✔ Don't just flip the power switch when you're done.

✔ In the same vein, don't use the reset button on your PC unless you absolutely have to. See Chapter 30 for such situations.

✔ Refer to Chapter 2 for proper PC shutdown instructions.

Buying Too Much Software

Your PC probably came out of the box with dozens of programs pre-installed. (No, you're not required to use them; see Chapter 19 on uninstalling software.) Even with all that software pre-installed, don't overwhelm yourself by getting *more* software right away.

Buying too much software isn't really the sin here. The sin is buying too much software and trying to learn it all at once. The buy-it-all-at-once habit probably comes from buying music, where it's okay to lug home a whole stack of CDs from the store. You can listen to several CDs over the course of a few days. They're enjoyable the first time, and they age well. Software, on the other hand, is gruesome on the first day and can take months to come to grips with.

Have mercy on yourself at the checkout counter and buy software at a moderate rate. Buy one package and learn it. Then move on and buy something else. You learn faster that way.

Buying Incompatible Hardware

Whoops! Did you forget to notice that that new keyboard you bought was for a Macintosh? Or maybe you thought you were getting a deal on that USB modem, and lo, your PC doesn't have a USB port. And the biggest disappointment: You buy a new AGP expansion card, but all you have available are PCI slots.

Always check your hardware before you buy it! Especially if you're shopping online; if you're not sure that the hardware is compatible, phone up the dealer and ask those folks specifically.

Not Buying Enough Supplies

Buy printer paper in those big boxes. You *will* run out. Buy extra floppy disks, Zip disks, Jaz disks, CD-Rs, and whatever type of disks your PC's disk drives eat.

Not Saving Your Work

Whenever you're creating something blazingly original, choose the Save command and save your document to the hard disk. When you write something dumb that you're going to patch up later, choose the Save command, too. The idea here is to choose Save whenever you think about it — hopefully, every four minutes or sooner.

You never know when your computer will meander off to watch Barney while you're hoping to finish the last few paragraphs of that report. Save your work as often as possible. And always save it whenever you get up from your computer — even if it's just to grab a Fig Newton from the other room.

Not Backing Up Files

Saving work on a computer is a many-tiered process. First, save the work to your hard drive as you create it. Then, at the end of the day, back up your work to floppy or Zip disks. Always keep a safety copy somewhere, because you never know.

At the end of the week (or monthly), run the backup program that came with your PC's tape backup drive. I know this is a pain, but it's much more automated and easier to do than in years past. If your PC lacks a tape backup unit, *buy one!* You can back up to Zip disks, but that's expensive; backing up to floppy disks is crazy; and backing up to a CD-R or a Jaz drive is okay, especially if you have software that can perform the backup for you.

Opening or Deleting Unknown Things

There are both hardware and software rules about opening or deleting unknown things. On the software side, I have a rule:

If you didn't create the file, don't delete it.

Windows is brimming with unusual and unknown files. Don't mess with 'em. Don't delete them. Don't move them. Don't rename them. And especially don't open them to see what they are. Sometimes opening an unknown icon can lead to trouble.

On the hardware side, don't open anything attached to your PC unless you absolutely know what you're doing. Some hardware is meant to open. New console cases actually have pop-off and flip-top lids for easy access. They make upgrading things a snap. And if you do open a console, remember to unplug it! It's okay to open your printer to undo a jam or install new ink or a toner cartridge. Even so, do not open the ink or toner cartridges.

Other hardware items have *do not open* written all over them: the monitor, keyboard, and modem.

Booting from an Alien Disk

The number-one way to get a computer virus is to start your computer from a strange floppy disk. I'm not talking about starting the PC using a boot disk that you create or one that comes in a hermetically sealed software box. I'm talking about that — wink, wink — *game* Earl slipped you last week. You know the one. (Heh, heh.) Boot from that disk, and you're inviting who-knows-what into your PC. Don't.

Replying to SPAM E-Mail

Do not reply to any SPAM e-mail unless you want more SPAM. A popular trick is for the spammers to put some text that says, "reply to this message if you do not want to receive any further messages. . . ." Don't! Replying to SPAM signals the spammer that they have a "live one," and you will get even more SPAM. Never ever reply to SPAM!

Opening a Program Attached to an E-Mail Message

You can receive photos via e-mail. You can receive sound files. You can receive any type of document. You can even receive ZIP file archives. These are all okay to receive. But if you receive a program (EXE) file, do not open it!

The only way to get a virus on a PC is to *run* an infected program file. You can receive the file okay. But if you open it, you're dead. My rule is: Don't open any EXE file you're sent through e-mail.

- ✔ ZIP files are okay to receive. You can open them and see what's in them. And if they contain programs you're unsure of, then just delete the whole deal, and you're safe.

- ✔ If you have to send a program file through e-mail, write or phone the recipient in advance to let them know it's coming.

- ✔ When in doubt, run antivirus software on the file before you run it.

- ✔ Some types of viruses can come in Microsoft Word documents. Antivirus software may catch these viruses, but in any case, confirm that the sender meant to send you the file before you open it.

Chapter 33

Ten Things Worth Buying for Your PC

I'm not trying to sell you anything, and I'm pretty sure that you're not ready to burst out and spend, spend, spend on something like a new computer (unless it's someone else's money). But you may want to consider buying some nifty little things for Mr. Computer. Like ten things worth buying for a dog (leash, cat-shaped squeeze toys, pooper-scooper, and so on), these ten things will make working with the beast more enjoyable.

Software

Never neglect software. Jillions of different types of software programs are available, each of them designed to perform a specific task for a certain type of user. If you ever find yourself frustrated by the way the computer does something, consider looking for a piece of software that does it better.

Mouse Pad and Wrist Pad

Rolling your mouse on your tabletop may work okay, but the best surface is a mouse pad, a screen-sized piece of foam rubber with a textured top ideal for rolling mice around. Avoid the mouse pads with a smooth finish. You pay more for pads with cute pictures or the new mood pads that react to temperature. The best mouse pad is one with your zodiac sign on it, a picture of various cheeses (which makes the mouse happy), or some clever sayings in Assyrian.

Like a mouse pad, the wrist pad fits right below your keyboard. It enables you to comfortably rest your wrists while you type. Some mouse pads even have wrist pads on them. (Yup, you're supposed to hold up your wrist when you move the mouse, too.)

Antiglare Screen

Tawdry as it may sound, an antiglare screen is nothing more than a nylon stocking stretched over the front of your monitor. Okay, these are *professional* nylons in fancy holders that adhere themselves to your screen. The net result is no garish glare from the lights in the room or outside. It's such a good idea that some monitors come with built-in antiglare screens.

Glare is the number-one cause of eyestrain while you're using a computer. Lights usually reflect in the glass, either from above or from a window. The antiglare screen cuts down on the reflections and makes the stuff on the monitor easier to see.

Some antiglare screens also incorporate anti-radiation shielding. I'm serious: They provide protection from the harmful electromagnetic rays that are spewing out of your monitor even as you read this! Is this necessary? No.

Keyboard Cover

If you're klutzy with a coffee cup or have small children or others with peanut butter–smudged fingers using the keyboard, the keyboard cover is a great idea. You may have even seen them used in department stores: They cover the keyboard snugly but still enable you to type. A great idea, because without a keyboard cover, all this disgusting gunk falls between the keys. Yech!

In the same vein, you can also buy a generic dust cover for your computer. This item preserves its appearance but has no other true value. Only use a computer cover when the computer is turned off (and I don't recommend turning it off). If you put the cover on the PC while it's on, you create a mini-greenhouse, and the computer will — sometimes — melt. Nasty. This result doesn't happen to the keyboard, which is a cool character anyway.

More Memory

Any PC works better with more memory installed. An upper limit is anywhere from 128 to 512MB or so, which is ridiculous — well, presently. Still, upgrading your system to 32 or 64 or 128MB of RAM is a good idea. Almost immediately you notice the improvement in Windows and various graphics applications and games. Make someone else do the upgrading for you; you just buy the memory.

Larger, Faster Hard Drive

Hard drives fill up quickly. The first time it's because you've kept a lot of junk on your hard drive: games, things people give you, old files, and old programs you don't use anymore. So you can delete those or copy them to Zip disks for long-term storage. Then, after a time, your hard drive fills up again. The second time, it has stuff you really use. Argh! What can you delete?

The answer is to buy a larger hard drive. If you can, install a second hard drive and start filling it up. Otherwise, replace your first hard drive with a larger, faster model. Actually, buying a faster model is a great way to improve the performance of any older PC without throwing it out entirely.

Ergonomic Keyboard

The traditional computer keyboard is based on the old typewriter keyboard (the IBM Selectric, by the way). Why? It doesn't have to be. No mechanics inside the keyboard require the keys to be laid out staggered or in a cascading style. Repetitive typing on such a keyboard can lead to various ugly motion disorders (VUMDs).

To help you type more comfortably, you can get an ergonomic keyboard, such as the Microsoft Natural Keyboard. These keyboards arrange the keys in a manner that's comfortable for your hands, keeping everything lined up and not tweaked out like on a regular computer keyboard.

My wife loves her Microsoft Natural keyboard. She raves about it. On the other hand, I'm a purist and refuse to use it. In fact, I use an old IBM 101-key keyboard on my typing computer because I love all the noise it makes.

Larger or Secondary Monitor

Ever see a 19-inch computer monitor? How about the 21-inch model? They're *wonderful*. The 17-inch monitor you have was probably a good choice for when you bought your computer. But check out the screen real estate on that larger monitor.

The nifty thing about Windows 98 and buying a new monitor is that you don't have to toss out the old one. You can use *both* monitors at once. You need a second video adapter to drive the second monitor, but it's absolutely wonderful.

See Chapter 12 for more information on dueling monitors.

USB Expansion Card

USB is the *thing* to have for expanding your PC. If your computer lacks a USB port, then you can buy a USB expansion card.

My advice: Get a two-port USB PCI card. (Sorry about all the acronyms and jargon.) Two ports is enough to start. If you get more than two USB devices, you can either swap them out or just buy a USB hub to continue expanding your system. See Chapter 9 for more USB information.

Scanner or Digital Camera

If you want the latest PC toy, then buy a scanner or digital camera.

Scanners are wonderful if you enjoy graphics and want to send pictures over the Internet. Digital cameras are great toys, but they're expensive. And they take some getting used to.

My advice: If you already have a nice camera and take lots of pictures, get a scanner. Wait for digital cameras to drop a bit in price before you make the investment. (See Chapter 18 for more information on scanners and digital cameras.)

Chapter 34

Ten Tips from a PC Guru

● ●

In This Chapter

▶ You're in charge

▶ Computer nerds love to help

▶ Get a UPS

▶ Don't fret over upgrading software

▶ Back up your files

▶ How to perfectly adjust your monitor

▶ Unplug the PC when you open the case

▶ Subscribe to a computer magazine

▶ Avoid the hype

▶ Don't take this computer stuff too seriously

● ●

I don't consider myself a computer expert or genius or guru, though many have called me all those terms. I'm just a guy who *understands* how computers work. Or, better than that, I understand how computer people think. They may not be able to express an idea, but I can see what they mean and translate it into English for you. Given that, here are some final tips and suggestions before you and your PC go off on your merry way.

You Control the Computer

You bought the computer. You clean up after its messes. You feed it floppy disks when it asks for them. You control the computer, simple as that. Don't let that computer try to boss you around with its bizarre conversations and funny idiosyncrasies. It's really pretty dopey; the computer is an idiot.

If somebody shoved a flattened can of motor oil in your mouth, would you try to taste it? Of course not. But stick a flattened can of motor oil into a disk drive, and the computer will try to read information from it, thinking it's a floppy disk. See? It's dumb.

You control that mindless computer just like you control an infant. You must treat it the same way, with respect and caring attention. Don't feel like the computer's bossing you around any more than you feel like a baby's bossing you around during 3 a.m. feedings. They're both helpless creatures, subject to your every whim. Be gentle. But be in charge.

Most Computer Nerds Love to Help Beginners

It's sad, but almost all computer nerds spend most of their waking hours in front of a computer. They know that's kind of an oddball thing to do, but they can't help it.

Their guilty consciences are what usually make them happy to help beginners. By passing on knowledge, they can legitimize the hours they whiled away on their computer stools. Plus, it gives them a chance to brush up on a social skill that's slowly slipping away: the art of actually talking to a person.

- ✔ Always be grateful when given help.

- ✔ Beware of False Nerds. These are people who don't love computers but who went to some sort of school to learn a few by-rote tricks. They may not be helpful nor know anything about computers other than what they're told. You can tell False Nerds because they lack the enthusiasm of the True Nerd, the one who will help you.

Get a UPS

The Uninterruptable Power Supply (UPS) is a boon to computing anywhere in the world where the power is less than reliable. Plug your console in the UPS. Plug your monitor in the UPS. If it has extra battery-backed-up sockets, plug your modem into the UPS as well.

- ✔ See Chapter 2 for information on using a UPS as well as using a power strip.

- ✔ Using a UPS does not affect the performance of your PC. The computer could care less whether it is plugged into the wall or a UPS.

Upgrading Software Isn't an Absolute Necessity

Just as the models on the cover of *Vogue* change their clothes each season (or maybe that should be change their *fashions* each season), software companies issue perpetual upgrades. Should you automatically buy the upgrade?

Of course not! If you're comfortable with your old software, there's no reason to buy the new version. None!

The software upgrade probably has a few new features in it (although you still haven't had a chance to check out all the features in the current version). And the upgrade probably has some new bugs in it, too, making it crash in new and different ways. Feel free to look at the box, just as you stare at the ladies on the cover of *Vogue*. But don't feel obliged to buy something you don't need. (And I apologize for all the parentheticals.)

Back Up

Backing up files is about as exciting as vacuuming under the couch. You know you should do it, but it's boring, and chances are good that it won't really matter whether you do it or not.

But accidents happen. Cats can drag dead roaches out from beneath the couch when Grandma's visiting. And your software can crash, leaving you with nothing but a blank screen.

Back up your files every time you're done working with your computer. If you back up your files every day, at the very worst you have lost only one day's worth of work. And train the cat to not only drag out the roaches but also to toss them in the trash before Grandma arrives.

Perfectly Adjusting Your Monitor

I don't have much explaining to do here. Keeping the monitor turned up too bright is bad for the eyes, and it wears out the monitor more quickly.

To adjust the monitor to pink perfection, turn the brightness (the button with the little sun) all the way up and adjust the contrast (the button with the half moon) until the display looks pleasing. Then turn the brightness down until the little square outside the picture's edges disappears. That's it!

Unplug Your PC When You Upgrade Hardware

The new PCs don't have a flippable on-off switch like the older models. When you open the case to upgrade or add an expansion card, your belly (if it's like my belly) may punch the power-on button, and lo, you're working in a hazardous electrical environment. To prevent that, unplug the console before you open it for upgrading.

You don't need to unplug the console or even turn off the PC when you add a USB device. (You do need to unplug it if you add a USB expansion card, however.)

Subscribe to a Computer Magazine

Oh, why not? Browse the stacks at your local coffeehouse-slash-music store-slash-bookstore. Try to find a computer magazine that matches your tastes.

- I haven't found a good beginner's magazine in a while. (One may be out there since I last looked.)
- What sells me on a magazine are the columns and the *newsy* stuff they put up front.
- Some magazines are all ads. That can be great if you like ads, or it can be boring.
- Avoid the nerdier magazines, but I probably didn't need to tell you that.

Avoid the Hype

The computer industry is rife with hype. Even if you subscribe to a family-oriented computer magazine, you'll still read about the latest this or the next-biggest-trend that. Ignore it!

My gauge for hype is whether or not the thing hyped is shipping as a standard part of a PC. I check the ads. Yes, FireWire is supposed to be the next big thing, bigger than USB. Did I write about it here? No. That's because it's not a standard on any new computer. It's still a wishy thing available mostly for the Mac.

- ✔ When hype becomes reality, you'll read about it here in this book.

- ✔ Former hype I've successfully ignored: Pen Windows; Push technology; Shockwave; Microsoft Bob; Windows CE.

- ✔ Hype the jury is still out on: wireless networking; the SuperDisk drive; FireWire; home networking.

- ✔ Hype that eventually became reality: USB; CD-R; Zip drives; shopping on the Web or *e-commerce;* DVD drives (but still no software on DVD discs); digital cameras.

Don't Take It So Seriously

Hey, simmer down. Computers aren't part of life. They're nothing more than mineral deposits and petroleum products. Close your eyes and take a few deep breaths. Listen to the ocean spray against the deck on the patio; listen to the gurgle of the marble Jacuzzi tub in the master bedroom.

Pretend you're driving the convertible through a grove of sequoias on a sunny day with the wind whipping through your hair and curling over your ears. Pretend you're lying on the deck under the sun as the Pacific Princess chugs south toward the islands with friendly, wide-eyed monkeys that eat coconut chunks from the palm of your hand.

You're up in a hot-air balloon, swirling the first sip of champagne and feeling the bubbles explode atop your tongue. Ahead, to the far left, the castle's spire rises through the clouds, and you can smell Chef Meisterbrau's waiting banquet.

Then slowly open your eyes. It's just a dumb computer. Really. Don't take it too seriously.

Index

Notes

Notes

Notes

Notes

Notes

YOUR ONLINE RESOURCE

WWW.DUMMIES.COM

Discover Dummies Online!

The Dummies Web Site is your fun and friendly online resource for the latest information about ...*For Dummies*® books and your favorite topics. The Web site is the place to communicate with us, exchange ideas with other ...*For Dummies* readers, chat with authors, and have fun!

Ten Fun and Useful Things You Can Do at www.dummies.com

1. Win free ...*For Dummies* books and more!
2. Register your book and be entered in a prize drawing.
3. Meet your favorite authors through the IDG Books Author Chat Series.
4. Exchange helpful information with other ...*For Dummies* readers.
5. Discover other great ...*For Dummies* books you must have!
6. Purchase Dummieswear™ exclusively from our Web site.
7. Buy ...*For Dummies* books online.
8. Talk to us. Make comments, ask questions, get answers!
9. Download free software.
10. Find additional useful resources from authors.

WWW.DUMMIES.COM

Link directly to these ten fun and useful things at
http://www.dummies.com/10useful

For other technology titles from IDG Books Worldwide, go to
www.idgbooks.com

Not on the Web yet? It's easy to get started with *Dummies 101*®: *The Internet For Windows*®*98* or *The Internet For Dummies*®, *6th Edition*, at local retailers everywhere.

IDG BOOKS WORLDWIDE

Find other ...*For Dummies* books on these topics:

Business • Career • Databases • Food & Beverage • Games • Gardening • Graphics • Hardware
Health & Fitness • Internet and the World Wide Web • Networking • Office Suites
Operating Systems • Personal Finance • Pets • Programming • Recreation • Sports
Spreadsheets • Teacher Resources • Test Prep • Word Processing

IDG BOOKS WORLDWIDE BOOK REGISTRATION

We want to hear from you!

Visit **http://my2cents.dummies.com** to register this book and tell us how you liked it!

- ✔ Get entered in our monthly prize giveaway.

- ✔ Give us feedback about this book — tell us what you like best, what you like least, or maybe what you'd like to ask the author and us to change!

- ✔ Let us know any other *...For Dummies*® topics that interest you.

Your feedback helps us determine what books to publish, tells us what coverage to add as we revise our books, and lets us know whether we're meeting your needs as a *...For Dummies* reader. You're our most valuable resource, and what you have to say is important to us!

Not on the Web yet? It's easy to get started with *Dummies 101*®: *The Internet For Windows*® *98* or *The Internet For Dummies*,® 6th Edition, at local retailers everywhere.

Or let us know what you think by sending us a letter at the following address:

...For Dummies Book Registration
Dummies Press
7260 Shadeland Station, Suite 100
Indianapolis, IN 46256-3917
Fax 317-596-5498

BESTSELLING
BOOK SERIES